D1519675

THE COLD WAR
AND
DEFENSE

The Cold War
and
Defense

Edited by
Keith Neilson
and
Ronald G. Haycock

PRAEGER

New York
Westport, Connecticut
London

355.033
C688

Library of Congress Cataloging-in-Publication Data

The Cold war and defense / edited by Keith Neilson and Ronald G.
  Haycock.
      p.   cm.
    ISBN 0-275-93556-6 (alk. paper)
      1. Armaments—Congresses. 2. Cold War—Congresses. 3. Military
policy—Congresses. 4. North Atlantic Treaty Organization—
Congresses.   I. Neilson, Keith. II. Haycock, Ronald G.
UA11.C575   1990
355'.033'0045—dc20   90-30926

Library of Congress Catalog Card Number: 90-30926
ISBN: 0-275-93556-6

First published in 1990

Praeger Publishers, One Madison Avenue, New York, NY 10010
An imprint of Greenwood Publishing Group, Inc.

Printed in the United States of America

The paper used in this book complies with the
Permanent Paper Standard issued by the National
Information Standards Organization (Z39.48-1984).

10 9 8 7 6 5 4 3 2 1

Contents

Acknowledgments   vii

Introduction   1
Keith Neilson and Ronald G. Haycock

1   Cold War and Defense   7
Ernest R. May

2   Balances of Power: The Strategic Dimensions of the Marshall Plan   75
Michael Hogan

3   Britain: The Defense of Western Europe and Its Overseas Role, 1945–68   99
Michael L. Dockrill

4   Rings and Flanks: The Defense of the Middle East in the Early Cold War   111
Bruce R. Kuniholm

5   Major and Minor: The Defense of Southeast Asia and the Cold War   137
Peter Dennis

6   Continental Defense and Arctic Sovereignty, 1945–50: Solving the Canadian Dilemma   153
David Bercuson

7   Canada and NATO: Adjusting the Balance   171
Denis Smith

Afterword: Foreign Policy and Military Planning—The Cold
War and National Defense, 1945–60   185
B. J. C. McKercher

Bibliography   195

Index   201

About the Contributors   205

Acknowledgments

The directors of the Fourteenth Military History Symposium are greatly indebted to the Royal Military College of Canada, which hosted the Symposium, assumed a portion of the expense, and provided support services and assistance in ways far too numerous to mention. Mrs. Karen Brown, the departmental secretary, who looked after the myriad details of organization, has our profound thanks for all that she has done. The Social Sciences and Humanities Research Council of Canada provided financial support which is gratefully acknowledged.

The day-to-day support and encouragement of colleagues within the Department of History, and particularly that of Professor Barry Hunt, chairman of the Department, was particularly appreciated and made the Symposium truly a collective enterprise. Finally, we must express our appreciation to the speakers for their thought-provoking and stimulating presentations.

THE COLD WAR
AND
DEFENSE

Introduction

Keith Neilson and Ronald G. Haycock

Until recently, it appeared that the Cold War, like the poor, would always be with us. Since the end of World War II, a kind of uneasy equipoise has existed between the two hostile ideological blocs generally referred to as the East and the West. Underpinning this division has been the issue of defense. The state of undeclared hostility—the phrase Cold *War* is not accidental—between the two groupings has meant that a perpetual state of military readiness has been maintained for more than 40 years. Defense, then, is inseparable from Cold War.

But when we speak of the Cold War, what do we mean? Generally, it is a generic term, used to cover the situation described above. But viewed from the perspective of different countries, in different regions, the concrete reality of the Cold War takes on varied aspects. Each country brought to the Cold War its own history. Traditional foreign policy and defense problems did not evaporate in 1945. Instead, they became the old wine that had to be poured into the new bottle called the Cold War. In this volume, consisting of the essays presented at the Fourteenth Military History Symposium, held at the Royal Military College of Canada on 24–25 March 1988, the diversity of that historical experience, and the differing ways in which it shaped the Cold War defense plans of a number of countries, is the central theme.[1] There are related issues. Much of the Cold War planning for defense took place in the context of alliances; some of it took the shape of economic planning. War planning in peacetime required new governmental bodies and had a domestic context. Such matters are inextricably linked to the Cold War and defense and, as such, are among the issues discussed below.

Defense policy is not always easy to pinpoint, even in retrospect. In a wide-ranging keynote address, Ernest May points out that such tangible manifestations of a nation's defense policy as public declarations, war plans, budgets, force postures, and deployments may all give contradictory indications of what actual defense plans are. Despite this, May argues that some degree of coherence may be found in the defense policies of the two superpowers in the years immediately following World War II.

Perhaps no country had to undergo as great a reorientation of its traditional position as a result of the onset of the Cold War as did the United States. The postwar world thrust that country into a position of global predominance, a position of which it had no previous experience. This resulted, May asserts, in large-scale changes in the U.S. government, changes matched in scope only by those experienced in the U.S. War of Independence and in the Civil War. The government of the United States changed in three particular ways: it became more oriented toward foreign, rather than domestic, affairs; it was run by a new group of leaders and managers whose formative experiences differed fundamentally from those of their predecessors; and it became more subject to extrinsic pressures, reflecting the growth of U.S. involvement overseas.

From 1945 to 1950, these changes resulted in a chaotic scene. The various branches of the armed forces struggled to make their version of defense— with the concomitant budgetary allocations—the accepted one. New bodies such as the National Security Council provided a forum in which the new men could deal with these varying ideas and their implications. But only events could provide a point around which these conflicting views could crystalize. The threatening international situation of the late 1940s–hostilities between East and West seemed very possible over Berlin—forced a coherence upon U.S. defense policy, a coherence increased by the outbreak of actual fighting in Korea in 1950. This coherence centered around the idea of a stable, peaceful, and prosperous Western Europe. By 1950, with the creation of NATO and the beginnings of various plans for European recovery, the flux in postwar U.S. defense policy was to some degree ended.

While U.S. defense policy was difficult to understand due to its conflicting manifestations, Soviet defense policy, May argues, remains obscure because of the closed nature of the society that produced it. It is almost impossible to know whether there was a Soviet threat to Western Europe immediately after 1945. At best, one may only speculate as to Stalin's thoughts concerning the international situation. Given the Soviet dictator's long tenure in office, however, May contends that Stalin's intention may have been to avoid a post–1945 Europe similar to that which emerged post–1918, wherein the Soviet Union was isolated. Whatever the case, it seems clear that Soviet policy was relatively aggressive in 1947–48 and less so after 1949.

If U.S. defense policy cohered around the idea of a stable, prosperous Western Europe, then the Marshall Plan was central to its achievement. Michael Hogan argues that the Marshall Plan must be thought of in the context of defense and that the conventional idea of "containment" of the Soviet Union is an inadequate explanation of the complexities of the Plan. For the Americans, the defense of Europe required the reconciliation of Germany and the rest of Western Europe. To do this, German reparations had to be pared and trade among the Western Europeans liberalized. Neither Britain nor France, for varying reasons, could accept these goals wholesale. The result was that the Marshall Plan became only part of European defense, and a separate but related initiative—the creation of NATO—was begun to supplement it.

Michael Dockrill explains why the British refused to accept U.S. plans for the defense of Europe. Shattered by the war, Britain preferred to focus on the reestablishment of its position as a world power rather than on the narrow issue of Europe. This reflected the British experience after World War I, when plans for the defense of Europe foundered on U.S. withdrawal from the Old World. The Marshall Plan let the British hope that they could utilize their own resources to restore themselves as a great power, while U.S. resources propped up Europe. Events challenged this approach. The outbreak of the Korean War and the Soviet explosion of an atomic bomb meant that a rearmed Germany was essential to the defense of Europe.

This shifted British attention away from empire and back to Europe. From 1949 to 1954, Dockrill demonstrates, the British worked in favor of some sort of pan-European defense scheme. When this scheme failed, due to French intransigence, Britain promised to maintain the British Army of the Rhine in Germany as a measure to reconcile the French to Germany's entrance into NATO. Paralleling this, Britain also began to consider defense by nuclear weapons as a cheap means of maintaining itself as a great power. By 1957, with the international situation improving after the end of hostilities in Korea, the accession of Germany into NATO, and the British debacle at Suez, nuclear weapons had become the centerpiece of British defense policy in Europe. However, British conventional commitments overseas did not decline until at least 1968. Thus, Dockrill concludes, in retrospect it is evident that only from about 1949 to 1954 was Britain's interest fixed on the continent. For the rest of the period from 1945 to 1968, Britain's Cold War was concerned with its traditional interests overseas.

The persistence of traditional interests, Bruce Kuniholm shows, was no less important in the Middle East. The new circumstances of such states as Turkey, Greece, Persia, and Iraq after 1945 required some rethinking of traditional foreign policy issues. With the Soviet Union coming to be thought of as the only potential enemy, such nineteenth-century preoccupations as the "Great Game," the Balkan issue, and the Eastern question had to be discarded as paradigms for diplomacy. Instead, this region as a whole had to be thought of as the "southern flank" of the defense of Europe. This reconsideration had to be done quickly, since the disintegration of British power eliminated for the states in that region their traditional policy of balancing between the British empire and Imperial Russia (and its Soviet successor). The creation of NATO, so important for Europe, worried Turkey and Greece because their own security was not clearly protected. Therefore, between 1948 and 1951 they, along with other Middle Eastern states, strove successfully to establish the belief that their region was essential to the defense of Europe as a whole. By so doing, they created a certain kind of special relationship with Europe. This new perception, Kuniholm argues, is central to an understanding of the diplomacy of the Middle East to the present day.

In Southeast Asia, Peter Dennis demonstrates, the Cold War became entangled with other historical circumstances. Although the United States had agreed at Potsdam to withdraw from the region, it found this difficult to do as it still was part of the Allied military command and as much U.S. military equipment was being used by the French in the latter's attempt to recreate its colonial position in Indochina. By 1948 the U.S. intention to withdraw had ended due to the state of emergency in Malaya, the worsening situation in Viet Nam, and the outbreak of the Cold War in Europe. In 1950 President Truman allocated $10 million to the French government for its war in Viet Nam.

In Australia, these events went hand-in-glove with a fundamental shift in posture. World War II had demonstrated to Australians that their relationship with Britain was not sufficient to guarantee their security. The alternative was to shift allegiance to the United States. But, despite the efforts of the Australian Labor Minister for External Affairs, H. V. Evatt, the United States was not eager to replace Britain as Australia's shield. Suspicious of Labor's politics and feeling that the Pacific was not vital to U.S. interests, the United States shied away until 1950. The outbreak of the Korean War, seven months after the defeat of Australia's Labour government, led to U.S. reconsideration. The result was the ANZUS agreement of September 1951.

But Australia's position was not determined solely by the decline of British power and the rise of the United States. The collapse of colonial empires in the region meant that Australia had to serve as a surrogate power in order to regulate the transition from European to local dominance. This meant that Australia's interests occasionally clashed with those of both Britain and the United States. Australia, for example, rejected the British proposal (itself based on traditional imperial thinking) that Australia focus its military efforts on the defense of the Middle East. Instead, the Australians looked to help the United States defend Southeast Asia. And while this relationship was relatively harmonious over Australian aid in Viet Nam, it was less so in Western New Guinea, where the United States viewed Australia's intervention as neocolonial. The Cold War in Southeast Asia was filtered through the lens of local historical circumstance.

The situation was similar in Canada. In two interrelated papers, David Bercuson and Denis Smith show how Canada came to terms with its own traditional defense concerns in the changed circumstances of the post–1945 world. The emergence of the United States and the Soviet Union as competing superpowers, Bercuson shows, forced a geographic reorientation of Canadian defense. With the high arctic now a potential front line, Canada faced a dilemma. Its own assertions of Arctic sovereignty were threatened by U.S. requirements for comprehensive air defense. From 1945 to 1948, Canadian officials and politicians worked hard to discover a way in which both concerns could be met. In a careful examination of U.S.–Canadian discussions, Bercuson shows that Mackenzie King shrewdly avoided being rushed into a premature decision and finally settled upon a formula where joint U.S.–Canadian participation could satisfy the priorities of both nations.

If Bercuson sees the settling of the intertwined issues of Arctic sovereignty and U.S. defense as a triumph of moderation, Denis Smith sees Canada's entry into, and continuing membership in, NATO differently. For Smith, Canada's joining NATO was a continuation of traditional foreign policy: Canada's foreign relations, he asserts, had always operated "with the approval and protection of the United Kingdom and the United States." Further, he asserts that the creation of NATO was the result of fear, postwar exhaustion, the misapplication of history, and opportunist political calculation. Given this, Smith argues, Canada should reconsider its position. The changed circumstances of the 1980s require a changed foreign policy for Canada.

As the above papers make clear, the Cold War and defense defy simplistic explanations. For every country and every region, the circumstances after 1945 required different responses if their security was to be guaranteed. New military and diplomatic problems required changed thinking. Old explanations and answers had to be reconsidered to see if they still were valid. But even when they were not, the persistence of the past meant that *de novo* solutions rarely were found. Instead, most of the old problems simply took on new coloration. The past, as always, is prologue.

NOTE

1. Publications resulting from previous symposia are as follows: Peter Dennis and Adrian Preston (eds.), *Soldiers as Statesmen* (London, 1976); Barry Hunt and Adrian Preston (eds.), *War Aims and Strategic Policy in the Great War* (London, 1977); Adrian Preston (ed.), *General Staffs and Diplomacy Before the Second World War* (London, 1978); Ronald Haycock (ed.), *Regular Armies and Insurgency* (London, 1979); Edgar Denton III (ed.), *Limits of Loyalty* (Waterloo, Ontario, 1980); N.F. Dreisziger (ed.), *Mobilization for Total War* (Waterloo, Ontario, 1981); Keith Neilson and Roy A. Prete (eds.), *Coalition Warfare* (Waterloo, Ontario, 1984); Roy A. Prete and A. Hamish Ion (eds.), *Armies of Occupation* (Waterloo, Ontario, 1984); A. Hamish Ion and Barry D. Hunt (eds.), *War and Diplomacy Across the Pacific 1919–1952* (Waterloo, Ontario, 1988); and Ronald Haycock and Keith Neilson (eds.) *Men, Machines and War* (Waterloo, Ontario, 1988).

1

Cold War and Defense

Ernest R. May

THE SEVERAL FACES OF POLICY

Foreign policy has at least three dimensions–what is said; what is planned; and what is done. Defense policy is even more complicated, with at least six dimensions. What is said may be in a speech, publication, or piece of testimony. Alternatively, "declaratory" defense policy (to borrow Paul Nitze's term) may appear in manuals of military or naval doctrine.[1] What is planned may be in a war plan or in a budget. What is done may show as force posture or as actual force deployments. None of these six elements need fit neatly with any of the others.

Consider statements and doctrine. In the 1950s, speeches, testimony, and such described U.S. nuclear forces as existing to "meet attack,"[2] In Strategic Air Command (SAC) doctrine, they existed for preemption. SAC's commander, General Curtis LeMay, explained: "If I see that the Russians are amassing their planes for an attack, I'm going to knock the shit out of them before they take off the ground." To the protest, "But General LeMay, that's not national policy!" LeMay replied, "I don't care. It's my policy. That's what I'm going to do."[3]

Consider plans and budgets. During 1947–49 U.S. war plans assigned the navy the primary task of securing and supplying forward bases for bombers. The chief of naval operations not only endorsed this assignment; he fought for it. These plans presupposed a navy equipped for landing operations, antisubmarine warfare, and patrol service in narrow seas. The navy's budgets, however, provided primarily for carrier task forces designed to move rapidly in open ocean. Plans implied a policy of preparing to fight a European war. Budgets implied instead a policy of getting ready for a second war with Japan.[4]

Finally, consider force posture versus deployments: in that same period, long-range bombers dominated U.S. force posture. LeMay's Strategic Air Command was growing. Almost all other service elements were shrinking—including other parts of the air force. However, LeMay's operational forces consisted mainly of medium-range World War II B–29s based in California, Texas, and Louisiana. No newer, longer-range B–36 was completely ready for action until 1950. No SAC bomber could drop an atomic bomb on the Soviet Union until more than two weeks after the beginning of a war—by which time it was assumed that the Red Army would be outside Paris.[5] Posture bespoke readiness for what would be called "massive retaliation." Deployments suggested something more like Britain's defense policy of the 1920s and early 1930s—one assuming no major war within the next ten years.

Discussion of defense policy can focus on any of these dimensions. Grand arguments can arise by pitting evidence about one dimension against evidence about another. Debates about Soviet defense policy, for example, often have one party citing articles from Soviet military journals, while the other points to actual Soviet deployments. At least in the past, Soviet writings and Soviet actions seldom seemed consistent.[6] Here, an attempt will be made to keep these dimensions distinct.

For the critical question about defense policy, as about foreign policy, has to do with coherence. Each dimension is likely to have its own features. What is said publicly is not likely to be the same as what is planned privately. Action, when called for, often differs from what was planned or promised. Still, some sets of words, thoughts, and actions have more coherence than others. I will explore here the degree to which one can find coherence of vision or purpose in the defense policies of the superpowers during the first half-decade after World War II. Partly because I know more about it, partly because of huge differences in documentation, I will deal at length with the United States and only briefly with the Soviet Union.

A GOVERNMENT UNDERGOING TRANSFORMATION

The years around World War II form one of the great periods of change in U.S. political history. The only comparable periods are those of the War for Independence and the War between the States. The institutions from which defense policy emerged underwent transformation in 1945–50; so did accepted definitions of the national interests defense policy was supposed to serve.[7]

In these years, the U.S. government changed in three important respects. It became a government more oriented toward foreign than domestic affairs. It acquired a new class of managers and leaders. And it became, at the same time, a government of, by, and for large numbers of people not eligible to vote in U.S. elections.

As recently as the beginning of the 1930s, the national government had been small and relatively insignificant. President Calvin Coolidge remarked in the 1920s, "If the Federal Government should go out of existence, the common run of people would not detect the difference in the affairs of their daily life for a considerable length of time."[8] He was right. The national government did little besides handle mail, regulate immigration, collect tariffs, and try to enforce Prohibition. Only during the Great Depression did the government begin systematically to support farmers, regulate markets, mediate labor disputes, and aid the helpless and aged.

Only after World War II did the United States arm itself to deal with foreign nations. Previously it had maintained a respectable navy, but its army had been small. (In 1938 the United States had had a smaller army than Rumania.[9]) The U.S. diplomatic corps was new and only partly professional. Most ambassadors in major capitals qualified by making large campaign contributions.[10] Apart from a few ingenious cryptanalysts in the armed forces, the United States had no secret intelligence services.[11] The barons in Washington were the Secretaries of Agriculture, Labor, the Interior, and the Treasury. They received far more public attention than did the Secretaries of State, War, and the Navy. With World War II, this changed. The military establishment expanded, as did organizations concerned with foreign affairs.

By the 1950s the potentates in Washington included the Secretaries of State and Defense, the chiefs of staff, and the head of the CIA. Except for the Secretary of the Treasury, the chiefs of domestic agencies had become second-level officials.[12]

As of 1945 the federal government and the attentive public were just beginning to change orientation. No one knew then that they would not go back quickly to being domestically focused. Well into the 1950s, close watchers of American trends kept expecting a reversion to isolationism.[13]

POLITICIANS AND OFFICIALS

The change in the orientation of the government was accompanied by a change, perhaps even more significant, in the composition of its leadership.

Prior to World War II, government in the United States was dominated by politicians. Cities, counties, and states had career civil servants,. So did the national government. But power, such as it was, belonged to men (occasionally women) who won elections. In Washington, authority belonged to Presidents, members of Congress, and those who helped them get and keep their offices.

After World War II, power in Washington was often exercised by men or women with no experience of, and frequently with disdain for, elective politics. Sometimes they were government careerists; more often they were businessmen, bankers, lawyers, professors, or professionals of some other type.

This change bore some resemblance to a change sweeping all developed nations. In his great 1918 lecture "Politics as a Vocation," Max Weber characterized this change. Government had earlier been the province of hereditary elites. Now, Weber said, it had become increasingly the province of two new groups—professional politicians, and bureaucrats or professional administrators. But the change in the United States was distinctive, for the United States had been governed from the beginning by professional politicians, and the new group rising to share power did not consist primarily of bureaucrats.

"Politician" is, of course a loose term. It describes an array from John Quincy Adams and Harry Hopkins to Joe McCarthy and the White House aides sent to the penitentiary after Watergate. Still, it has some meaning. For the newly empowered nonpoliticians, we have no term at all. "Establishment" will not do. If the United States had an "establishment," it surely included such politicians as Franklin Roosevelt, Herbert Lehman, and Nelson Rockefeller. Another British category—the "official" as distinguished from the "minister"—comes closer. "Officials" think of themselves as servants of the crown or the state, above politics. They look down on "ministers," who are creatures of parties and elections.[14]

While British officials are civil servants, the Americans most nearly their equivalents are mostly what Richard Neustadt labels "in-and-outers." They are independent of, but at the same time dependent on, politicians. They have careers outside government. They qualify for office through expertise or business or professional reputation. If not in office, they have other, usually more profitable, ways of earning a living. They achieve office, however, because politicians appoint them. They can lose office if they side with the wrong politicians. And they cannot get knighthood. Nevertheless, for want of better, I borrow here the term "official" to designate American policymakers who cannot be classed as politicians.[15]

I do not wish to exaggerate either the precision of the distinction or the contrast with the past. I have in mind a difference as much in attitude as in personal history. Most politicians discussed in this essay had some engagement in political campaigning. All of them thought policy inseparable from electoral politics. They might talk about politics stopping at the water's edge, but they did not act as if they believed it. They seemed to regard approval by the electorate, sometimes just approval in public opinion polls, as an important test of policy—not necessarily the only or final test, but an important test.

Officials, by contrast, were not involved in elective politics—at least not zestfully so. If they took part in campaigns, it was as "issues" advisers. They believed that policy could and should be "above politics." They assumed that there were discernible national interests which politicians were likely to ignore or sacrifice for the sake of short-term domestic advantage. They thought the proper role for politicians and ordinary citizens was to be persuaded by officials, not to exercise persuasion of their own.

In a few cases, careers and attitudes were at odds. George Marshall was an official who thought much like a politician. A professional soldier, he never took part in a political campaign. He never would have. As Secretary of State in 1947–49, he sometimes seemed a prototypical official. He opposed the recognition of the state of Israel on the ground that doing so would injure U.S. interests in the Middle East. Attending a White House meeting where Presidential Counsel Clark Clifford argued the case for recognition, Marshall attacked the proposal as a "transparent dodge to win a few votes." In what Clifford characterized as "a righteous, goddamned Baptist tone," Marshall said, "Unless politics were involved, Mr. Clifford would not even be at this meeting."[16]

Most of the time, however, Marshall gauged decisions and policies less in terms of national interest than in terms of public support. He thought that a Communist victory in the Chinese civil war would be a calamity. He nevertheless opposed giving military aid to the Chinese Nationalists, saying: "It involves obligations and responsibilities on the part of this Government which I am convinced the American people would never knowingly accept."[17] Similarly, although he acknowledged strategic bombing to be almost the only immediate threat the United States could offer against the Soviet Union, he testified publicly to doubts about brandishing such a threat. He explained:

I think one of the great difficulties in regard to air power, and the American people, and their attitude toward life, is that its application involves so much of the loss of life of nonmilitary persons, children as well as grown people. That is almost unavoidable, and yet that is very, very terrible.

We reached the point in the last war, when we were so infuriated over the practices of the Japanese and of the Germans that the American people were willing to go through with it. I thought it was vital that they should, but it was a terrible thing to have to use that type of power. If you are confronted with the use of that type of power in the beginning of the war you are also confronted with a very certain reaction of the American people. They have to be driven very hard before they will agree to such a drastic use of force.[18]

Marshall later had second thoughts about this position. What provoked those thoughts was John Foster Dulles's argument that "the American people would crucify you if you did not use the bomb."[19] Most of the time— perhaps even when arguing that recognition of Israel seemed a bid for Jewish votes—Marshall exemplified what I think of as the perspective of the politician.

Richard Nixon took to the presidency some of the attitudes I associate with officials. His memoirs and those of his adviser, Henry Kissinger, have as a main theme the insensitivity of Congress and the public to national interests. One can perhaps argue that Nixon, although a professional politician, always had an official's attitude toward politics. He *earned* the nickname "Tricky Dick." The habits of his career contributed to his impeachment.

In general, however, an appetite for politics and a politician's attitude toward policy seem to me to have gone together. A distaste for politics (and politicians) has gone normally with the attitudes of an official.[20] One can see the contrast in men who are similar in other respects. Clark Clifford and Dean Acheson were both Washington lawyers; both served Harry Truman and professed to like him. But Clifford relished politics while Acheson did not, and the difference sometimes showed in policy advice.

In 1946, when Republican candidates such as Richard Nixon were trumpeting their anti-Communism, Clifford presented Truman a long memorandum. It argued that the President should tell the public that U.S. policy toward the Soviet Union "may determine whether or not there will be a third World War." The President should ask public support for maintaining the military power to deter further Soviet aggression, explaining that this military power consisted primarily of high technology—bombers and atomic and biological weapons. He should propose that the United States "support and assist all democratic countries which are in any way menaced or endangered by the U.S.S.R." He should make clear that this meant military support only in a last resort. He should emphasize forms of economic support serving as "effective demonstrations that capitalism is at least the equal of communism."[21]

The data in Clifford's memorandum came largely from officials. The recommendations were those of a politician: oversimplify the issue, excite the public, minimize potential costs, outflank the Republicans by being dramatically anti-Communist and pro-capitalist. There is no reason to think that Clifford said anything he did not believe. However, he could have written what he did without being utterly convinced of its truth.

Acheson, then Under-Secretary of State, was concurrently at work on a plan for voluntarily surrendering the U.S. atomic monopoly to the United Nations.[22] The plan may have been statesman-like. Had the Russians not turned it down, it would, however, have faced rough going in the Republican-dominated Congress that Clifford had feared and predicted.

Two decades later, Clifford would caution President Lyndon Johnson against Americanizing the Vietnam War. He did not couch his argument in national interest terms. He said to Johnson very privately, "I don't believe we can win in South Viet Nam. . . . If we lose 50,000 men there, it will be catastrophic in this country. Five years, billions of dollars, hundreds of thousands of men—this is not for us. . . . I cannot see anything but catastrophe for our nation in this area."[23] Acheson was among those arguing that national interest required defense of South Vietnam, almost regardless of U.S. domestic opinion. Among the "wise old boys" whom Johnson periodically consulted, Acheson was almost the last to conclude that the war's costs exceeded its benefits.[24]

Another illustrative pair are two of the Harvard professors who went to Washington with John Kennedy. Arthur Schlesinger, Jr., had something of a politician's outlook. He had earlier been an organizer, speechwriter, and campaigner. McGeorge Bundy had the outlook of an official. His previous exposure to electoral politics had been solely that of a behind-the-scenes adviser or platform-drafter. Schlesinger worried about what the public would think when and if it became known that Cuban exiles landing at the Bay of Pigs had been armed and trained by the CIA. It mattered to him that the chairman of the Senate Foreign Relations committee opposed the operation. Bundy worried lest revelations of CIA involvement create complications for pro-American elements in other Latin American governments. Once sure that the CIA had reframed the landing plan "so as to make it unspectacular and quiet, and plausibly Cuban in its essentials," he became a champion of it. Doubts voiced by a Senator did not impress him. Other officials, including Bundy's brother, felt indignant at being asked by the President to register reactions to the Senator's views.[25]

The gulf between politicians and officials is perhaps best evidenced by the example of W. Averell Harriman, a man who crossed the line. Ambassador to Britain, then Russia, during World War II, Harriman managed the vast European aid program of the Truman administration. He had all the attributes and attitudes of an official. In 1954 he ran for governor of New York and was elected. He tried unsuccessfully to become the Democratic candidate against Eisenhower in 1956. Under Kennedy and Johnson, he again held appointive posts in the State Department, but to the end of his days, the title he liked best was "governor."

Walter Isaacson and Evan Thomas, both of *Time* magazine, have written a collective biography entitled *The Wise Men*. Two of its central characters are Acheson and Harriman. The others are all prominent officials—Charles E. Bohlen and George F. Kennan, professional diplomats expert on the Soviet Union; Robert A. Lovett, a Wall Street banker who succeeded Acheson as Under-Secretary of State and was later Secretary of Defense; and John J. McCloy, a Wall Street lawyer who headed the World Bank, then was U.S. High Commissioner in occupied Germany, and who would later be called "chairman" of the U.S. Establishment. Isaacson and Thomas report what was said to them by the others about Harriman:

Most of Harriman's old colleagues . . . felt that he was cheapening himself, letting hubris compromise his principles. They believed that his moderate views on the Cold War came not from a sophisticated understanding of Soviet behavior but rather out of a desire to win over the liberal wing of the Democratic Party . . . McCloy attributed a 'definite change in [Harriman's] attitude' on the Cold War largely to 'political ambition.'... Lovett, determinedly apolitical himself, was privately contemptuous of his old friend's desire for elected office. 'Averell's a Democrat,' he would say, 'and a fool.' Acheson would tease Harriman about his career in politics, but, recalls his son-in-law..., there was a slight edge to his voice.[26]

The politician–official distinction is not uniquely applicable to the postwar era. In some respects, Alexander Hamilton had the outlook of an official. Certainly, John Hay did when, as ambassador to Britain and then Secretary of State, he bemoaned, at the turn of the century, the inability of politicians and the public to see the identity of interest between the United States and the United Kingdom. But, in Washington before World War II, officials were sports. During and after the war, they became a numerous and powerful class.

Some politicians perceived themselves in danger of being manipulated by officials. Harry Truman observed that "the General and the Admirals and the career men in government look upon the occupant of the White House as only a temporary nuisance who soon will be succeeded by another temporary occupant who won't find out what it is all about for a long time and then it will be too late to do anything about it."[27] The fear had basis, for most officials thought most politicians selfish, short-sighted, and unintelligent. But they could not do without each other. The politicians needed advice. They also needed competent agents to act for them. Officials needed delegations of authority and appropriations from public funds.

Postwar U.S. foreign and defense policy was partly a product of mutually suspicious interaction between politicians and officials. This essay describes some of that interaction.

NEW ROLES FOR NON-AMERICANS

A third change that came over the United States in this period was more remarkable and, in the long run, probably more important. Before World War II, the U.S. government had been a government of, for, and by people who for the most part lived in the United States or its territories. By the second half of the 1950s, it had become a government much more of, for, and by people inhabiting a global commonwealth-empire. To what extent the U.S. government had been or was to be an instrument of elites rather than of mass publics can be debated. Whatever the case, the constituencies to which the government responded broadened dramatically after 1945.

The United States had been recognized as a great power since the late nineteenth century. By the 1920s it was already by some margin the wealthiest country in the world. Owing to this fact, governments elsewhere paid close attention to what happened in Washington. In some respects, the United States, though formally nonentangled, was actually in the 1920s a dominant factor not only in western hemisphere affairs but in Western Europe and the Western Pacific. Up to World War II, the relations between other governments and the U.S. government nevertheless remained inter-governmental (or interinstitutional, as, for example, between European central banks and the Federal Reserve Bank of New York).[28]

After World War II an additional set of relationships developed. Some noncitizens began to play active and important roles in Washington decision-making. In part this was because U.S. voters took interest in foreign places. The *New York Times* index is suggestive. For 1955 that index had three times as many entries for Otto Suhr, then lord mayor of Berlin, as for Elmer Robinson, the mayor of San Francisco, a U.S. city of comparable size. It had a third again more entries for Ngo Dinh Diem, the prime minister of South Vietnam, than for George M. Leader, the governor of Pennsylvania, even though Pennsylvania was nearby and had about the population of South Vietnam and Leader was talked of as a possible presidential nominee.

In larger part, the new relationships existed because of the new roles of officials. Career diplomats, military and naval officers, intelligence officers, and in-and-outers from banks and big law firms generally knew and cared more about the likes of Suhr and Diem than the likes of Robinson and Leader.

In still larger part, however, the new relationships resulted from initiatives by foreigners taking advantage of a political system that was comparatively open. The U.S. government had its origins, after all, in a treaty of alliance. The Articles of Confederation had been a compact of sovereign states fighting a common enemy. The Constitution of 1789 retained characteristics of a treaty. Although Article V made acts of the national government "the supreme law of the land," most of the attributes of sovereignty stayed with individual states. One effect of federalism was to legitimize political action by non-voters or noncitizens. New Yorkers were entitled to meddle in the affairs of Pennsylvania, and vice versa.

Though statesmen of the new United States worried about foreign powers worming into U.S. councils, they could not find satisfactory safeguards. For a time, pro-British and pro-French Americans neutralized one another. The Alien and Sedition Acts produced reactions that discredited most efforts at statutory control. The comparative isolation of the United States after the Napoleonic Wars made the original problem seem academic. Then the arrival of large numbers of immigrants confused distinctions between domestic and foreign politics. The Irish question, for example, became a subject of debate not only in Congress but in state legislatures and city councils. Upper-class Americans, generally not partial to the Irish, saw nothing wrong with British subjects lobbying to block resolutions for Irish independence. Despite periodic manifestations of xenophobia, neither the national government nor state or local governments significantly limited political activity by noncitizens. It was to be 1975, for example, before Congress forbade presidential candidates to accept campaign contributions from foreign citizens or governments.[29]

After 1945 many people in many parts of the world perceived that their lives could be affected significantly by actions of the United States. Some discovered (or rediscovered) the extraordinary openness of the U.S. political system. American diplomats tended to become advocates for the countries in which they were stationed—nearly all diplomats do. But some U.S. diplomats had unusual opportunities for advocacy. In-and-outers could lobby "ministers" in ways not open to diplomats confined within traditional Foreign Offices.

Neither were diplomats the only channels. In occupied countries, military governors became advocates. Soon, economic aid missions began to proliferate. Alliances then bred military missions. Members of these missions began to behave, like diplomats, as spokesmen for their clients. The new U.S. "intelligence community" established foreign stations. These stations became points of contact for foreigners outside the normal intergovernmental ambit—members of opposition parties, labor organizers, student leaders, dissidents, and the like.[30] Not all Americans abroad were officials. The American Federation of Labor, for example, developed a network of relationships with non–Communist labor unions in Europe.[31] These various missions, public and private, all served as nerve endings, communicating to Washington the wishes and feelings of foreigners who cared about what Washington did.

More and more U.S. newspapers, magazines, and broadcasting networks either established foreign bureaus or increased their budgets of foreign news. For foreigners, the U.S. news media provided means of getting directly to the central nervous system of the U.S. government. If the embassy, aid mission, military mission, or CIA station could not get the attention of decision-makers, a well-placed story in *The New York Times* or *Time* or *Newsweek* would. With U.S. newspapers and news broadcasts increasingly featuring stories from abroad, Congressmen and other politicians increasingly traveled to those places, not only to see them at first hand but to be reported doing so. This greatly enlarged access to the U.S. decision-making system by foreigners.

It was, of course, reciprocal. Even when most amiable and most unselfish, these Americans represented what Barbara Ward Jackson would later characterize as the elephant in the bathtub. The other bathers had to be sensitive to every move. But, at least from evidence thus far open, it does not appear that the new relationships were often those of dictators and dictated-to. In fact, Europeans probably had more influence on U.S. policies than the reverse. Apart from the comparative openness of the U.S. political system, there was the fact that Europeans cared more. London spent more hours thinking about Washington than Washington did about London. The disproportion widened with disproportions in power.

U.S. foreign and defense policies were products of interaction between American politicians and officials. The ways in which both groups perceived issues and options were greatly influenced by non-Americans who became, for practical purposes, participants in U.S. governmental processes.

NEW DEFINERS OF NATIONAL INTEREST

Harry Truman's presidency magnified the transitional character of the period. He had been Senator from Missouri before becoming Vice-President and then, suddenly, President. His constituents had not traditionally shown much interest in national, let alone foreign, affairs. His own interests matched better the earlier, domestically-oriented government than the newer one growing up around him. He had been 50 years old when he first saw federal programs touch the lives of large numbers of people whom he knew. Until 1950 he continued to cherish the hope of concentrating on expansion of those programs. His preferred agenda was his "Fair Deal." He disclosed what he most cared about in foreign affairs by "Point Four" of his 1949 inaugural address, calling for efforts to lift levels of production and standards of living in less developed countries.[32]

Although the National Security Act of 1947 created a National Security Council to coordinate policy and strategy, not much coordination took place until after 1950. Truman himself had doubts about the wisdom of creating the Council. He suspected that it might infringe on presidential prerogatives. He acquiesced because it came to him as part of a package that offered hope of making the military budget more manageable. He did not for some time allow the Council to develop independent staff; neither did he have any of his White House staff become expert on issues in foreign policy or defense.

Truman did use the budget as a management tool. Although the Bureau of the Budget provided him systematic staff support, this helped him more in dealing with domestic programs than with foreign policies or defense policies.[33] In contrast to FDR, Truman liked tidiness. He appreciated officials putting before him issues he could decide. That gave officials more initiative and control than in FDR's time, when no one—sometimes not even the President—knew when or how or by whom decisions might be made. The national government turning more toward external affairs was headed by a politician old-fashioned in outlook but with a managerial style congenial to officials.[34]

CONGRESSIONAL POLITICIANS

For the most part, the other elected politicians in key posts shared Truman's outlook. On Capitol Hill, the outside world concerned chiefly the Senate Foreign Relations and House Foreign Affairs committees. Defense belonged to Military Affairs and Naval Affairs committees in each of the two houses. (These merged after 1947 into Armed Services committees.) Scores of other committees competed for legislative time and for money. A few cared about aspects of foreign or defense policy—tariffs, shipping, and immigration, for example. Traditionally powerful committees interested themselves only in matters domestic—post offices, public works, the judiciary, and so on. Appropriations committees looked hard at all spending.

Since Congress obeyed a strict seniority system, the dominant members of committees tended to be those with long service. This meant that most leaders of committees concerned with foreign and defense affairs had joined them before World War II. In those days, foreign affairs had not attracted a lot of press or constituent interest; Senators and Representatives had not competed vigorously for seats.

On the Senate Foreign Relations Committee, the senior Republican was Arthur Vandenberg of Michigan. A one-time arch-isolationist, he had been born again after Pearl Harbor. Heavy in body, humor, speech, and every other dimension, Vandenberg alternately bored and exasperated the officials who had to deal with him. A sketch of the Senator, written by Acheson, is revealing of both men.[35] In it, Acheson describes

a ritual of statesmanship that I was to experience many times and always with fascination: Senator Vandenberg, faced with a proposal to take a step into the strange and frightening postwar world, invariably began by resisting the proposal. He declared the end unattainable, the means harebrained, and the cost staggering. . . . [T]his first phase, the phase of opposition, usually lasted through one meeting and sometimes longer. . . . Then followed the period of gestation. The proposal grew and developed within him. . . . [T]his gave time for the country, the Republicans, and the Senator to get used to the idea and for the weight of supporting fact to have its effect.

At this stage Senator Vandenberg was convinced but not committed. Before that occurred, one further step remained to be taken. We called it variously 'applying the trademark,' or 'determining the price.' This meant either stamping the proposal with a Vandenberg brand, or exacting from the administration a concession which he thought politically important.

Lavishly flattered and constantly cajoled by Acheson, Lovett, and other officials, Vandenberg became legislative sponsor for many of their proposals. He did so only after applying to them, as Acheson perceived, tests as to their acceptability in his caucus, chamber, party, and country. In the process, he often not only simplified the rationale but shifted its emphasis toward visible short-term threats or benefits.

This was partly a matter of calculation. Partly, however, it was a result of Vandenberg's having internalized the criteria of judgment he supposed to be prevalent among the voters to whom he answered. Early in the Cold War, he wrote, not to a constituent, but to his wife of 30 years:

I want to be scrupulously fair and reasonable with [the Russians] . . . : but I want to be relentlessly firm in our insistence upon these American positions. No more Munichs! If it is impossible for us to get along with the Soviets on such a basis, the quicker we find it out the better. America must behave like the *Number One World Power* which she is. Ours must be the world's moral leadership—or the world won't have any.[36]

The senior Democrat on the Foreign Relations Committee was Tom Connally of Texas. He let his white hair curl over his collar and affected a wide black hat, black string tie, and oversize black jacket. Physically, he was the model for "Senator Throttlebottom" in Al Capp's contemporaneous "Lil' Abner" comic strip.

Connally's vanity matched Vandenberg's. A constant trial for officials trying to butter up both men was the fact that either would take offense if he learned that the other had been consulted first. As compared with Vandenberg, Connally had a sharper and lighter sense of humor. Acheson records that, at the annual dinner of a private club, he once heard Connally parody one of his own Senate speeches.[37] But Connally behaved and thought much as did Vandenberg. Explaining why the United States should lend money to Britain after the war, Connally described Britain as "all crippled up, got one eye half gouged out and one ear bit off,." Before the wincing eyes of Europe-centered officials, Connally advertised the North Atlantic Treaty as "but the logical extension of the principle of the Monroe Doctrine."[38]

Because of all the coaching they received, Vandenberg and Connally probably came closer than any of the older Congressional generation to appropriating the logic of officialdom. Their committee colleagues were more given than they to justifying action either in terms of averting immediate danger (usually war or Communism—in the United States) or winning more or less immediate gain.

SECRETARIES OF STATE: BYRNES TO MARSHALL TO ACHESON

At the beginning of the postwar era, prewar conditions seemed likely to return, at least in respect to the roles of politicians and officials. Truman, the politician in the White House, answerable to those politicians on the Hill, named James F. Byrnes his vicar for foreign affairs. The then British ambassador advised London that Byrnes was "a born politician . . . responsive to the smallest variation of the popular, Congressional, and sectional mood of his country."[39] While Byrnes abhorred Communism and disliked the Russians he met, he assumed that the U.S. public would soon lose interest in foreign affairs. So he sought the best deals available.

This irritated officials. They believed that U.S. national interests required sustained concern with European affairs. Congress and the masses needed, in their view, to be educated and led, not followed. Worse yet, Byrnes paid little deference to official expertise. He refused to cable home reports on conferences aboard. "I might tell the President sometime what happened," he explained to an aide, "but I'm never going to tell those little bastards in the State Department anything about it."[40]

Byrnes failed, however, to keep Truman's confidence. His secretiveness led him sometimes to keep the President as well as the State Department in the dark. His frequent absences from Washington to attend foreign ministers' meetings meant that he could not keep watch on his officials. They used every opportunity to hint to the President, members of the White House staff, and members of Congress that, while Byrnes might have been a success as a Senator and as FDR's "deputy President," he was not up to the complexities of being Secretary of State.

Travel abroad meanwhile dulled Byrnes's sense of domestic currents. He was late in perceiving the anti-Communist tide. Although he began quickly to sound tougher toward the Soviets, it was too late. Both Vandenberg and Connally had begun to warn Truman that they thought Byrnes was about to "give away . . . our 'trading stock'."[41] When the Republicans swept into control of Congress, Byrnes would probably have had to go, even had Truman continued to think of him as his "able and conniving Secretary of State" and to feel, as in 1945, that the "smart boys in the State Department, as usual, are against the best interests of the U.S."[42]

Facing those large Republican majorities and that anti-Communist tide, Truman decided to replace Byrnes with General Marshall. Chief of staff of the U.S. Army during World War II, Marshall had recently led an unsuccessful effort to mediate the Chinese civil war. Truman, in company with many others, venerated Marshall. He called him "the greatest living American," then went even farther, saying he was "the great one of the age."[43] For two years, Truman displayed his decisiveness by resolutely supporting practically every recommendation that Marshall made. (The only major exception was recognition of Israel.)[44]

After being elected in his own right, Truman accepted Marshall's pleas of ill health and allowed him to retire. He replaced him with Acheson. A polished, stylish, profoundly Anglophile Washington lawyer, Acheson got along well with other officials but not, as a rule, with men who had been elected to office. As one of his biographers writes, he "looked on Congress as a necessary distraction—necessary because only Congress could provide the dollars for the nation's defense, a distraction because of the need to take valuable time explaining to Congress why particular steps in foreign policy were essential."[45]

Acheson excepted President Truman. He respected not only the office but the man. "I have a constituency of one," he would say. He showed a loyalty that Truman repaid in kind.[46] But the counsel Acheson took and the counsel he gave Truman derived from other officials. This was the implication of his often-quoted observation that "the springs of policy bubble up; they do not trickle down."[47] For the balance of his administration, Truman followed Acheson's advice, much as he had earlier followed Marshall's.

FRONTIERS IN THE EASTERN MEDITERRANEAN

To a much greater extent than before the war, officials defined national interests. The ones who did so were mostly in the State Department. Soviet experts led by Kennan and Bohlen, Europeanists, and other Foreign Service officers concerned with the Middle East developed the thesis that the United States had an important interest in preventing the expansion of the Soviet empire.

It would not have been easy to predict that Truman would follow this advice. The British had long held a line against Russia in the Eastern Mediterranean and Middle East. The United States had traditionally done little in that area apart from defending U.S. companies—mostly against Britain. Straight-line projection suggested postwar Washington–London rows over British discrimination against U.S. oil companies. Instead, when officials advised Truman that the historic British strategic interests in the region were now U.S. interests, he accepted this appraisal and acted on it.[48]

Truman did not accept the advice blindly. Acheson tells in his memoirs of taking to Truman a State Department–Pentagon recommendation for a near-ultimatum to Moscow. Some general present asked in Acheson's ear whether the President understood that the note could lead to war. Acheson describes what happened when he asked the question aloud:

The President took from a drawer of his desk a large map of the Middle East and Eastern Mediterranean and asked us to gather around behind him. He then gave us a brief lecture on the strategic importance of the area and the extent to which we must be prepared to go to keep it free from Soviet domination. When he finished none of us doubted he understood fully all the implications of our recommendations.[49]

Though not easily impressed by anyone, Acheson later declared himself "awed" by Truman's knowledge. He remarks in his memoir that the Soviets "followed the route of invasion by barbarians against classical Greece and Rome and later of the czars to warm water." He closes: "From Thermopylae to the Crimea the responses to pressure at these points had been traditional. If some Americans found their history rusty, neither the British nor the President did."[50] The episode helped cement the Acheson—Truman relationship.

Although Truman did know the history to which Acheson referred, his reading of it may not have been the same. He felt that throughout history a major cause of war had been competition for waterways. Growing up near the Mississippi not long after the Civil War may have had an influence. At Potsdam he had expressed a Wilsonian-Rooseveltian interest in free international waterways. He had spoken for Russia's having access to the sea. It outraged him that the Soviets not only gave him no support but seemed bent now on closing the Dardanelles and monopolizing the mouth of the Danube. That accounted at least in part for his telling Acheson and the others, that he was prepared to oppose the Soviets "to the end."[51]

A month later, after the Soviets had begun to back down, Truman read and approved a speech to be given by his Secretary of Commerce, Henry Wallace. In that speech, delivered before a largely pro-Soviet audience in Madison Square Garden, Wallace said:

[T]o make Britain the key to our foreign policy would be, in my opinion, the height of folly. . . .

Make no mistake about it—the British imperialistic policy in the Near East alone, combined with Russian retaliation, would lead the United States straight to war unless we have a clearly-defined and realistic policy of our own. . . .

[W]e are reckoning with a force which cannot be handled successfully by a 'Get tough with Russia' policy. 'Getting tough' never brought anything real and lasting— whether for schoolyard bullies or businessmen or world powers. The tougher we get, the tougher the Russians will get. . . .

On our part, we should recognize that we have no more business in the *political* affairs of Eastern Europe than Russia has in the *political* affairs of Latin America, Western Europe, and the United States.[52]

When officials protested and newspaper and magazine editorials asked if the administration were reversing policy, Truman claimed not to have read the speech carefully. He fired Wallace. However, Wallace had probably reported truthfully when he said that Truman had, in fact, read the text carefully and commented frequently, "That's right" or "Yes, that is what I believe." Until others pointed it out, the President could well have failed to see anything wrong with Wallace's sentiments. It is unlikely, however, that he would have failed to take exception had the text expressed equally clearly the sentiments of the State Department's Near Eastern experts: that in the Near and Middle East, "British and American interests . . . were synonymous."[53] Truman, the politician, had reacted against what he saw as Soviet bullying, inconsistent with UN principles. He was still far from accepting the officials' notion that the United States now had, like Britain earlier, a permanent frontier in the Eastern Mediterranean.

In 1947 Truman moved a step farther in that direction. He proclaimed publicly that the United States had a major interest in protecting both Turkey and Greece from Soviet encroachment and from Communist subversion. One sees in the process the new roles of both officials and foreigners. Officials put forward the same arguments as before. They now added Greece, where Communist-led guerrillas, supplied from neighboring Yugoslavia, were trying to unseat a British-backed monarchy. These officials proposed that the President go to Congress and ask for money so that the United States could replace Britain as chief outside financier for the Turkish and Greek regimes.

U.S. officials made this proposal in large part at the prompting of friends and acquaintances in London. In Britain, both officials and ministers had begun to see more clearly the toll taken by six years of war. A government White Paper acknowledged early in 1946, "The central fact is that we have not enough resources to do all that we want to do. We have barely enough to do what we must do."[54] The Treasury pressed for cutting foreign commitments—for example, to Turkey and Greece. The Foreign Office resisted. Worsening economic conditions, aggravated by winter storms, made increasingly attractive the alternatives of pushing the burden onto an ally. For almost three centuries, Britain had had a tradition of using her always limited resources primarily for leverage within coalitions. Not since the thirteenth century had Britons made up more than 10 percent of the armies fighting British wars on the continent.

By January 1947, Treasury, Foreign Office, and Cabinet had come together. Prime Minister Clement Attlee and his inner Cabinet had just agreed that Britain's future as a great power depended on its having nuclear weapons of its own. The cost of nuclear independence promised to be horrendous. There was almost no question of also carrying on support of Turkey and Greece. The Foreign Office proceeded along lines suggested earlier by the Joint Planning Staff of the Chiefs of Staff Committee—that it should be "an essential feature of our general policy to associate the Americans as closely as possible in the defence of our interests throughout the world, and particularly in the defence of the Middle East."[55] British representatives in Washington called the State Department to say that if Turkey and Greece were to get money and military aid in future, it would have to be from the United States.

When U.S. officials concluded that the British were in earnest, they developed the proposal that went to the White House. One result was the famous Truman Doctrine message of March 12, 1947. The other result was eventual action by Congress granting $400 million in aid funds and authorizing military advisers.

The drafting of the Truman Doctrine illustrates some of the problems inherent in the transition from a government dominated by politicians to one in which politicians shared power with officials. Memoranda exchanged among officials took for granted the identity of U.S. and British interests. The surviving documents include notes on a meeting of Marshall and Acheson with the Secretaries of War and the Navy. All the department heads were officials, and all were accompanied by officials. They agreed without debate that "the independence of Greece and Turkey were of vital importance to the U.S. strategic position." The problem on which they focused was "the general difficulty being encountered in obtaining necessary appropriations from Congress to back up U.S. world responsibilities."[56]

The President seems not to have questioned his officials about their reasoning. The fact that Marshall endorsed the proposal may have been enough in itself to convince Truman. The alternative of saying that Turkey and Greece were Britain's smoldering chestnuts had pretty much disappeared, given the outcry against the Wallace speech and the sweep by anti-Communist candidates in the 1946 elections. There remained, however, questions about the reasoning to be laid before Congress and the public.

An illuminating moment came when, in a morning meeting at the White House, Congressional leaders were given the administration's proposals. Marshall, seldom given to overstatement, told the legislators that, if the United States did not aid Greece and Turkey,

Soviet domination might . . . extend over the entire Middle East to the borders of India. The effect of this upon Hungary, Austria, Italy and France cannot be overestimated. It is not alarmist to say that we are faced with the first crisis of a series which might extend Soviet domination to Europe, the Middle East and Asia.[57]

Even with such a warning from such a source, the legislators remained unmoved. Or so Acheson thought. "No time was left for measured appraisal," he says in his memoirs. With passion, he declared that, if Greece were allowed to fall, the "infection" would spread throughout Europe and Africa: "The Soviet Union was playing one of the greatest gambles in history at minimal cost. . . . We and we alone were in a position to break up the play." The Republican leaders then promised to support the program, provided it was presented to the public as Acheson had presented it to them.[58] Politicians liked to have national interests defined in terms of great and immediate peril.

Truman couched his message to Congress in universalistic terms—of support for freedom against tyranny. Acheson and Clifford had been the principal drafters. The language made some officials uncomfortable (notably George Kennan), but this seemed the price that officials had to pay to get politicians to act in the national interest. And it had to be paid over and over, for before Congress acted, officials had to sound the Truman Doctrine theme not only in hearings but in countless specially organized meetings with editors, businessmen, and others supposed to influence or speak for the public from which politicians derived their authority.

The differences between officials' reasoning and politicians' reasoning is evident in records of secret executive sessions of the Senate Foreign Relations Committee. They show Senators sympathetic to officials' recommendations but groping for grounds on which to give approval. Vandenberg said to his colleagues that the fall of Greece and Turkey "would establish a chain reaction around the world which could very easily leave us isolated in a Communist-dominated earth." Connally said, "Unless we do something there we might as well just tell them [the Russians] to go to it wherever they can." Walter George, a Democrat from Georgia, floated the suggestion that the United States and the Soviet Union were in a worldwide contest for raw materials. Bourke Hickenlooper, a Republican from Iowa, talked of Communism, like Nazism, "beginning this thrusting movement, this feeling movement." Hickenlooper asked, "Are we not up against the question of resisting this thing wherever it begins to poke its finger?" Elbert Thomas, a Democrat from Utah, declared, "I am opposed to any bottling up theory. . . . [W]e want to do for Turkey and for Greece what is good for the Turkish people and for the Greek people, and what is good for ourselves." Henry Cabot Lodge, Jr., a Republican from Massachusetts, used the terminology of officials but in his own way: "I think 'strategic' measure is a good word for it," he said of the administration recommendation, "and in my experience, whenever you put it to the American people that this is a policy that is in their national interest, you will get support." To illustrate, however, Lodge jumped immediately to the observation that "with modern weapons we are not far away from anybody any more."[59]

Officials and politicians agreed about what to do. It is not clear that, as yet at least, they agreed why.

FRONTIERS IN EUROPE AND BEYOND

Officials also redefined U.S. interests in Europe. In 1944 Roosevelt and Churchill had initialed the Morgenthau Plan, calling for the permanent emasculation of Germany. Roosevelt had backed off in face of protests from some of the nonpoliticians whom he had recruited for his wartime national government. Secretary of War Henry Stimson actually shook his finger in the President's face, reproaching him for disregarding how much postwar Europe would need what Germany could produce.[60] Just how much economic rebuilding the Germans would be allowed nevertheless remained unclear. Even within the State Department and army bureaucracies, tension persisted between men bent on prosecuting war criminals and breaking up cartels and other men coping with legions of the hungry and homeless.

Gradually, the consensus began to favor pushing German economic recovery. Major Nazi leaders had been tried and either executed or jailed. Americans on the scene thought less about what had happened in the past and more about problems of the present. Their concern increased as they saw a distant Congress reduce appropriations for occupied areas and as they saw the French and Russians strip their occupation zones of food, tools, and other necessities.

Appeals from the U.S. military commanders in Germany jibed with the strategic reasoning of officials at home. Some officials in Washington held that Europe had suffered a series of civil wars. The United States had been drawn into both of the last such wars. Europeans and Americans shared an interest that no such war occur again, but previous wars taught that victory bred vengefulness. Europe needed now a peace that would not beget grievances—one that would knit Western Europe together.

Again, one sees both officials and foreigners playing large roles. The theme of European unity had been sounded for years by Jean Monnet. In travels through North America before the war, representing his family's wine and brandy interests, Monnet had made friends with men who were to be powerful officials in postwar America, among them Acheson, Lovett, McCloy, and Harriman. In 1947 and afterward, Monnet badgered these friends to promote European unity. They agreed with his goal, as did most Europeanists in the U.S. bureaucracy.

When the severe winter of 1946–47 exposed the feebleness of Western Europe, the idea of the Marshall Plan began to take form in the State Department. British Foreign Secretary Ernest Bevin organized a European response which, when analyzed, added up to a request for between $15 and $20 billion in aid.[61]

Tendencies in U.S. electoral politics were still unclear. Henry Wallace had declared himself a presidential candidate. He criticized the whole of U.S. foreign policy since the death of FDR. The government would better serve the interests of Americans, Wallace argued, if it left Europeans to work out their own accommodations with the Soviet Union. Senator Robert A. Taft of Ohio, the leading figure on the right wing of the Republican Party, also argued against aiding Europeans. He took the ground that they were no longer worth rescuing. The United States, Taft said, should concern itself primarily with the western hemisphere.

While no one expected Wallace to win, some forecasters thought he might get enough votes to affect the outcome. An early 1948 Gallup poll gave him 7 percent of the prospective vote. On the Republican side, many expected Taft to be the nominee. That possibility remained lively until the third ballot of the Party convention in Philadelphia in June. Given the Republican congressional sweep in 1946 and plummeting poll ratings for Truman and other Democrats, the Republican nominee seemed almost sure to be the next President.[62] In the winter of 1947–48, well-informed Washingtonians had reason to be skeptical about the administration's ability to get the enormous appropriations required to fund the Marshall Plan.

A series of events then helped the administration's cause. After Communists in February seized complete control of Czechoslovakia, Truman went in person before a joint session of Congress to deliver a "Special Message on the Threat to the Freedom of Europe." Abandoning the generalities of the Truman Doctrine, he accused "the Soviet Union and its agents" of having "destroyed the independence and democratic character of a whole series of nations in Eastern and Central Europe." He continued: "It is this ruthless course of action, and the clear design to extend it to the remaining free nations of Europe, that have brought about the critical situation in Europe today." So saying, he asked for prompt action on funding the Marshall Plan. Noting Western European moves toward a defensive military alliance, Truman also asked for gestures showing willingness to support that alliance if war came.[63]

Congress voted almost everything the administration requested. It provided money for the European Recovery Program, gave the Pentagon a supplemental appropriation, and endorsed a resolution not only applauding the European alliance but promising "association . . . by constitutional process."[64]

With regard to Germany, the French had meanwhile begun to cooperate with the Americans and British. The three Western powers issued new currency. They in other ways acted to boost German agricultural and industrial production and to show that they would not let the Soviets frustrate this effort. The Soviets showed their continuing opposition most dramatically by cutting off land communication with West Berlin. For ten months, from June 1948 to April 1949, until Stalin finally ended this blockade, Westerners airlifted supplies to their zones in the city.

By 1949 U.S. national interest had come to be defined as more than just the prevention of another Western European civil war. That, to be sure, remained central. It underpinned everything done in 1949–50 to give West Germany self-government, to make it a full participant in the European recovery program, and to foster economic and political cooperation. Most U.S. officials would have urged that the United States so define its national interest, even had there been no East–West conflict. Some older hands had actually urged such a definition of national interest back in the 1920s, when the Soviet Union had been pursuing "socialism in one country." But the extent of active U.S. involvement—the guiding role in Bonn first of General Lucius Clay and then of McCloy; the assistance lent Monnet and his allies by Harriman, David Bruce, and others in U.S. diplomatic and aid missions in Paris and London; and the provision of billions of dollars—was justified to politicians by themselves, and by politicians to the electorate, less in terms of simply preserving peace and order in Western Europe than in terms of fending off a Soviet or Communist threat to the United States itself.

In general the new definitions of U.S. interests corresponded exactly with those of Europe-centered and more or less Anglophile officials. Despite conferences and treaties and a good deal of high-level visitation, Latin America lost the prominence it had had prior to World War II. Despite special missions by Marshall and others and a great deal of rhetoric invoking "the open door," Asia also got short shrift. When Mao's victory over Chiang produced the greatest-ever increase in the world's number of Communists, politicians pressed officials as to why they seemed so unconcerned. By 1950 officials had begun to respond. Statements by Acheson and lesser State Department spokesmen reintroduced some of the universalism of the Truman Doctrine message. Acheson's famous National Press Club speech of early 1950, remembered chiefly for putting South Korea outside the U.S. "security perimeter," was actually intended as proof of administration concern about Asia.[65]

There was some incongruity between words and actions. Words aimed primarily at domestic audiences stressed ideological differences and dangers to Americans themselves. Actions reflected the perceptions of interests dominant among officials. The first interest was a balance of power in Europe much as Britain might have maintained had it not been so weakened by the war. The objective was to prevent any continental nation—in this case, the Soviet Union—from controlling the continent of Europe or the seas bordering it. The second interest and objective was a reconstructed Europe at peace with itself.

What created an appearance of harmony was the increased use by both politicians and officials of the phrase "national security." Politicians usually eschewed terms such as "balance of power" and "strategic interest," Lodge's example to the contrary notwithstanding. Officials for the most part found it uncomfortable to talk, at least among themselves, about defending democracy, freedom, or capitalism. Clifford had wanted the Truman Doctrine message to call for protecting free enterprise and to say that Americans' own freedoms were in immediate peril, but Acheson had edited out all such lines. "National security" could have one set of meanings for politicians, and another for officials. It gave them common ground without requiring that they confront their differences. The term only began to cause trouble if turned around, for the possibility of national *insecurity* brought in questions of defense policy. And postwar U.S. defense policy took form much more slowly than foreign policy.

THE PENTAGON'S PREOCCUPATIONS

During the early postwar years, all forms of defense policy were by-products. U.S. military leaders had other preoccupations. They had to disassemble wartime forces and establish new routines for peacetime. At the same time, they debated both the creation of a separate Air Force and "unification." They faced daunting questions about service roles and missions. Worst of all, they had to make decisions, large and small, about money. How much? For which service? From whom within each service?

Demobilizing the armed forces was almost as hard as mobilizing them, yet it had to be done in months, not years. The navy, for example, had to sell off nearly 4,000 ships and mothball 2,000 others. It also had to shut down 84 shipyards.[66] Of 12 million men and women in uniform, 11 million had to be released. The ones most needed, not only to run occupation regimes but to manage demobilization, were long-serving veterans. They, however, had the best claims for preference in being sent home. Even though the services had given high priority to making demobilization more orderly than it had been after World War I, soldiers and sailors in all theaters protested its slowness. There were reports of riots, even of mutinies. Servicemen sent letters to U.S. newspapers; some took out paid ads.[67] Until mid–1946, when most draftees had been mustered out, demobilization dominated thinking in the War and Navy Departments.

In the transition from war to peace, the men at the top of the armed services had to deal with details that at another time they might have delegated to others. General Dwight D. Eisenhower succeeded Marshall as chief of staff of the army. Partly lest he be seen to favor his own theater, he had to spend inordinate amounts of time deciding personally on the location of battle monuments. He also had to take on himself decisions involving breaks with prewar traditions. One example was his ruling that "the time has come to eliminate animals from the Army."[68] Also, he and his navy, army, and air force counterparts were war heroes. Eisenhower received every day an average of 700 personal letters that he thought deserved responses. Chester W. Nimitz, who had led the naval war against Japan and was now chief of naval operations, was so often asked for his autograph that he carried pocketfuls of pre-signed cards. He could not go out in public without being mobbed. Once, a crowd—mostly female—pursued him into a men's room. He had to give a speech of thanks standing on a toilet. Little wonder that, as Eisenhower lamented to his staff, no one had time to think about policy.[69]

After demobilization ceased to be such a preoccupation and the war became more and more a matter of memory, the service chiefs still found it hard to focus on policy. Too much of their time and thought had to go to controversy over how the military establishment should be organized.

One question was whether there should be an independent air force. Army fliers wanted a separate service, equal (at least) to the army and navy. During the 1920s General William ("Billy") Mitchell had been courtmartialed and forced out of uniform partly for overzealousness in this cause. Other, more tactful officers had succeeded in getting the army's air service upgraded. It became the army air corps, then in World War II the army air forces (AAF). In addition to supporting ground forces, the AAF had waged its own strategic bombing campaigns. Now, its officers believed it was entitled to independence like that of the British Royal Air Force.

Most ground force generals no longer objected. Many of them hoped, however, that the new service would be part of a unified Department of National Defense. Some army officers had championed unification even before the time of "Billy" Mitchell. Pearl Harbor had helped this cause. Many Americans thought the surprise attack had succeeded because the U.S. army and navy did not cooperate. Congressional investigations of the war effort also helped. Time and again, they uncovered inefficiency and waste attributable to a lack of coordination between the services. The chairman of the chief investigating committee had been Senator Harry S. Truman. As President, Truman not only supported unification; he put high on his priority list reshaping "the antiquated defense setup."[70]

Although most army fliers were willing to accept some type of unification if that were part of the price for independence, naval officers, without notable exception, denounced the idea. Some did so with "Billy" Mitchell passion. The result was an interservice war that consumed nearly all the energies not consumed by demobilization. This war went on with intermittent fury through most of 1945–50.

THE SERVICES' QUARRELS WITH EACH OTHER

While most specifics of the unification controversy can be ignored here, the themes cannot. Officers began with differing views about the weapons and tactics best suited for uncertain contingencies. Debate intensified these differences. Opinion became matters of dogma. Openmindedness became heresy, punishable at promotion or assignment time. Every element in every type of policy—statements, doctrines, plans, budgets, postures, deployments—felt the effects of the war the services waged against one another.

The most ferocious fighting concerned airplanes at sea. Many army fliers believed that the new air force should control all aircraft, whether on land or at sea. One of the Congressional committees studying unification took testimony from General George C. Kenney, who had commanded bomber forces in the Southwest Pacific. Kenney said:

Any arbitrary assignment of air responsibility over water areas to the Navy and over land areas to the Army or the Air Arm, completely negates the experience gained in this war and the performance of aircraft to come. Primary responsibility for air warfare must rest with the coequal, coordinate Air Force, whatever the character of the earth's surface underneath.[71]

The threat of annexation by the air force alarmed both navy fliers and naval officers who did not fly. Before the war, navy fliers had been, like army fliers, an exotic caste. The best billets had gone to captains of surface ships, especially battleships. The Pacific War changed this. By the time of Japan's surrender, the aircraft carrier had become the centerpiece of the navy. Officers wearing wings could reasonably assume that, in future, the navy would be run primarily for them. They had no interest in being a minority in an air force dominated by ground force pilots. Other navy officers wanted to keep aviators in the navy because the aircraft carrier had become the core of the fleet. James Forrestal, Secretary of the Navy at the end of the war, said to Congress:

The carrier task forces of this war . . . are a unique creation of the United States. . . . These carrier task forces . . . are one of the most powerful forces in existence in the world today. They have a remarkable mobility and an enormous reach. In my judgment, these great carrier task forces, backed up by the surface power of the fleet and by the amphibious striking force of the Marine Corps, constitute an all-purpose weapon which . . . give this Nation and the world a swift and effective means of dealing with arrogance wherever it might raise its head.[72]

If all pilots went to the air force, most of the rest of the navy would be reduced to the status of a service force.

In defending their service, naval officers became increasingly dogmatic. They had long had scripture and doctrine in the form of Mahan's texts preaching the supreme importance of sea power. They now found Mahan's logic appropriated by army fliers, who claimed that air power had taken the place of sea power. Unable flatly to dispute this claim, naval officers constructed a new doctrine, the core of which was the principle of flexibility. A navy pamphlet of 1945, summarizing lessons of the Pacific War, said: "Any exclusive adoption of a single weapon or type of weapon immediately limits freedom of action and greatly simplifies the enemy's problem of defense. War is a phenomenon of great complexity whose problems are solved pragmatically."[73] This doctrine was as comforting to submariners and surface ship officers as to aviators. By the time the army air forces became an independent air force, nearly all naval officers had come to accept as true something like the following syllogism:

• The nation's ability to protect itself against mortal threats depends on its having several types of ready military forces.

• Anyone who opposes the nation's having a variety of ready military forces is inimical to the nation's safety.

- The air force opposes the nation's having a variety of ready military forces.
- The air force therefore is inimical to the nation's safety.

In the late 1950s Admiral Arleigh Burke, a man of considerable sophistication and learning, would say to an aide that having an air force as a rival service was "just like Communism being here in this country."[74] In the mid–1970s I myself heard two different admirals, on two different occasions, commit an identical Freudian slip. "The AIR FORCE!" each said with vehemence, "er . . . I mean, the Soviet Union."

Other issues divided the services. The army questioned the navy's having a marine corps with units above regimental size. The marines pointed to the accomplishments of marine divisions in the Pacific War. Army and AAF officers differed as to which service should have chief responsibility for air defense. In some cases, issues concerned functions that services did not want. The army assumed, for example, that the mission of transporting troops across water belonged to the navy. Eisenhower discovered to his surprise that this was not true. Nimitz told him "the Army was trying to make a 'service organization' out of the Navy."[75] But air force–navy differences over aviation dominated.

Some service differences could be traced back to particular experiences. Eisenhower, looking on more or less detachedly, explained to a Congressman:

All advocates of every theory of American security turn back to the experiences of World War II for historical example—for illustration—to prove the soundness of their own arguments. The difficulty is that these experiences were frequently as different, one from the other, as is the center of a continent from an ocean expanse. They were as varied as the climates and territorial characteristics of the different quarters of the globe—almost as diverse as the personalities of the participants in the fighting of World War II.

The obvious lessons of the war are not the same to the men who conducted an island-hopping campaign through the far reaches of the Pacific . . . as they are to men who, day after day, carried the destructiveness of American bombing into the heart of Hitler's homeland.

It was only human that each man would gain a tremendous respect for the particular weapon, machine or type of unit with which he personally was identified in the war, and that he should tend later to magnify or at least support the importance of that particular weapon, machine or unit in considering the future of our country's security.[76]

In some instances, experiences were personal and embittering. While Eisenhower in the European theater had given considerable autonomy to subordinate commanders, whether army, navy, or AAF, Douglas MacArthur in the Southwest Pacific had insisted on direct control of all force elements. Forrest Sherman, one of the most broad-minded admirals, said tactfully to a Congressional committee that service under MacArthur had "disillusioned naval officers who had given support to the theories of a single department."[77] And MacArthur continued to act as an irritant. He argued unsuccessfully but unrelentingly that, as occupation commander in Japan, he should have under him all land, air, and naval forces in the Pacific.[78] AAF officers often crossed the bounds of civility in arguing the unity of air power. Naval officers did likewise in contradicting them. In too many cases, disagreement hardened into personal hatred.

In 1947 the services agreed to a National Security Act that made the air force independent and created a Secretary of Defense. (This was the same Act that created the National Security Council and the CIA.) It solved no basic issues, for it left open all questions as to how the services would divide functions. The new Secretary seemed little more than chairman of a committee of service Secretaries, each better staffed than he. And the price for even these compromises had been a promise by Truman to name Forrestal the first Secretary of Defense even though, as Secretary of the Navy, Forrestal had been one of the most artful opponents of unification. A White House aide noted:

President's intention was merger.

We are not getting merger. . . .

We have three services, headed nominally by a 'Secretary' with no staff, no tools, no control.[79]

Forrestal himself recognized the meagerness of his powers. He commented to a friend that the new secretaryship "will probably be the greatest cemetery for dead cats in history."[80]

KEY WEST AND NEWPORT

Hoping that passage of the National Security Act might have cooled tempers, Forrestal tried to get the service chiefs to agree on workable divisions of responsibility. He first arranged for review of the subject by a committee of key second-level officers. He counted particularly on General Lauris Norstad, who had been chief planner for the army before transferring to a similar post in the new air force. But the apparent navy victory in the legislative battle had in no way quieted naval officers' anxieties. Nimitz's successor as chief of naval operations, Admiral Louis E. Denfield, refused to accept any part of formulas recommended by Norstad; "the Army and the Air Force," he declared, "seek to shackle, restrict, or otherwise prevent the Navy from exploiting its intrinsic capabilities."[81]

In March 1948 Forrestal tried a different tack. He had at least two reasons for feeling that the services should somehow adjust their differences: he had to appear on Capitol Hill and state the general case for defense spending.

He wanted to be better able to answer questions about why funds were divided as they were between the air force, the navy, and the army.

Forrestal also feared that questions as to which service should have what responsibility might soon need practical answers. He had seen a top-secret "eyes only" cable sent by General Lucius Clay, the occupation commander in Germany, to the chief of army intelligence. "Within the last few weeks," said Clay, "I have felt a subtle change in Soviet attitude which I cannot define but which now gives me a feeling that [war] may come with dramatic suddenness."[82] We now have reason to suspect that the dispatch of this cable had been cooked up between Clay and the army staff as part of their preparation for testifying before Congress, but Forrestal seems not to have known or sensed this. He took Clay's cable at face value, as did officials in the State Department.[83]

On his personal authority, Forrestal summoned the service chiefs and their deputies to the naval base at Key West, Florida. He told reporters in Washington that he would press them to decide "who will do what with what." If that failed, he said, "I shall have to make my own decisions."[84]

Forrestal kept the chiefs at Key West for four days. They eventually agreed to a text. In each major area of dispute, one service received "primary" responsibility. Its chief was to act as agent for the Joint Chiefs. Other services, however, retained "collateral" responsibilities. On the most touchy subject, that of strategic bombing, the Key West agreement assigned "primary" responsibility to the air force. It specified also, however, that the navy had a "right . . . to proceed with the development of weapons the Navy considers essential to its function" and "the right to attack inland targets."[85] The document had as many loopholes as a lace doily.

The inadequacy of the Key West accord became apparent even before the final language had been adjusted. General Carl Spaatz, the chief of staff of the new Air Force, asked that he be designated the Joint Chiefs' agent for matters concerning nuclear weapons. This was a corollary, he argued, of his "primary" responsibility for strategic bombing. Denfield disagreed emphatically. To General Hoyt Vandenberg, who was about to succeed Spaatz, Forrestal voiced exasperation with "(1) the Navy belief, very firmly held and deeply rooted, that the Air Force wants to get control of *all* aviation; (2) the corresponding psychosis of the Air Force that the Navy is trying to encroach upon the strategic prerogatives of the Air Force."[86]

After trying other expedients, Forrestal resorted once again to making the chiefs sit down with one another, this time at the Naval War College in Newport, Rhode Island. After three days of debate, the service chiefs amended the Key West accords. The new document said that the service with primary responsibility for a mission "must have exclusive responsibility for programming and planning." It also said, however, that "in the execution of any mission . . . all available resources must be used. . . . For this reason, the exclusive responsibility and authority in a given field do not imply preclusive participation."[87] In their first published annual report, the Joint Chiefs of Staff spoke of the Newport conference as having produced "further clarification." In his own annual report, Forrestal was more candid: "There are still great areas where the viewpoints of the services have not come together."[88]

Neither Forrestal nor his immediate successor tried again to get written agreement regarding service roles and missions. The efforts made at Key West and Newport had done at least as much harm as good. Previous debates among the services had at least been debates about principles or procedures. After Key West and Newport they often resembled theologians' quarrels about holy texts. The negotiations and subsequent debates strengthened each service's tendency to make its own defense policy.

QUESTIONS OF MONEY

At the heart of interservice debates was the question: who will get money for what?

Before passage of the National Security Act, the army and navy prepared their budgets separately. Competition for marginal dollars took place within each service—artillery versus armor, submarines versus surface ships, and so on. Each service then made its case to its own Congressional committees. Army witnesses appeared before Senate and House Military Affairs committees, then before military affairs subcommittees of the Senate and House Appropriations committees. Navy witnesses appeared before Naval Affairs committees and subcommittees. Army and navy programs were rarely compared with each other.

"Unification" changed everything. The Secretary of Defense had to present a spending estimate for national defense. The Bureau of the Budget, reorganized after the war, had a Military Division. This Division would ask the Secretary and the services to explain and justify this estimate. The Budget Director would then give the President advice on what to recommend to Congress. On Capitol Hill, the Senate and House had meanwhile merged committees so that each branch now had a single Armed Services Committee, and each Appropriations Committee had an Armed Services subcommittee. Here, too, spokesmen for the military establishment would have to answer questions about why money should be allocated as proposed.[89]

The timetable ensured that serious differences among the services would nearly always be exposed to debate, for the budget process was continuous and unrelenting. Congress voted money for a fiscal year running from July 1 until the next June 30. Fiscal 1949 thus began on July 1, 1948 and ended June 30, 1949. Fiscal 1950 covered 1949–50; fiscal 1951, 1950–51; and so on..Each service had to work out its own spending proposals during the spring of the preceding year. The navy, for example, would expect bureaus

and operating units to have ready by April of one year their recommendations for spending to begin 15 months later, in July of the next year.
During the summer and early autumn, the Secretary of Defense and his
aides would question service proposals. The chiefs of staff would debate
among themselves and the services would make adjustments internally. By
late autumn, the Secretary of Defense would have numbers to discuss with
the Bureau of the Budget. The Bureau would give its advice to the President.
The Secretary and the services would get one last opportunity for appeal.
In early January, the President's budget message would go to Congress.
Committee hearings would occupy the spring. Final votes by Congress
would come at or near the last moment. Sometimes Congress would allow
spending to continue at previous-year levels and not vote funds for the
current fiscal year until after it had begun.

This meant not only that budgeting went on year-round but that the services would be testifying in defense of budgets for the upcoming fiscal year
at the same time that they were framing budgets for the fiscal year to follow.
After unification, the service chiefs were always occupied with dollars.

During the transition to this new system, the services had been in nearly
complete uncertainty about what to plan for. During the war, the army
staff had come up with a proposal for a peacetime establishment of more
than a million men, many of them assigned to an army air forces of 75
groups. This proposal horrified General Marshall, then chief of staff, who
ordered all copies destroyed. Following Marshall's guidance, the staff then
proposed an establishment only a third as large, making provision for only
16 air groups.[90]

The navy differed from the army only in having no Marshall. Its staff
recommended a standing navy of over half a million men, with carrier task
forces, surface ships, and submarines sufficient "to suppress any incipient
war by joint action with other powers or, if necessary, by independent
action."[91] Publicity for the navy's carrier planning then excited an army air
forces rebellion against Marshall. If the army did not aim for more than 16
air groups, protested the air staff, the navy might take over the strategic
bombing mission.[92] Subsequent study by the air staff produced a reasoned
argument for a seventy-group force, assuming that the Soviet Union would
be the prospective enemy.[93]

No one had more than vague notions as to how much money the President
and Congress would commit. The army staff guessed $3 billion a year for
the army and air forces, with the costs of universal military training included. The air staff voiced hope for postwar spending—on all services—
of around $8 billion a year.[94]

Truman proved more generous than even the air staff had hoped. His
investigations during World War II, together with army service in World
War I, gave him, to say no more, a skeptical attitude toward the military.
He warned his budget director that they "would spend every nickel they

could get their hands on."[95] But Truman prided himself on heeding lessons of history. He believed that World War II demonstrated the folly both of "isolationism" and of military unpreparedness. His first postwar speech about defense epitomized what Michael Sherry has termed "the ideology of preparedness." Truman said:

In our desire to leave the tragedy of war behind us, we must not make the same mistake that we made after the first World War when we sank back into helplessness. . . . Until we are sure that our peace machinery is functioning adequately, we must relentlessly preserve our superiority on land and sea and in the air.[96]

Holding this view, Truman was willing to spend on military forces almost every dollar he thought the nation could afford. Before he became President, Congress had already passed tax laws designed to bridge the transition from war to peace. Prewar legislation fixed the basic terms for many domestic programs, as, for example, agricultural price support. Wartime legislation committed money to the World Bank and other such organizations. The war also left the Truman administration with a national debt exceeding $250 billion—six times what it had been in 1940. The Treasury forecast that taxes would bring in between $31 billion and $32 billion. Nondefense commitments would claim two-thirds of those receipts. Partly on principle but also partly to stem inflation, the President hoped to put about $4 billion toward retirement of the debt. Having recommended to Congress new programs in health, housing, and public works, Truman could have set aside some of the remainder to cover their costs. He chose instead to insist that new programs carry their own financing. He assigned all the balance of anticipated revenues to the armed services—$15 billion for fiscal 1947.[97]

Acting similarly in his second full year in office but providing almost nothing for debt reduction, Truman allocated $11.3 billion to defense. The new Republican-dominated Congress voted cuts in taxes. Twice during 1947 Truman vetoed such cuts. Eventually, he had to accept a bill that reduced prospective revenue by $4 billion. In the beginning of 1948, he proposed spending $11 billion on defense, even though asking $7 billion to underwrite the Marshall Plan.[98] Later, Truman would receive harsh criticism for his "remainder" method of allocating money to the armed services: critics called it a poor way of measuring national security needs.[99] In Truman's own opinion, he was stretching to ensure that defense would not be underfunded.[100] Given what the wartime service staffs had projected as postwar spending, Truman's opinion seems not entirely groundless.

SERVICE CONCERNS

The services nevertheless had reason, quite apart from their competition with one another, to feel uncomfortable under any spending limits permitted by "remainder" budgeting. Although particulars differed widely, all service planners faced four problems.

First, military technology was undergoing potentially revolutionary change. The atomic bomb was the most momentous scientific and engineering achievement of the war, but it was by no means alone. The prospect of harnessing nuclear fission as a source of power carried with it the promise of ships, submarines, perhaps aircraft and rockets, vastly different from those of World War II. Jet-powered aircraft had just begun to appear in the late months of the war. It was obvious that manufacturers would be able to produce much more powerful jet engines, enabling planes routinely to exceed the speed of sound. The German V–1 and V–2 rockets showed in primitive form the potentialities of aerodynamic and ballistic missiles. Visionaries foresaw missiles able accurately to deliver nuclear warheads even at intercontinental ranges. And these were but the most publicized technologies. Scores of other new developments had occurred in electronics, chemistry, and other fields. In the aftermath of World War II, military planners had to anticipate that their arsenals were going to become obsolete at increasingly shorter intervals.

Second, the unit cost of weaponry promised to skyrocket. In part, this was because new technology usually cost more. In part, it was because increased demand on equipment usually required a geometric increase in capabilities—for example, greater speed or reduced vulnerability. The first army air forces jet fighter was the Lockheed P–80, which first came into service in 1947. It cost a little over $100,000 a copy. The Republic F–84, which began to come into service in 1947, cost almost three times as much. Essential differences between the P–80 and the F–84 was that the P–80 had a top speed of 502 knots; the F–84 did 592 and could climb a little more rapidly. The North American F–86, which arrived a year after the F–84, cost 40 percent more. Its only advantage was 26 knots more in top speed.[101] The differences were not trivial. In combat in Korea in the early 1950s, F–84s and F–86s could outperform Soviet-built MiG–15s; P–80s could not. But the cost differences were steep—and were usually steeper than service planners had originally estimated.

The third problem was "lead time"—the lengthening interval between the ordering of a new weapon and its actual delivery. The example of the B–36 bomber illustrates. The army announced in April 1941, eight months before Pearl Harbor, that it wanted a long-range bomber. Contractors submitted bids and in October 1941 Convair won. By mid–1943 Convair had a workable design. The army air forces provisionally ordered 100 planes. By mid–1944 a firm contract existed. In August 1946 a test version made its first flight. In December an AAF evaluation board expressed disappointment at the plane's slowness. Convair proposed modifications. By March 1947 a slightly faster test version flew. In August the new air force decided that it would go ahead with the 100-plane order. By December, Convair had a production prototype. In the spring of 1948 the Air Force ordered actual delivery of 61 planes. The process had taken seven years. It would be another two years—after the outbreak of the Korean War—before the first fully outfitted B–36 joined the operating forces.[102]

Such delays were neither uncommon nor peculiar to aircraft. The army stated a requirement for a new heavy tank in June 1945. Chrysler produced the first test model of a T–43 in June 1951. Large-scale delivery commenced a year later—again after an interval of seven years.[103] And the B–36 and T–43 were comparatively crude. It was a near certainty that lead times would lengthen as aircrafts, ships, tanks, and other weapons became more sophisticated.

The fourth problem was the difference between the timetables for military planning and for governmental action. Planners needed authority and money now to order weapons for delivery five, seven, or perhaps ten years in the future. They did not know what the world would be like then. But the government, officials and politicians alike, did not operate in the long term. Department heads and their immediate subordinates tended to be preoccupied with current problems. The military forces of most interest to them were those currently available. Politicians felt the need to have some justification in the here and now for spending large quantities of taxpayers' dollars.

These linked problems made it hard, in the best of circumstances, for officials in the military establishment to come up with coherent defense policies. Public statements had to embody rationales appealing to politicians and ordinary citizens. Internal definitions of doctrine had to address instead questions of how military forces might be used in some indistinct future. Budgets had to be constructed and defended in the present, while plans had to look ahead. Force posture resulted from budgets. No one could know exactly what forces would exist until each fiscal year's processes ran their course. Deployments, on the other hand, could answer to immediate demands. Officials of the Truman administration would have found it difficult to frame defense policies even if there had been no interservice rivalries. Those rivalries multiplied the difficulties.

PROGRAMS FOR 1948–50

When the new system first went into effect in the spring of 1948, service rivalries nevertheless dominated. The fiscal 1949 budget, presented to Congress by Truman in January 1948, came from the old system. The defense component simply added together the independent service budgets. Two months later came the Communist takeover in Czechoslovakia, Clay's "war may come" cable, and Truman's decision to make a fiery speech to Congress. The President pressed for Marshall Plan appropriations. The army had meanwhile raised an alarm about a level of staffing below even minimal estimates of need. Truman agreed to ask Congress for supplemental money and also to revive the appeal for universal military training.

Forrestal feared that special action on behalf of the army would make it harder for him to work up a defense-wide budget for fiscal 1950. He was equally concerned lest the new Congressional Armed Services committees take that function away from the Secretary of Defense.

Not long before, a presidentially appointed Air Policy Commission had published its report. Entitled *Survival in the Air Age*, it emphatically endorsed the air staff argument for a seventy-group air force. This, it said, would provide "the very minimum number" of air defense interceptors together with "a counteroffensive air force in being . . . so powerful that if an aggressor does attack, we will be able to retaliate with the utmost violence and to seize and hold the advanced positions from which we can divert the destruction from our homeland to his."[104] The report mentioned the navy, including carriers, as having a role for the time being in seizing and holding those advanced positions, but it was primarily a brief for the air force. A Congressionally created committee, covering the same ground, also issued a report calling for a massive air build-up.[105]

Forrestal, who defended publicly the concept of "balanced" armed forces, could see a possibility of Congress's taking upon itself the role of turning service budgets into a defense budget. He asked the chiefs of staff to make a joint recommendation on what the President should ask Congress in the way of supplemental defense funds. For the first time, the Joint Chiefs of Staff, as a body, discussed budgets. Thereafter, as Mr. Dooley would have said, "they were to the flure."[106]

General Vandenberg and other air force officers insisted that progress toward a seventy-group air force should take precedence over all else. Admiral Denfield and naval officers argued that the navy's target of 14,474 planes was equally important. New money, the navy argued, should be divided equally among the services. General Bradley and army officers agreed. Meanwhile, Vandenberg and his cohort carried their case to the House Armed Services Committee. The committee, on its own, added $922 million for air force aircraft procurement. With this, and navy representatives working on members of other committees in hopes of getting a share of any such money, the Joint Chiefs could not come close to agreeing on figures to give the President.

The outcome was confusion, embarrassing to both Truman and Forrestal. With advice from both Forrestal and the Budget Bureau, Truman asked Congress for $3 billion, approximately half for new staffing and other purposes, and the other half for aircraft. The chiefs could work out no compromise within those numbers. Forrestal thought—and said publicly—that "balance" could be maintained with supplemental appropriations near $3.5 billion. The chiefs then gave him their numbers for achieving a seventy-group air force and "balance." They ran as follows:[107]

$ billion

	FY1949	FY1950	FY1951	FY1952
Army	6.3	7.2	7.2	7.3
Navy	7.6	8.0	8.0	8.0
Air Force	5.4	6.6	7.3	7.5
Totals	19.3	21.8	22.5	22.8

Sensing that some such numbers might be implied even by the $3 billion supplemental, Truman refused the extra $500 million Forrestal asked. He raised his original request by only $100 million. He then told Forrestal and the chiefs that they could expect no more than $14.5 billion in fiscal 1950. When both houses ended up voting an additional $822 million for aircraft—almost what the Armed Services Committee had recommended—Truman declined to spend the money.

Work on the fiscal 1950 budget was all the while under way. When service estimates were added up, they totaled almost $29 billion—twice what the President had allotted.

Under Forrestal's goading, the chiefs appointed a Budget Advisory Committee composed of senior officers. The committee's chairman was Air Force General Joseph McNarney. As Marshall's deputy in the early part of the war and as commander in the Mediterranean later, McNarney had a reputation for cold, ruthless decisiveness.[108] At first, he did not show these qualities. The committee reported that it could not arrive at a total below $23.6 billion. Acting on his own rather than as committee chairman, McNarney then suggested a solution. If the United States were prepared to abandon the Eastern Mediterranean in the event of war, McNarney said, the navy's requirements for aircraft carriers could be cut in half.

Bradley and Vandenberg accepted this formula. On this basis, they recommended to Forrestal a budget totaling $15.8 billion. Denfield protested vehemently but came in with an alternative budget of $16.5 billion, all the extra $800 million earmarked for the navy. Under Forrestal's lash, the Joint Chiefs finally supplied figures within the President's ceiling. Their totals, however, were arbitrary. They continued to disagree about the desirable number of navy carriers.

Forrestal tried hard to get help in pressing the President to raise his budget ceiling. He appealed to Secretary of State Marshall to say to Truman that the armed forces were inadequate. Marshall declined.[109] Truman meanwhile was told by his Budget Director that Forrestal had lost control of the Pentagon. He also saw newspaper rumors that Forrestal, expecting a Republican victory in the presidential race, was building alliances with Republicans. After his surprise success in the election, Truman notified Forrestal, with little warning, that his fiscal 1950 budget would provide only $13.4 billion for defense. The Bureau of the Budget had stripped close to $500 million from the air force and half as much from the other services.

THE FISCAL 1950 BUDGET BATTLE

The President's decisions did not end debate over the fiscal 1950 budget; the struggle continued through most of 1949. Much of it took place in front of reporters, microphones, and newsreel cameras.

Long before Truman fixed final figures, the air force and navy began preparing for battles that would take place afterward on Capitol Hill. Before a commission studying government organization, navy witnesses asserted that, at present, carriers were the only bases from which the Soviet Union could be effectively bombed. Air force witnesses said the exact contrary. Secretary of the Air Force Stuart Symington told the committee that the chief organizational problem in the Pentagon was the existence of an independent, backward-looking navy.

Hanson Baldwin, military analyst for *The New York Times*, used his columns to champion the navy's case for flexible forces. With air force encouragement, if not sponsorship, the popular writer William Bradford Huie published a series of articles for *Reader's Digest*, the most widely circulated monthly periodical in the United States, portraying the carrier fleet as a modern equivalent of the horse cavalry.[110] Eisenhower, called back into service to mediate interservice negotiations about the next budget, wrote in his diary. "The bitterness of the fight between Air and Navy is so noticeable that it is never absent from any discussion."[111]

Air force leaders counted on Congress's at least putting back the last half-billion dollars taken away by Truman and the Budget Bureau. They hoped for more. Although the President's budget called for a forty-eight-group air force, Symington said that he continued to regard seventy groups as minimal. Otherwise, he said publicly, the United States would within three years cede air superiority to the Soviets.[112] Gallup polls reported 74 percent of the public as believing that the air force would be the most important service in a future war; only 4 percent believed this to be true of the navy.[113] At the opening of Congress, the chairmen of the House and Senate Armed Services committees introduced in their houses resolutions endorsing in principle the seventy-group goal. They had read public opinion. So had other Representatives and Senators.

The November 1948 election had been a victory not just for Truman but for Democrats across the country. The Republicans had had 51–45 and 245–188 majorities in the Senate and House. Now the Democrats had majorities of 54–42 and 263–171. Senator Millard Tydings of Maryland and Representative Carl Vinson of Georgia now chaired the Armed Services committees. Both were old-timers with long records of independence from the executive branch. Tydings had successfully survived Franklin Roosevelt's attempt in 1938 to purge the Senate of conservative Democrats.

Tydings, Vinson, and other Congressional elders remembered well the prewar era in which the Military and Naval Affairs committees had collaborated with the services in determining budgets, with the President little more than a bystander. It was in no way strange for them to think of redoing the figures of Forrestal and Truman. They would have been well ahead of their time had they thought otherwise. Not for another decade would even the shrewdest outside analysts notice that the increasingly complex relationship between defense programs and national strategy made it harder for Congress to handle defense appropriations as it handled appropriations for public works and post offices.[114]

When hearings commenced, air force witnesses did not openly criticize the administration's proposals. They claimed to be loyally cutting back to mandated levels. In order to meet the highest priority, they said, the air force was continuing the build-up of the long-range bomber force but reducing other forces. The Strategic Air Command ordered 39 additional B–36 bombers. Other elements of the air force announced cancellation of contracts for jet fighter-bombers, fighters, and transport helicopters.[115] This was in part an internal victory for LeMay, who had just become commander of SAC. It said to everyone that bomber pilots ruled the air force. It also had the effect of producing constituent pressure in states and districts affected by the cancellations.[116] When questioning Symington, Vandenberg, and others from the air force, most members of the Armed Services committees sounded like lawyers taking testimony from friendly expert witnesses: "Wouldn't you say, general, . . . ?" "Yes, sir."

The navy had to follow the air force lead. Even with the cuts made in the Pentagon and by the Budget Bureau, the navy came to Capitol Hill asking funds for 288 combatant ships in a fleet to be organized around eight aircraft carriers.

Leading the array was a "supercarrier," the *USS United States*. Displacing 65,000 tons empty and 80,000 tons when loaded—twice as much as the *Essex* class carriers that had won the Pacific war—it was advertised as able to carry bombers as big and heavy as B–29s. Navy witnesses always denied that the ship was designed primarily to carry nuclear-armed bombers. They pointed out that the requirement for such a ship had been defined before Hiroshima, and ticked off many other missions for which it would be suited. Nevertheless, the *United States* was generally thought to symbolize the navy's claim to a role in strategic bombing. When questioning navy spokesmen about the super carrier, members of the Armed Services and Appropriations committees often sounded like lawyers confronting hostile witnesses. To stave off any committee recommendation for canceling the project, the Secretary of the Navy announced that he would instead deactivate three lesser carriers and mothball 400 aircraft.[117]

The Armed Services and Appropriations committees concluded by recommending only modest changes in the President's budget. Stalin had meanwhile ended the Berlin blockade. Communists and fellow travelers in Europe had become less militant. Instead of battling police, they were parading under Picasso doves. While reporters and columnists characterized the Communist "peace offensive" as phony, many took it as a sign that the Soviets were backing away from the Cold War. Gallup polls suggested a diminishing public fear of war. In August 1948 almost 60 percent of those polled expected war within ten years. In May 1949 only 50 percent said they expected war within the next 30 years.[118] Opinion among members of Congress probably followed a similar pattern. With the economy in recession, government tax receipts seemed likely to fall well below Truman's estimates. When the Appropriations Committees finally reported and the two houses worked out their differences, the military establishment received less than Truman had asked. By voting no funds for universal military training, Congress managed to provide a little more for the Air Force, but not much, and with no guarantee that the President would spend it.[119]

LOUIS JOHNSON, THE SUPER CARRIER, AND THE B–36

In the meantime, Truman moved to strengthen his own—and the executive branch's—control over defense spending. The commission studying government organization had issued its report and Truman accepted some of its recommendations. After mid–1949, when these became law, the Secretary of Defense would be head of a Department of Defense, not just a coordinator. The Joint Chiefs would have a formal chairman. In these and other ways, responsibility would become more centralized.

Truman meanwhile let Forrestal go. Always a high-strung workaholic, Forrestal had begun to show signs of heading for a breakdown. Less than three months after leaving office, he would commit suicide. To replace him, Truman chose Louis Johnson. A onetime leader in the West Virginia legislature, Johnson was a politician, not an official. As head of the American Legion in the 1930s, he had been chief lobbyist for World War I veterans. In 1948, when few prominent Democrats bothered to turn a hand for Truman, Johnson took the cheerless job of finance chairman. He raised most of the money that made possible Truman's "whistle-stop" campaign. Although Truman did not particularly like or trust Johnson, he was much obligated to him, and he could count on his not becoming a captive of the generals and admirals. Burly, crude, blustering, with dreams of being the Democrats' candidate for President in 1952, Johnson seemed much better fitted than Forrestal to axe service budgets and push toward defense spending of $5 to $7 billion a year.[120]

Johnson started by seizing a block of Pentagon offices from the army. He told the press that he expected to save a billion dollars just by "cutting out wastage, duplication, and . . . unnecessary civilian employment."[121] After just seven weeks in office, with only token consultation of defense officials, Johnson announced that he was canceling the navy's supercarrier. He knew that the air force and army opposed the project and that it had tepid support on Capitol Hill. He almost certainly knew that the President questioned its worth. Truman's recall of Eisenhower had come at about the same time as the appointment of Johnson, and Truman's instructions to Eisenhower had been "to support strongest possible Air Force . . . [and] to cut certain of the Navy's assumed missions in order to obtain more money for Air."[122] His guidance to Johnson must have been similar. Although Truman regretted Johnson's highhandedness and tried to mollify some of those whose feelings were hurt, he backed the decision itself.[123]

There ensued an open brawl between the navy and air force, the likes of which Washington has seldom seen. Navy partisans charged Johnson with having a financial interest in the B–36. A Congressional committee looked into the charges and reported finding "not one scintilla of evidence."[124] By that time, however, naval officers had begun publicly to denounce the B–36 as "a billion dollar blunder." The House Armed Services Committee conducted a new round of hearings. There, navy witnesses alleged that the B–36 was too big and slow to get through Soviet air defenses. In mock encounters, they said, navy fighters easily downed B–36s. Some naval officers argued, in addition, against the whole concept of massive nuclear attacks on enemy cities. Such attacks would be inhumane; neither would they defeat the enemy's armed forces. The public simply beguiled itself by believing that big bombers provided military security.[125]

Air Force witnesses retaliated by defending the B–36, denouncing the navy for airing issues of strategy better debated in secrecy, and charging "sour grapes." The super carrier had been intended to carry city-busting nuclear bombers, they said. Having lost that carrier, the navy now wanted to say that no one should have the role. "An immoral weapon," said an air force general, "is one too big for your service to deliver."[126] General Bradley capped the hearing by siding with the air force. Venting some of the anger accumulated during budget debates, Bradley accused the navy of refusing to accept any degree of unification. The admirals, he said, were "fancy dans" unwilling to play on a team "unless they can call the signals."[127]

After the hearings, the Secretary of the Navy fired Admiral Denfield. On the ground that officers should not be punished for speaking their minds, many members of Congress protested. Outcries came even from partisans of the air force. Johnson backed off from reprisals against others and the storm subsided. The Armed Services Committee finally issued a report in March 1950. Taking no sides, the report recommended that all the services cooperate more closely in strategic planning. It laid on the Secretary of Defense the onus for guiding this planning. It urged him to keep the appropriate committees of Congress "fully informed."[128]

In the meantime, with Eisenhower on temporary duty as nonstatutory Chairman and Bradley still Army Chief of Staff, the Joint Chiefs had tried to work out a budget for fiscal 1951. Eisenhower first had each service identify what it regarded as the minimum needs of the other services. He proposed that these figures be the "red bricks" of the budget. Any difference between the total and the ceiling set by the President could be divided up, he suggested. Each service would then have a little money for "blue bricks" or "purple bricks."[129] When the air force and army included only minimal carrier forces among "red bricks," the navy refused to continue the exercise.

Eisenhower next tried the tactic of setting his own ceilings. Again, the navy called the results unacceptable. A new Budget Advisory Committee, headed this time by an admiral, future Chief of Naval Operations Robert B. Carney, tried its hand but gave up. The air force member of the committee said that its failure proved the impossibility of providing adequately for three services within the President's $15 billion ceiling; therefore, the air force should be given the lion's share.

Eisenhower finally divided the hypothetical funds three ways by fiat, with the air force getting about 20 percent more than the army and 25 percent more than the navy. When the President gave notice that he would give the services only $13 billion, Eisenhower made proportional cuts. Secretary Johnson then made marginal adjustments, chiefly for the benefit of the army and navy. By that time, the B–36 brouhaha had passed. Forrest Sherman, a much more political admiral, had become CNO. Reporters could find few signs of new struggles like those over the fiscal 1950 budget. On the surface, it seemed that Louis Johnson ruled the Pentagon and that defense officials were doing the bidding of politicians, just as in prewar days. The reality underneath the surface was quite different.

PLANS—THE BUDGETEERS' AND CURTIS LEMAY'S

Defense officials, whatever their biases, agreed on one point: the United States did not have the military power necessary to defend all the interests it had defined for itself. They seldom questioned the definitions of national interest being developed primarily by officials in the State Department. The major exception was Korea. The State Department's Asian hands held that a unified, democratic Korea ought to be an objective of U.S. diplomacy. The chiefs of staff warned that, in a war, Korea would be a liability—costly to defend and of no use as a base for any type of military operations. The result was a compromise, the ambiguity of which was apparent in Acheson's celebrated 1950 speech, which put Korea outside the U.S. "security perimeter" but said that, as a signer of the UN Charter, the United States nevertheless cared about Korea.[130] With regard to the Eastern Mediterranean, Middle East, West Germany, and Western Europe, there had been no such differences of opinion. The Truman Doctrine, declarations concerning Berlin, and the North Atlantic Treaty were designed to leave no misunderstanding about U.S. willingness to use force. Defense officials had not only agreed to these commitments, but had also helped sell them to Congress and the country.

At the time, most men in the Pentagon assumed that, because of these commitments, the military establishment would get more muscle. In 1948, when the most serious commitments were made, this assumption seemed warranted. Truman had gone to Congress, asking restoration of selective service and a $3 billion defense supplemental when the chiefs of staff formally endorsed military guarantees for Western European and "other selected non-communist nations." They had emphasized, when giving this endorsement, "the extreme importance . . . of keeping our military capabilities abreast of our military commitments."[131]

Only after the commitments had been announced did defense officials learn that, in fact, they would not get much more money. Senior officials in the services, both uniformed and civilian, then became so busy battling each other that they could not take time to think about what they might do if one of these commitments were tested. Officers supposedly engaged in war planning were trying most of the time to improve their services' claims for funds. Officers and civilians at the top of the services seemed, as we have seen, to think of little else.

A basic joint war plan had been drafted in 1947. Given that it envisioned the use of nuclear weapons, it had an apt, if crude, codename—"Broiler." It assumed that the Soviets would quickly capture Western Europe. The Red Army would be in Amsterdam within a week, at the Pyrenees and the toe of Italy within ten weeks. The objective of the United States would be to "destroy the war-making capacity of the U.S.S.R." In part, this was to be done by bombers flying from the United Kingdom, some of them carrying atomic bombs. In part, it was to be done by air operations out of the Eastern Mediterranean, either from carriers or from bases in the Cairo-Suez area, the latter to be secured and supplied by seaborne forces. In part, it was to be an outcome of "such later operations as may be necessary." The plan thus gave each service a basis for claiming priority funding.[132]

Air force planners tried repeatedly to reduce the role assigned to the navy. They raised questions about the cost and difficulty of trying to hold the Eastern Mediterranean. They argued that the Soviets were likely to occupy Spain, thus closing all access to the Mediterranean. Navy planners insisted that the Soviets would stop at the Pyrenees or at least fail to reach Gibraltar. Air force planners proposed that bombers be based at Karachi in Pakistan instead of Cairo-Suez. This brought support from the army, for the establishment of a Karachi base would depend on airborne troops. Navy planners continued to defend the merits of a Cairo-Suez base. Similar wrangling continued all through 1948.[133]

Officials not completely engaged in the budget brawl came close to ridiculing these plans. The Army-Navy Munitions Board, a partly civilian organization designed for mobilization planning, questioned whether U.S. industry could meet the implied supply requirements.[134] Logistics planners told the service chiefs that "Broiler" was "mounted on a logistical shoe-string." Looking at a follow-on version, they added up the requisite skilled staff levels and aircraft and said that they did not exist.[135]

In the absence of serious central planning, service branches and commands developed their own concepts of what to do in case war came. In most cases, the plans were simply schedules for remobilizing forces of World War II.

The major exception was the Air Force Strategic Air Command. LeMay, who had taken charge of SAC in October 1948, proceeded to plan for winning a war with little or no help from any other element of the air force, let alone from the navy or army. He believed that strategic bombing could have won World War II if enough bombers had been built. He had even greater faith concerning World War III. Air force scouts supplied him with information about the quantities and types of nuclear weapons Atomic Energy Commission laboratories could produce. He asked for all—and then some. With well-cultivated connections in Congress and the aircraft industry, he got top priority, within the air force budget, for the bombers he wanted.

Within weeks of taking command, LeMay had a plan for nuclear strikes on 70 Soviet cities. Six months later, he had 220 targets and the confident expectation "that additional intelligence will result in an increase in the number of targets found to justify atomic attack."[136] "[W]e could have destroyed all of Russia . . . without losing a man to their defenses," LeMay would later write.[137]

At the end of 1948, when U.S. foreign policy seemed to have greater coherence and direction than at almost any other time, U.S. defense policy was almost perfectly incoherent. In public statements, defense officials contradicted one another. Not only did the services have no common doctrine, none had a service-wide doctrine. They had competing plans. They were at one another's throats about budgets. Posture and deployments were in flux. No person inside or outside the U.S. government could have given an intelligible summary of the country's defense policy.

A TURN TOWARD COHERENCE

During 1949 the higher levels of the service moved toward new consensus. This may seem odd, given the fury of contemporaneous fights over the budget, the B–36, and the super carrier. It can probably be explained by six different factors, all interacting.

First, there was a fear that war might actually occur. The Soviet blockade of Berlin had scared Washington. Though Clay professed certainty that the Russians were bluffing, CIA sources said otherwise. "[T]he Soviets mean business in the present crisis," the Berlin station reported. When Clay recommended forcing the blockade with an armed convoy, the service chiefs united in advising the President against such action—"in view of the risk of war involved."[138] Although the sense of crisis dissipated and intelligence analysts became more optimistic, fear lingered.[139] News in 1949 of the Soviet nuclear test provided additional fuel.

Second, the services faced a number of common problems created by the negotiation and ratification of the North Atlantic Treaty. Having given support in principle to a defensive alliance with the West Europeans and Canadians, the chiefs of staff agreed to let a few U.S. officers sit in with the West European Union military planning committee. These officers had no function except to show the flag. They were instructed to participate only as observers and to disclose nothing about U.S. plans—especially the fact that those plans called for getting out of Europe posthaste if the Russians struck.[140]

Learning subsequently that the President and Secretary of State envisioned a very large military assistance program for Europe, perhaps on a par with the $17 billion economic recovery program, the service chiefs concluded that they could not afford to be so standoffish. They issued new orders, permitting their representatives to take full part in any talks that concerned either U.S. forces or military assistance.[141] This meant that the chiefs had to think more seriously about an answer for European generals who asked, "And what do *you* plan to do?"

Third, the service chiefs faced a need to think more seriously and comprehensively about the implication of nuclear weapons. Bombs of the Hiroshima and Nagasaki type had been handmade laboratory products. They could not be turned out in quantity, and, for all their immense destructive power, they had poor qualities as weapons. They had to be transported in parts, and with many precautions. Before one bomb could be used against one target, a team of 77 specialists had to work for a week on its final assembly. The bomb had to be carried by a uniquely engineered plane. And it had to be dropped on an urban industrial center, for it could not be relied on to hit any more precise target. A test bomb aimed at an island in the Pacific in 1946 had missed by two miles.[142] Since uranium was thought to be scarce and the process of winnowing its fissionable matter both slow and expensive, military planners assumed that atomic bombs would be few and would have very special purposes. Even SAC planners assumed that strategic bombing would use mostly TNT and incendiaries, as in World War II.[143]

In April 1948 the Atomic Energy Commission conducted a new series of tests, code-named "Sandstone." These tests demonstrated the feasibility of mass-producible weapons in a variety of shapes and with a variety of yields. New finds of uranium, combined with improved processing techniques, meanwhile opened the possibility that nuclear weapons could be manufactured in quantity. The Atomic Energy Commission (AEC) could promise bombs almost as easily handled as TNT bombs. It could even offer the prospect of nuclear weapons that could be carried by fighter bombers or fitted to rockets, torpedoes, or artillery shells.[144] At the other end of the spectrum, just after news that the Soviets had learned how to make atomic bombs, came the prospect of a U.S., and eventually a Soviet, "super-bomb"—a thermonuclear weapon with destructive power a thousand times that of the Hiroshima bomb.[145] Planners in almost all branches of all services had to begin thinking about using—and facing—nuclear firepower.

Fourth, despite their bitter quarrels with one another, leaders in the services increasingly shared a common view that their problems were not understood by the politicians to whom they answered. They all regarded the President's Budget Bureau as a hostile agency. They all saw Louis Johnson as an antagonist. They all felt dismay when Congress in 1949 effectively ratified the Truman-Johnson fiscal 1950 budget. Previously, defense officials had been fighting over shares. Even while publicly saying that a seventy-group air force was minimal, Symington expressed in private the opinion that defense spending need not exceed $10 billion a year. The problem, as he saw it then, was simply wasteful spending on the navy.[146] As fiscal 1950 spending limits became firm, defense officials came more and more to agree that, whatever the sharing formula, the total was too small. By early 1950 the Joint Chiefs were declaring formally and unanimously that available forces were "not strong enough to accomplish effectively" the missions assigned them. the chief of staff of the air force, despite his service's favored position, said that the existing budget entailed "risks beyond the maximum acceptable."[147]

Fifth, defense officials saw evidence of active sympathy among officials elsewhere in the government, particularly in the State Department. Marshall, despite his military background (perhaps because of it) had lent little support to the Pentagon. He had even gone on record saying that, at the margin, it was better to spend money on European armies than on the U.S. army.[148] His chief policy planner, George Kennan, thought an actual war highly unlikely. The general direction of Kennan's advice ran toward minimizing military aspects of the U.S.–Soviet competition.[149] Acheson had more sympathy than Marshall for the arguments of defense officials. This sympathy intensified after run-ins with Louis Johnson, for Acheson came quickly to loathe Johnson and to support almost any of Johnson's ill-wishers.

The potential for effective aid to defense officials was greatly increased when, in the course of 1949, Acheson made Paul Nitze his department's chief planner. Nitze had once been a Wall Street associate of Forrestal. That gave him an extra reason for disliking Louis Johnson. But Nitze's sympathy for defense officials was more than personal. He had once taken a year's sabbatical from banking in order to ponder theories on the rise and fall of civilizations. Experience on the postwar Strategic Bombing Survey had equipped him with some knowledge concerning modern weaponry, nuclear weapons in particular. Just before being chosen to succeed Kennan, he made a study of Western Europe. He concluded that recovery and stability required a greater sense of security against possible Soviet attack. He also concluded that the Europeans could not afford the requisite investment in military forces.[150] Nitze thus had several reasons of his own for being a champion of greater U.S. military preparedness. He was tenacious and adroit.

The final, and by no means least important, factor was the personal influence of Eisenhower. His stint as acting chairman of the Joint Chiefs lasted only six months. He left with the services still wrangling. The public outbursts of the B–36 hearings occurred after he had gone back to fretful exile as president of Columbia University. Nevertheless, in his forceful, commonsense way, Eisenhower had persuaded his Pentagon colleagues to begin raising their sights above service differences in order to focus on common concerns and objectives.[151]

TO NSC 68—AND BEYOND

When Eisenhower agreed to serve as acting Joint Chiefs of Staff (JCS) chairman, he wrote in his diary: "Basic & firm strategic concept is 1st requirement. Once this is achieved much else will fall in line."[152] At session after session, he pressed the service chiefs to think not just about programs and budgets but about objectives and priorities. After a couple of months of exploratory discussion, Eisenhower put to the Chiefs the simple but powerful proposition that the primary objective of the United States, after the preservation of the homeland, was to prevent the Soviets from taking over Western Europe.[153] Questions such as Cairo-Suez versus Karachi, it followed, were second-order. They concerned means, not ends.

Eisenhower's formula did not win immediate acceptance. Admiral Denfield had criticized plans in the "Broiler" series for assuming too readily that Europe could not be held. He criticized Eisenhower for implying the reverse, warning against the danger of becoming committed to a new Maginot Line.[154] Nevertheless, with practical questions pressing because of the new North Atlantic Treaty, other defense officials, including some in the navy, began to come around. In July 1949 an interdepartmental committee, representing the State Department, the military establishment, and the Economic Cooperation Administration, circulated a paper designed to guide testimony before Congress on the Treaty and military aid to the European allies. It said:

The United States cannot, without dealing a mortal blow to the civilized world, and risk of vastly increased U.S. and Allied casualties and cost, abandon Western Europe to enemy occupation with the later promise of liberation. Military strategy, in the long view, must, in the event of war, envisage the containment and thereafter the defeat of any aggressor.[155]

By the early autumn of 1949 this had become agreed declaratory policy. When the Treaty's Defense Committee held its first meeting, Secretary Johnson opened with a text drafted for him by Eisenhower. Johnson said that the United States rejected completely "the policy of desertion and reconquest." He voiced "unswerving determination to protect ourselves and our associates . . . no matter from what quarter aggression may be launched or where it may strike." He spoke, he said, on behalf of the President, Eisenhower's formally installed successor, General Bradley, and congressional leaders.[156]

This new strategic concept ran in a different direction from the "Broiler" plans and LeMay's planning at SAC headquarters. The "Broiler" plans spoke of "maximum systematic destruction of elements vital to the Soviet war effort." It was possible that such destruction would have the effect of keeping the Red Army out of Western Europe. It was not self-evidently so. A committee headed by Air Force General Hubert R. Harmon analyzed the question for the Joint Chiefs. It reported that, while SAC might be able to destroy 40 percent of Soviet industry, its attack would not stall a Soviet ground offensive. There would still be a long war to fight.

Air force officers challenged these conclusions.[157] Even the army and navy chiefs questioned them. (Harmon had the reputation of being a raucous-voiced, Patton-like "bull in the china shop.")[158] The Joint Chiefs agreed to have a second review made by a new, quasi-independent Weapons System Evaluation Group. Reporting early in 1950, it effectively affirmed the Harmon board's conclusions.[159] At the beginning of 1949, the chief of staff of the air force had been completely of LeMay's view. He had argued that there would be no "worthwhile strategic objective after the completion of the atomic air offensive."[160] By the spring of 1950, he was saying that SAC, if adequately funded, could "collapse" the Soviet economy, but that it would only "retard" a Soviet advance into Western Europe.

The new strategic concept did not imply giving up strategic bombing. Everyone saw a bombing campaign as a necessary immediate response to a Soviet attack on Europe. Except for LeMay and his disciples, no one continued to argue that the United States could achieve its objectives in a war by strategic bombing alone.

Doctrine began slowly to follow declaratory policy. The Tactical Air

Command and elements of both the army and navy launched studies of the operating rules that might be needed for forces using precisely aimed, relatively low-yield nuclear weapons against an enemy's maneuver forces.[161] Joint planning addressed the question of how, in the near term or in some longer term, to hold at least a Rhine frontier.[162] With Nitze taking the lead, officials from the State Department and the military establishment set about to maneuver Truman and congressional leaders into providing appropriate additional funds for the services. Force posture and deployments were expected to follow behind.

Nitze's opportunity came in a charge from Acheson to organize for the President and the National Security Council a basic review of national security policy. Understanding the pressures likely to affect politicians, Nitze enlisted as many constituencies as possible. He worked to ensure a united front among officials. He then consulted industrialists, financiers, scientists, and college presidents. He tailored the text of the report to reflect what they said. Because some of them favored reprogramming defense funds rather than increasing the total, Nitze avoided recommending explicitly that more be spent.

The final document, NSC 68, nevertheless challenged almost every premise invoked by Truman and members of Congress when setting limits on spending for the military. It argued that nothing less than human freedom was at stake, that a critical test was near at hand, and that the essential choices were surrender, a desperate immediate preventive war, or "a rapid and sustained build-up of the political, economic, and military strength of the free world."[163]

For its purpose, the document was stunningly well designed. It spoke authoritatively for officialdom and all of officialdom's admirers. At the same time, it was couched in universalist, moralistic language like that of revivalists, "boosters," and candidates for office. No politician could look at the document and not ask himself what questions he would have to answer if it were published and he were charged with having ignored it. Truman's first response was to order—with underlining—that the document *"be handled with special security precautions . . . [and] that no publicity be given this report or its contents."*[164] Just what his response would be still remained uncertain when, on June 25, 1950, a shooting war started between Communist North Korea and non-Communist South Korea.

At that time, U.S. defense policy was not easy to read. Speeches, doctrine, plans, budgets, force posture, and deployments were beginning nevertheless to seem a little more harmonious—and a little more in tune with foreign policy. What might have happened, absent the Korean conflict, is impossible to judge. The Korean conflict turned everything upside down. NSC 68 had called for "recognition . . . that the cold war is in fact a real war in which the survival of the free world is at stake." After June 1950 this came to be accepted not as hyperbole, but as truth.

For 20 years thereafter, defense policy issues would dominate the American political agenda. Much, however, would carry over from these early, formative years. The armed services would never see much more eye-to-eye than in 1949–50. SAC and most of the rest of the military establishment would continue to follow separate lines. Questions of purpose and priority would often be obscured by questions having to do with this year's or next year's budget. One cannot understand the 1950s and 1960s without understanding the chaotic history of U.S. defense policy in the first half-decade after World War II.

AND THE RUSSIANS?

Looking only at the United States or even the West, one can conjure up many larger explanations for the trends in U.S. foreign and defense policies. A good argument can be made against disaggregating national behavior, even into big disaggregates like politicians and officials. Doing so can, by highlighting differences, obscure properties that are common, particularly those due to shared ideology or shared interest.

To do justice to the subject and period, one must ask to what external reality Americans and their foreign friends were reacting. Was there a Soviet or Communist threat? Or did Western elites, ideologically capitalist, even if Socialist or Labourite, imagine—perhaps even invent—an external enemy? Even at the disaggregated level, did members of particular elites fantasize a Soviet enemy because of political, bureaucratic, or even personal needs? To the extent that one can judge in hindsight, what was the Soviet Union actually up to in 1945–50?

Unfortunately, the question cannot be answered much better now than it could at the time. For both foreign and defense policies, our chief evidence consists of contemporaneous public utterances and contemporaneous actions, most of them designed to be heard or seen. A few memoirs, particularly those of Nikita Khrushchev, together with testimony by emigres, give glimpses of Kremlin decision-making. Pirated copies of the classified Soviet military journal, *Voennaya Mysl'*, say something about debates over doctrine. We know almost nothing about Soviet war planning. We have only estimates by Western analysts about Soviet budgets or force posture. These vary, and none is, on its face, better than any other. We know what Western intelligence agencies surmised regarding Soviet military and naval deployments. We have reason to believe that some of those surmises were widely off the mark not only because of errors on the Western side but also because of deliberate Soviet efforts to deceive. Given all these difficulties, any discussion of actual Soviet policies can only be speculative.

The Soviet government must have been undergoing its own transition in 1945–50. After the German attack in 1941, the regime had had to halt forced industrialization. For the sake of a unified war effort, it appealed to nationalism. It tolerated potential deviation that earlier would have been stamped out. Some military men were allowed to become national heroes even at the risk of Bonapartism. After the war, party documents and the press called again for public sacrifice in order to build industry. They also called for tighter discipline and vigilance against counterrevolutionary tendencies. From 1945 to the early 1950s the Soviet regime was engaged in a constant effort to become again what it had been in the 1930s.

At present, that observation cannot be amplified. We learned only recently, through the patient labor of a Scandinavian scholar, that Stalin used a large personal secretariat as a management device.[165] The fact was never revealed by the Soviet government or Soviet scholars. Similarly, only in recent years have Soviet publications begun glancingly to confirm Western speculation that, from World War II onward, the Soviet Council of Ministers had a military-political subcommittee more or less comparable to the U.S. National Security Council or at least to the British Committee of Imperial Defence.[166] The bizarre secretiveness of the Soviet government makes it very difficult even to speculate about institutional evolution and how, if at all, that may have affected Soviet strategy.

In the transition from war to peace, Stalin seems clearly to have remained unchallenged master of both party and government. During the 1920s he had done away with nearly all rivals. During the 1930s, the Great Purge had killed off millions of potential dissidents (along with many complete innocents). The memoirs of officials and military men who survived that period and the war testify to the awe of Stalin felt by almost everyone in the Soviet Union and the terror of him common among men and women of any stature or rank.[167] Extrapolating from Western models, one can hypothesize the existence of political or bureaucratic factions that competed for influence or advantage, but it would be absurd to suppose that anyone acted with independence comparable to that of contemporaneous Americans or West Europeans, or even with the independence of political leaders in Western-occupied Germany, Austria, Japan, or Korea.[168]

In these circumstances, and absent any additional evidence, it seems reasonable to assume that it was Stalin who defined Soviet objectives and strategy. Several questions therefore invite speculation. What were Stalin's own perceptions? And to whom did he listen? Was his uppermost concern the reconstruction of the Soviet Union and progress toward socialism in one country? Had experience since the 1930s convinced him instead that national security had to have overriding priority? Or had military success since 1943, combined with evidence of weakness or fecklessness among potential adversaries, led him to envision a Russian empire beyond the imagination of the Tsars? If the three perceptions competed in his mind, which held sway when? And to whom did he therefore pay most attention? To men pleading for resources for domestic use? To police agents and military men describing threats near and far? Or to dedicated Communists talking of opportunities abroad? If one group at one time, another at another, which? When?

The meticulous work of Vojtech Mastny, drawing heavily on disclosures by East European party officials, indicates that Stalin came gradually during World War II to see opportunities for the Soviet Union safely to establish postwar spheres of influence beyond the prewar boundaries.[169] Remembering events after World War I, he anticipated British efforts to hem the Soviet Union in behind a *cordon sanitaire*. Churchill, Eden, and other British leaders proved less resolute than expected. Roosevelt, Cordell Hull, Harry Hopkins, and most Americans who visited Moscow did not seem disposed to bolster the British position. Some of them, indeed, appeared at least as much anti-British as anti-Russian. Soviet generals and commissars advancing into Poland, Rumania, and Bulgaria installed regimes dominated by Communist minorities returning from long exile. (In Yugoslavia the new regime was also Communist, but largely because Communists had dominated the partisan Resistance; the regime took and held power without direct backing from the Red Army.) When faced with both British and U.S. protests, Stalin made cosmetic alterations in the Polish cabinet. These sufficed to secure Western diplomatic recognition. In Finland, Czechoslovakia, and Hungary, as in their occupation zones in Germany and Austria, the Soviets showed greater caution, giving Communists encouragement and some advantages in comparison with other political groups, but not all-out support. In some respects, Soviet behavior in these areas paralleled British and U.S. behavior in Italy.

In 1946 the Soviet Union adopted its first postwar Five-Year Plan. From announced details, some post hoc testimony, and evidence of what actually came off production lines, we can infer its character. Highest priority went, as publicly stated, to heavy industry. The populace was openly informed that, toward this end, it would have to wait until later for more abundant food, services, or consumer goods. Although the published budget assigned only a small percentage to defense, the scarcest of all resources—construction materials, machine tools, and skilled engineers—seem to have been consecrated primarily to large-scale production of new military equipment.

Before the war ended, Stalin forced the pace of efforts to produce long-range bombers. Three U.S. B–29s crash-landed in the Soviet Union in 1944 after raids on Japan. They were sufficiently undamaged to allow Soviet engineers to dismantle them and reconstruct their complete architecture. Stalin gave Andrei N. Tupelov, his principal bomber designer, just 36 months to produce a working copy. The result was the TU–4 bomber, with exactly the dimensions of the B–29, a range in excess of 3,000 miles, and the ability to carry a 12,000-ton bomb load. The postwar Five-Year Plan called for large-scale production of the TU–4.[170]

The long-range bomber was by no means the only military plane given high priority; Stalin also ordered an all-out effort to develop jet fighters and interceptors. But he did not insist on the earliest possible delivery. After hearing debate among designers, he agreed not to take the fastest course, which would have been to produce copies of captured German Messer-schmidt ME–262s. He listened instead to Aleksandr S. Yakovlev and other designers, who argued that it would be better for the morale of Soviet engineers if the first Soviet jet were their own creation. One consequence was a requirement for heavier investment of scarce resources, for several design bureaus would be working on competing models. Stalin also ordered a concerted effort to develop rockets, including rockets for air defense, but gave more emphasis to their eventual range and accuracy than to speed of delivery.[171]

Combined with evidence that Stalin insisted on earliest possible produc-tion of a nuclear device, whatever the cost, the fact that Stalin was willing to wait for new ground support and air defense aircraft but not for long-range bombers suggests that he gave priority to being able to demonstrate offensive military might. This is further supported by evidence that other extremely scarce resources were poured into building large numbers of copies of German oceangoing submarines.

The results of Stalin's budgetary decisions began to be visible to the West in 1947. Earlier, the Red Army had seemed to remain on a war footing. Western observers estimated its strength at between four million and five million. Some historians have argued that these estimates were exaggerated. Khrushchev later alleged that the army had actually been reduced below three million; whether or not this is so is still uncertain. One possibility is that the Soviets deliberately planted evidence designed to make Western intelligence analysts overestimate their ground force strength.[172]

At the Tushino air show in August 1947, three TU–4s were put on display. At succeeding anniversaries of the Revolution, May Days, and other such occasions, larger and larger flotillas of these bombers were flown over the heads of attending foreign observers. Before long, Western intel-ligence agencies could calculate accurately that the Soviet TU–4 force would exceed a thousand. (In fact, it reached 1,500.) Meanwhile, voyages by the new oceangoing submarines caused Western analysts to conclude that these, too, were being produced in quantity, perhaps at a rate of 50 to 70 a year.[173]

Until 1947 the Soviet government continued to tolerate Czechoslovakian and Hungarian regimes not totally dominated by Communists. Although it also left Finland alone, it pressed Turkey for concessions comparable to those the Finns had already made, and Stalin did not discourage the Com-munist regimes bordering Greece from actively supporting Communist-led guerrillas battling the British-backed Greek monarchy.

Although Soviet authorities promoted the fortunes of Communists in their zones of occupied Germany and Austria (and suppressed most other parties), Soviet actions suggested an expectation that these Communists would eventually be abandoned. Elsewhere, Communists were given credit for winning concessions from Moscow. Not all oil-drilling equipment was removed from Rumania, for example. In Germany, nothing of the sort was done. Anything and everything of economic value was removed to the Soviet Union. Engineers, technicians, and skilled workers were methodically rounded up and transported far into Russia. German industrial plants were taken apart, shipped to Russia, and reassembled there. The Soviet occupying army gave no indication of preparing for German reconstruction.[174]

Taken all together, this fragmentary evidence seems best accommodated by a hypothesis that Stalin's foreign policy objectives remained indefinite. He clearly expected to retain control of Poland, Rumania, and Bulgaria. He seemed equally to expect that Marshal Tito of Yugoslavia would follow his orders and ask no questions.[175] With regard to Czechoslovakia and Hungary, however, Stalin seemed not to know whether the Soviets would stay or go. In Austria and Germany his agents on the spot acted as if their instructions were to prepare for early withdrawal. Several historians have concluded that, at this time, the Soviet government may have been prepared to cut a bargain over Germany and Austria, perhaps even agreeing to peace treaties in return for substantial reparations payments.[176]

If this is the case, one has to seek some explanation for the furious contemporaneous pace of Soviet military modernization. The Western powers seemed to have accepted Soviet predominance in most of Eastern Europe. If the Soviet government had no plans to enlarge this sphere substantially, why sacrifice so much in order to get bomber and submarine forces? The question acquires a sharper edge given the background. The Soviet Union's great champion of strategic bombing, Vasili V. Khripin, had been a victim of the Great Purge. His long-range air force, though remaining directly under the high command, had played a wartime role as a minor adjunct of the Red Army. The prewar and wartime Soviet navy had been little more than a coast guard force.[177] Postwar Soviet military forces seemed designed for distant power projection. Why?

One might hypothesize that in the Soviet Union, as in the United States, diplomacy and military planning proceeded more or less independently. This must have been partially true. Stalin could not possibly have regulated every detail. It seems unlikely, however, that anyone in the Soviet system would have taken any action without the reasonably sure expectation that, if Stalin learned of it, he would approve. There was too much danger otherwise of hearing "that irrevocable Stalinist phrase, 'I do not need this worker—remove him.' "[178]

One might hypothesize that Stalin spent money for military forces because he wanted to appease generals who might otherwise become contenders for power, spending money on different types of forces in order to create rivalry and division among them. This seems so unlikely as to be hardly worth consideration, given that Stalin was able to send into limbo even the most popular military heroes of the war.

The hypothesis that Stalin wanted large offensive military forces for foreign policy purposes is far more compelling. It does not necessarily follow, however, that Western officials were right that he had in mind extending the Soviet empire. Like Truman and others in the West, Stalin may have been possessed by a desire to avoid a repetition of the events that led to World War II. But Stalin's sense of what had gone wrong was not the same as theirs. He could remember the rapid German recovery of the 1920s. He had seen Britain and France, with blessings from the United States, join Germany in the Locarno Pact. From the Soviet vantage point, Locarno had seemed the framework for a hostile alliance, for it guaranteed frontiers in Western Europe but not those in the East. Stalin probably thought that the hostile alliance had not materialized in part because of his own adroit maneuvering and in larger part because the Great Depression had intensified contradictions within the bourgeois capitalist world.

If Stalin anticipated similar developments in the decade or two after World War II, it might have made sense to him to consolidate the Soviet sphere and meanwhile ready the military forces needed to deter a new Locarno alliance from attempting to penetrate that sphere. Bombers and submarines could have seemed particularly suitable for this purpose if he supposed that the impetus for turning the alliance against the Soviets would come again, as in the 1920s, from London, for long-range bombers and submarines could directly threaten Britain, as ground forces could not. In other words, one can construe Soviet behavior before 1947 as consistent, if one assumes that Soviet leaders doubted their capacity to remain dominant among Czechs, Hungarians, and Germans and feared a repetition of patterns of the previous interwar period.

After 1947, Soviet behavior changed. Stalin created the Cominform, Communists took over Hungary and Czechoslovakia, and Moscow ordered West European Communists to take to the streets. Soviet representatives in occupied areas changed course. Before instituting the Berlin blockade, Soviet authorities had already stopped removals from their zone of Germany. They began organizing there a *Volkspolizei* with all the features necessary to be, with an occupying Red Army near at hand, an organ of permanent control.

All this can be, and has been, interpreted as responsive to actions by the West: the Truman Doctrine and the Marshall Plan; Anglo-American moves to build up western Germany; Truman's speech in response to the Czechoslovakian coup, and so on. Changes in Soviet behavior were accompanied by indications of changes within the Soviet regime. Georgi Malenkov, who had been in charge of removals from liberated and occupied areas, seemed to lose status. Andrei Zhdanov, who looked after the interests of foreign

Communist parties, gained status. Some Kremlinologists surmise that these internal shifts were a cause, not a consequence, of the changes in outward behavior.[179] The fact is that we do not have enough real evidence to judge between these hypotheses or even to arrive at a firm conclusion as to whether Soviet leaders saw themselves as on the defensive or, on the contrary, thought they faced opportunities created by confusion or weakness in the West. The only point about which we can be reasonably sure is that Soviet leaders now focused on the United States more than on Britain. From mid–1946 onward the Soviet press put the United States at the head of capitalist-imperialist conspiracies.[180]

Whatever the case in 1947–48, there was yet another turn in 1949. On the surface, Soviet behavior toward the West became, if not conciliatory, at least less provocative. One can surmise reasons. The outcome of the 1948 U.S. election must have surprised Soviets at least as much as Americans. If commentary in the Party press provided any clues to real thinking within the Soviet government, there had been expectation of a much better showing by Henry Wallace. He received less than 2 percent of the total vote and no electoral votes. In any case, Truman rather than Dewey was the President with whom the Soviets would have to deal.

Calculations in Moscow, to the extent that they centered on the United States, may have supposed that Truman would be easier to get along with than in the past. He no longer faced a Congress controlled by the Republican right. As already noted, his own rhetoric emphasized domestic programs and "Point Four." A commentator in *Pravda* noted with satisfaction the Democratic leader's "promises to avoid war, to promote the consolidation of peace, and to follow the line of Roosevelt's foreign, as well as domestic policy."[181]

Equally, however, observers in Moscow may have worried lest they face a more bold and confident Truman. Though U.S. military men despaired over the mere $14.3 billion allowed them in the budget presented by Truman in January 1949, the Soviet press cried alarm. The authoritative "Observer" alleged in *Izvestiya* that there was actually still more money for the military hidden within the civil budget. *Pravda* spoke of an "arsenal of aggression."[182] And the Soviet press never ceased crying alarm about the newly negotiated North Atlantic Treaty.[183]

To make matters still more complicated, there are scraps of evidence suggesting that the outwardly nonprovocative behavior of the Soviet regime expressed neither hope for detente nor fear of the West, but was only a mask. Tito's defection from the Soviet bloc in the spring of 1948 had infuriated Stalin. Between that time and the early 1950s, Stalin seems to have discussed with Soviet and East European Party leaders the possibility of massive military action at least against Yugoslavia and perhaps against Western Europe. Some of this evidence has come to light only recently; some of it was contemporaneous.[184]

We cannot now say with confidence what Stalin hoped, planned, or prepared for. All we can say, even in retrospect, is that Soviet purposes were so darkly hidden that it was neither unreasonable nor imprudent for Americans and other Westerners to worry about possible military aggression.

In summary, U.S. foreign and defense policies began gradually to cohere around a concept of, above all, preserving a peaceful and non-Communist Western Europe. These policies were largely the handiwork of a new class of U.S. leaders whom I have chosen to label "officials." These officials were encouraged, sometimes influenced, by non-Americans, particularly in Britain and Western Europe. These non-Americans increasingly became participants in the complicated processes of U.S. decision-making. Under the rubric of "national security," these policies won approval from politicians and the attentive U.S. public. "National security" did not always have the same meaning for officials, politicians, and the public. The extent of divergence would become apparent during the 1950s.

What gave coherence to Soviet foreign and defense policies—if anything other than the whims of Stalin—remains indecipherable. What can be said is that the visible elements of those policies—Soviet words and actions— were such as to make it difficult for observers in the West not to infer hostile purposes and worry about aggression. This became even more difficult— impossible even for many leaders of the non-Communist left in the United States and Britain—after June 1950, when Stalin's Asian satellite, North Korea, launched a surprise military offensive against South Korea.

NOTES

1. Paul H. Nitze, "Atoms, Strategy, and Policy," *Foreign Affairs*, 34, January 1956, 187–98, distinguished between *declaratory* foreign policy and *action* foreign policy. He was criticizing the Eisenhower administration for blustering about nuclear "massive retaliation" but showing no real sign of meaning what it said.

2. See, for example, the Eisenhower-Adenauer joint statement, May 28, 1957, in *Public Papers of the Presidents: Dwight D. Eisenhower* (Washington, 1958), 420–24.

3. Fred Kaplan, *The Wizards of Armageddon* (New York, 1983), 134. The protestor was Robert Sprague, deputy chairman of the presidentially appointed panel looking at continental defense. Sprague's testimony to LeMay's words, and supporting testimony from Jerome Wiesner, who accompanied Sprague, can be seen and heard on part three of the videotape series, *War and Peace, in the Nuclear Age*, produced in 1989 by WGBH-TV of Boston (available through the Annenberg Project for Public Broadcasting, Washington, DC). In fairness to LeMay, it should be said that he did not necessarily plan on acting without presidential authority; he could have assumed that, given evidence of Soviet preparation for an attack, the President would authorize SAC to act. For a less colloquially phrased statement of SAC doctrine, see Curtis E. LeMay (with Dale O. Smith), *America is in Danger* (New York, 1968), 82–83. On the general subject, see Kaplan, chapters 18 and 22; Robert Frank Futtrell, *Ideas, Concepts, Doctrine: A History of Basic Thinking in the*

United States Air Force (Maxwell Air Force Base, 1971), especially pages 438–42; Desmond Ball, "The Development of SIOP, 1960–1983," and Jeffrey Richelson, "The Dilemmas of Counterpower Targeting," pages 57–83 and 159–70 in Ball and Richelson (eds.), *Strategic Nuclear Targeting* (Ithaca, 1986).

4. Chief of naval operations to Secretary of the Navy, February 9, 1947, Paolo E. Coletta, *The United States Navy and Defense Unification, 1947–1953* (Newark, 1981), 45; JSPG 496/4, " 'Broiler': Joint Outline War Plan for FY 1949," December 18, 1947, *Records of the Joint Chiefs of Staff, Part II: 1946–1953* (Microfilm Project of University Publications of America, 1981) [hereafter cited as JCS Microfilm], *The Soviet Union*, reel 4; Edward A. Kolodziej, *The Uncommon Defense and Congress, 1945–1963* (Columbus, 1966), 111–23.

5. On B–36 readiness and SAC aircraft deployments, see *Aviation Week*, June 5, 1950, 12–13; on expectations regarding Soviet capabilities for moving against Western Europe and SAC's inability to launch a major strike before D + 16, see JSPG 500/2, " 'Bushwhacker': Outline War Plan for a War Forced on or about January 1, 1952," March 8, 1948 (92), JCS Microfilm: *The Soviet Union*, reel 4; JCS 1745/20, JSPC Report: Atomic Bomb Assembly Teams, September 9, 1949, JCS Microfilm: *Strategic Issues: Atomic Warfare*, reel 1; JCS 1958/2, JSPC: Directives for the Implementation of "Offtackle" [later "Crasspiece"], February 18, 1950, JCS Microfilm: *Strategic Issues: Atomic Warfare*, reel 6.

6. See Raymond L. Garthoff, *Soviet Military Doctrine* (Glencoe, 1953) and *Soviet Strategy in the Nuclear Age* (New York, 1958); Herbert S. Dinerstein, *War and the Soviet Union: Nuclear Weapons and the Revolution in the Soviet Military and Political Thinking* (New York, 1958); Benjamin S. Lambeth, "The Sources of Soviet Military Doctrine," and Edward L. Warner, III, "Soviet Strategic Force Posture: Some Alternative Explanations," pages 200–15 and 310–25 in Frank B. Horton, III et al. (eds.), *Comparative Defense Policy* (Baltimore, 1974); William R. Van Cleave, "Soviet Doctrine and Strategy, a Developing American View," pages 41–71 in Lawrence L. Whetten (ed.), *The Future of Soviet Military Power* (New York, 1976); Van Cleave, "A Garthoff-Pipes Debate on Soviet Strategic Doctrine," *Strategic Review*, 10 (Fall 1982), 36–63; Albert L. Weeks, "The Garthoff-Pipes Debate on Soviet Doctrine: Another Perspective," *Strategic Review*, 11 (Winter 1983), 57–64; Gerhard Wettig, "The Garthoff-Pipes Debate on Soviet Strategic Doctrine, A European Perspective," *Strategic Review*, 11 (Spring 1983), 68–78; Harriet Fast Scott and William F. Scott, *The Armed Forces of the USSR* (3rd edn) (Boulder, 1984), chapter 2; John C. Baker, "Continuity and Change in Soviet Nuclear Strategy," pages 636–60 in Kenneth M. Currie and Gregory Varhall (eds.), *The Soviet Union: What Lies Ahead?* (Washington, 1985); and Michael McGwire, *Military Objectives in Soviet Foreign Policy* (Washington, 1987), chapter 2.

7. The notion of "national security" as a unifying myth for postwar America was first developed in Daniel Yergin's elegant *Shattered Peace: The Origins of the Cold War and the National Security State* (Boston, 1977). Although not quite in those terms, the theme has been further developed in various writings of Melvyn Leffler, particularly "The American Conception of National Security and the Beginnings of the Cold War, 1945–1948," *American Historical Review*, 89 (April 1984), 346–81. The best general account of both policy history and institutional history for this period remains John Lewis Gaddis, *The United States and the Origins of the Cold War, 1941–1947* (New York, 1972).

8. Arthur M. Schlesinger, Jr., *The Age of Roosevelt, I: The Crisis of the Old Order, 1919–1933* (Boston, 1957), 57.

9. *The World Almanac and Book of Facts, 1938* (New York, 1938), 706. In fact, U.S. ground and air forces, including reserves, totaling 474,378 men, were numerically fewer than the forces of, among other countries, Argentina, Belgium, Greece, Portugal, Sweden, and Switzerland; ibid.

10. A good summary is Thomas H. Etzold, *The Conduct of American Foreign Relations: The Other Side of Diplomacy* (New York, 1977), chapters 1 and 2.

11. See Thomas F. Troy, *Donovan and the CIA: A History of the Establishment of the Central Intelligence Agency* (U.S. Central Intelligence Agency, 1981), 3–23.

12. *The New York Times* index for 1935 had listed 115 stories featuring Secretary of Agriculture Henry A. Wallace but only 24 concerning Secretary of the Navy Claude Swanson. (Fewer still were listed on the uniformed chiefs of the army and navy, whose names were little known then and hardly remembered now.) For 1955, the Times index was to list 203 stories on Secretary of Defense Charles E. Wilson and 117 on Admiral Arthur W. Radford, the chairman of the Joint Chiefs of Staff. It listed only 35 stories about Secretary of Agriculture Ezra Taft Benson. The suitability of *The New York Times* as an index of public opinion can be debated. The changes in gross magnitudes nevertheless seem large enough to evidence something more than just shifts of interest at the *Times*.

13. Lloyd C. Gardner, "Lost Empires," *Diplomatic History*, 13 (Winter 1989), 1–14, argues that this expectation was so strong as to be the equivalent of hysterical fixation.

14. See Robert D. Putnam, *The Beliefs of Politicians: Ideology, Conflict, and Democracy in Britain and Italy* (New Haven, 1973) and, for indications of the Canadian counterpart, Colin Campbell and George J. Szablowski, *The Super-Bureaucrats: Structure and Behavior in Central Agencies* (Toronto, 1979).

15. The alternative term, "political executive," is used in Joel D. Aberback, Robert D. Putnam, and Bert A. Rockman, *Bureaucrats and Politicians in Western Democracies* (Cambridge, MA, 1981) as a label for Americans holding managerial office by appointment. I do not borrow that term because it does not distinguish between men and women who come to office because they take part in electoral politics and those who come to office because of status, expertise, or other such attributes. For similar reasons, I do not use the term "super bureaucrat" coined by Campbell and Szablowski (see Note 14 above). But I freely admit that "official," as used here, is a less clear defining term.

16. The best account is Peter Grose, *Israel in the Mind of America* (New York, 1983), 288–93.

17. Executive Session Testimony before the Senate Foreign Relations Committee and House Foreign Affairs Committee, February 21, 1948, United States Department of State, *United States Relations with China, with Special Reference to the Period 1944–49* (Washington, 1949), 380–84.

18. Testimony of March 17, 1948, 80 Cong., 2 sess., United States Senate, Committee on Armed Services, Hearings: *Universal Military Training*, 21.

19. Forrest C. Pogue, *George C. Marshall, III: Statesman, 1945–1959* (New York, 1987), 315.

20. To put the argument a little less categorically and a little more schematically, imagine a horizontal *x*-axis representing some combination of experience and oc-

cupation. Career elective officer-holder is at one end; nonpolitical expert is at the other. Imagine an intersecting vertical *y*-axis representing beliefs about what legitimates a foreign policy, defense policy, or "national security policy" decision. Popular endorsement is at one end; long-term strategic interest measurable only by experts is at the other:

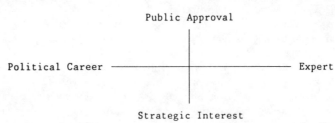

My hypothesis is that if one could measure these attributes, U.S. leaders after World War II would cluster near the upper lefthand and lower righthand corners.

21. The entire document is printed in Arthur Krock, *Memoirs: Sixty Years on the Firing Lane* (New York, 1968). The document is authentic. The original is in the Papers of Clark Clifford, Harry S. Truman Library, Independence, MO.

22. On the Acheson-Lilienthal Plan (which became the Baruch plan), see Dean G. Acheson, *Present at the Creation: My Years in the State Department* (New York, 1969), chapter 17; and *A History of the United States Atomic Energy Commission*, vol. 1: Richard G. Hewlett and Oscar E. Anderson, Jr., *The New World, 1939/1946* (University Park, PA, 1962), chapters 15–16.

23. "Views of Clark Clifford," taken down by Jack Valenti, Camp David, July 25, 1965, Office Files of the President, Clark Clifford File, Lyndon B. Johnson Library, Austin, TX. For an earlier caution from Clifford to Johnson, see Larry M. Berman, *Planning a Tragedy: The Americanization of the War in Vietnam* (New York, 1982), 371.

24. See David S. McLellan, *Dean Acheson: The State Department Years* (New York, 1976), 416–30; Walter Isaacson and Evan Thomas, *The Wise Men: Six Friends and the World They Made—Acheson, Bohlen, Harriman, Kennan, Lovett, McCloy* (New York, 1986), 678–79, 692–702.

25. The most up-to-date account is Peter Wyden, *Bay of Pigs, The Untold Story* (New York, 1979). His account of reactions to Fulbright appears on pages 146–51. The quotation from Bundy is from a memorandum from him to the President, March 15, 1961, Declassified Documents Microfiche (1984), no. 55. [These documents can be located through the *Declassified Documents Quarterly Catalogue,* published by the Carrollton Press of Washington, DC.]

26. Isaacson and Thomas, *The Wise Men,* 585.

27. Unsent letter to Arthur Krock, October 7, 1951, Robert H. Ferrell (ed.), *Off the Record: The Private Papers of Harry S. Truman* (New York, 1980), 218.

28. In *Imperial Democracy: The Emergence of the United States as a Great Power* (New York, 1961), I described the beginning of this process. The global role of the United States in the interwar years is expertly surveyed in Melvyn P. Leffler, "Expansionist Impulses and Domestic Constraints," and Robert M. Hathaway, "Economic Diplomacy in a Time of Crisis," pages 225–76 and 277–332 in William H. Becker and Samuel F. Wells, Jr. (eds.), *Economics and World Order: An Assessment of American Diplomacy Since 1789* (New York, 1984).

29. See Ernest R. May, "Changing International Stakes in Presidential Selection," pages 32–52 in Alexander Heard and Michael Nelson (eds.), *Presidential Selection* (Durham, NC, 1987).

30. See the memoir/history by Ray S. Cline, *Secrets, Spies and Scholars, The Essential CIA* (Washington, 1976), 128–33.

31. Traced in Roy Godson, *American Labor and European Politics: The AFL as a Transnational Force* (New York, 1976). See also sections on the AFL and the CIO in Peter Weiler, *British Labour and the Cold War* (Stanford, 1988). The seminal analytical work on this theme is to be found in Robert O. Keohane and Joseph Nye (eds.), *Transnational Relations and World Politics* (Cambridge, MA, 1972).

32. Robert A. Pastor, *Congress and the Politics of U.S. Foreign Economic Policy* (Berkeley, 1980), 269, points out, accurately, that Truman went on to ask $7 billion for aid to Europe and only $45 million for all "Point Four" programs. He is probably not right, however, in saying that the difference showed the relatively low priority of Point Four. Robert J. Donovan, *The Presidency of Harry S. Truman, 1949–1953: Tumultuous Years* (New York, 1982), 28–29, shows that the President and his staff insisted on keeping Point Four in the inaugural address even though the State Department argued against doing so. In 1950 Truman made Point Four the centerpiece of his commencement address at the University of Missouri: *Public Papers of Harry S. Truman, 1950* (Washington, 1965), 464–68. In a letter to his wife, Truman characterized that address as "a complete resume of the foreign policy of the United States," adding, "It has taken five years to get to this point. I am hoping two more will wind it up." Ferrell, *Off the Record*, 180.

33. See Anna K. Nelson, "President Truman and the Evolution of the National Security Council," *Journal of American History*, 72 (1985), 360–78; and Larry Berman, *The Office of Management and Budget and the Presidency, 1921–1979* (Princeton, 1979), 34–46. The George M. Elsey and Richard E. Neustadt interviews in the oral history collection at the Truman Library provide details.

34. Richard E. Neustadt, *Presidential Power: The Politics of Leadership from FDR to Carter* (New York, 1980) is an analytical work particularly rich in observations and insights on the Roosevelt and Truman presidencies.

35. Dean G. Acheson, *Sketches from Life of Men I Have Known* (New York, 1961), 123–46.

36. April 28, 1946, Arthur H. Vandenberg, Jr., with the collaboration of Joe Alex Morris (eds.), *The Private Papers of Senator Vandenberg* (Boston, 1952), 267.

37. Acheson, *Sketches from Life*, 142–45.

38. Tom Connally, as told to Alfred Steinberg, *My Name is Tom Connally* (New York, 1954), 322, 337. For indications of the rivalry with Vandenberg, see ibid., 269–70, 290–91.

39. Robert L. Messer, *The End of an Alliance: James F. Byrnes, Roosevelt, Truman, and the Origins of the Cold War* (Chapel Hill, 1982), 7.

40. Charles E. Bohlen, *Witness to History* (New York, 1969), 248; see Hugh De Santis, *The Diplomacy of Silence: The American Foreign Service, the Soviet Union, and the Cold War, 1933–1947* (Chicago, 1980), 207. The liveliest description of the antagonism between Byrnes and the "officials" is in Martin Weil, *A Pretty Good Club: The Founding Fathers of the U.S. Foreign Service* (New York, 1978), 228–66.

41. Messer, *End of an Alliance*, 144; Connally, *My Name is Tom Connally*, 290.

42. Diary entry of July 7, 1945: Ferrell, *Off the Record*, 49.

43. Robert J. Donovan, *The Presidency of Harry S. Truman, 1945–1948: Conflict and Crisis* (New York, 1977), 142; Ferrell, *Off the Record*, 109.

44. The authoritative summary is Pogue, *Marshall*, III, 144–412.

45. Gaddis Smith, *Dean Acheson* (New York, 1972), 404–5.

46. Isaacson and Thomas, *The Wise Men*, especially pp. 370–71, 392–93, and 463–65.

47. Acheson, "The President and the Secretary of State," pages 27–50 in Don K. Price (ed.), *The Secretary of State* (Englewood Cliffs, 1960), 41. (Oft-quoted begins here, for Acheson was, in fact, quoting from an article by himself that had appeared in *The New York Times*, October 11, 1959).

48. Bruce R. Kuniholm, *The Origins of the Cold War in the Near East: Great Power Conflict and Diplomacy in Iran, Turkey, and Greece* (Princeton, 1980), gives a detailed analysis of prewar as well as postwar trends. See also David J. Alvarez, *Bureaucracy and Cold War Diplomacy: The United States and Turkey, 1943–1946* (Thessaloniki, 1980).

49. Acheson, *Present at the Creation*, 195–96.

50. Ibid., 197. The information about Truman's map comes from Deborah Welch Larson, *Origins of Containment: A Psychological Explanation* (Princeton, 1985), 202–7, 231–32; "awed," from Isaacson and Thomas, *The Wise Men*, 371.

51. Acting Secretary of State to Secretary of State, August 15, 1946, United States Department of State, *Foreign Relations of the United States* [hereafter FRUS], *1946*, VII, 840.

52. Delivered September 12, 1946, *Vital Speeches*, XII (October 1, 1946), 738–41. See J. Samuel Walker, *Henry A. Wallace and American Foreign Policy* (Westport, 1976), 149–59.

53. Kuniholm, *Origins of the Cold War in the Near East*, 301.

54. Command Paper 7046 of February 22, 1946, quoted in Terry H. Anderson, *The United States, Great Britain, and the Cold War, 1944–1947* (Columbia, 1981), 167.

55. Foreign Office 371/591683, June 21, 1946, quoted in Richard A. Best, Jr., *"Cooperation with Like Minded Peoples": British Influences on American Security Policy, 1945–1949* (Westport, 1986), 96.

56. *FRUS, 1947*, V, 56–57.

57. Ibid., 61.

58. Acheson, *Present at the Creation*, 219. Pogue, *Marshall*, III, 164–65, suggests that Marshall's statement alone may have produced this effect. He also indicates that, in retrospect, Marshall thought everyone had been "too shrill."

59. United States Senate, Committee on Foreign Relations, *Historical Series: Legislative Origins of the Truman Doctrine*; 80 Cong., 1 sess., Hearings Held in Executive Session on S.938, A Bill to Provide for Assistance to Greece and Turkey (Washington, 1973), 128, 131–33, 135, 141–42.

60. Interview with John J. McCloy, December 12, 1985.

61. Michael J. Hogan, *The Marshall Plan: America, Britain, and the Reconstruction of Western Europe, 1947–1952* (Cambridge, MA, 1987) supersedes all earlier works.

62. See Irwin Ross, *The Loneliest Campaign* (New York, 1968). (The Wallace poll is reported on page 149.)

63. *Public Papers of Harry S. Truman, 1948* (Washington, DC: Government Printing Office, 1965), no. 52.

64. Senate Resolution 239, 80th Congress, June 11, 1948, 81 Cong., 1 sess.,

United States Senate, Committee on Foreign Relations, *A Decade of American Foreign Policy: Basic Documents, 1941–1949* (Washington, 1950), 197.

65. See William Whitney Stueck, Jr., *Road to Confrontation: American Policy Toward China and Korea, 1947–1950* (Chapel Hill, 1981), chapters 4 and 5.

66. Robert William Love (ed.), *The Chiefs of Naval Operations* (Annapolis, 1980), 188.

67. On the seriousness of efforts to ensure orderly demobilization, see Michael S. Sherry, *Preparing for the Next War: American Plans for Postwar Defense, 1941–45* (New Haven, 1977), chapters 1–2; on the riots, see R. Alton Lee, "The Army 'Mutiny' of 1946," Journal of American History, 52 (1966), 555–71.

68. Alfred D. Chandler, et al. (eds.), *The Papers of Dwight D. Eisenhower* (11 vols. in progress); (Baltimore, 1970—), vol. 8, 1634–35.

69. E. B. Potter, *Nimitz* (Annapolis, 1976), 413–14; Chandler, *Eisenhower Papers*, vol. 7, 850, n.3.

70. Harry S. Truman, *Memoirs: Years of Trial and Hope* (Garden City, NY, 1955), 46. See Demetrios Caraley, *The Politics of Military Unification: A Study of Conflict and the Policy Process* (New York, 1966); Paul Y. Hammond, *Organizing for Defense* (Princeton, 1961), chapters 8–9; Gordon W. Keiser, *The U.S. Marine Corps and Defense Unification, 1944–47: The Politics of Survival* (Washington, 1982); and John C. Ries, *The Management of Defense: Organization and Control of the U.S. Armed Services* (Baltimore, 1964), chapters 1–7.

71. Quoted in Vincent C. Davis, *The Admirals Lobby* (Chapel Hill, 1967), 197.

72. 79 Cong., 1 sess., House of Representatives, Committee on Naval Affairs, Hearings on the Composition of the Postwar Navy, 1168–69, quoted in Vincent Davis, *Postwar Defense Policy and the U.S. Navy, 1943–1946* (Chapel Hill, 1966), 194–95.

73. Quoted ibid., 206–7. My argument here merely echoes Davis's.

74. Kaplan, *Wizards of Armageddon*, 26.5.

75. Chandler, *Eisenhower Papers*, vol. 10, 722.

76. Letter to Representative Carl Vinson, January 3, 1950, Chandler, *Eisenhower Papers*, vol. 11, 892.

77. Vincent Davis, *Postwar Defense Policy and the U.S. Navy*, 146.

78. See Chandler, *Eisenhower Papers*, vol. 7, 858–962, and vol. 8, 1258–60.

79. Donovan, *Conflict and Crisis*, 265, quoting a note by George Elsey.

80. Letter to Robert Sherwood, August 27, 1947, Walter Millis (ed.), *The Forrestal Diaries* (New York, 1951), 299. See also Robert Greenhalgh Albion and Robert Howe Connery (eds.), *Forrestal and the Navy* (New York, 1962), 284–86.

81. Alfred Goldberg, (ed.), *History of the Office of the Secretary of Defense*, vol. 1: Steven L. Rearden, *The Formative Years, 1947–1950* (Washington, 1984), 395.

82. Jean Edward Smith (ed.), *The Papers of General Lucius D. Clay: Germany, 1945–1949* (2 vols.) (Bloomington, 1974), 568–69.

83. Millis, *Forrestal Diaries*, 387; George F. Kennan, *Memoirs, 1925–1950* (Boston, 1967), 400–1. On the motives for Clay's cable, see Smith, *Clay Papers: Germany*, vol. 2, 564–68; Jean Edward Smith, "The View from USFET: General Clay's and Washington's Interpretation of Soviet Intentions in Germany, 1945–1948," in Hans A. Schmitt (ed.), *U.S. Occupation in Europe after World War II* (Lawrence, 1978), 75–76; Avi Shlaim, *The United States and the Berlin Blockade, 1948–1949: A Study in*

Crisis Decision-Making (Berkeley, 1983), 106–8; and John H. Backer, *Winds of History: The German Years of Lucius DuBignon Clay* (New York, 1983), 224–28.

84. Millis, *Forrestal Diaries*, 389–90.

85. Millis, *Forrestal Diaries*, 392–93; Rearden, *Formative Years*, 395–97; *The History of the Joint Chiefs of Staff*, vol. 2: Kenneth W. Condit, *The Joint Chiefs of Staff and National Policy, 1947–1949* (Wilmington, 1979), 181–84.

86. Coletta, *The United States Navy and Defense Unification*, 80.

87. Millis, *Forrestal Diaries*, 476–77.

88. *First Report of the Secretary of Defense, 1948* (Washington, 1948), 9, 80.

89. See Berman, *Office of Management and Budget*, chapter 2; William E. Pemberton, *Bureaucratic Politics: Executive Reorganization during the Truman Administration* (Columbia, 1979); Elias Huzar, *The Purse and the Sword: Control of the Army by Congress through Military Appropriations* (Ithaca, 1950); and Samuel P. Huntington, *The Common Defense* (New York, 1961).

90. Sherry, *Preparing for the Next War*, 94–108.

91. Davis, *Postwar Defense Policy and the U.S. Navy*, 110–18.

92. Sherry, *Preparing for the Next War*, 226–27.

93. Alfred Goldberg, *A History of the United States Air Force, 1907–1957* (Princeton, 1957), 106.

94. Sherry, *Preparing for the Next War*, 106–9.

95. Ibid., 221.

96. "Address before a Joint Session of the Congress on Universal Military Training," October 23, 1945, *Public Papers of Harry S. Truman, 1945*, 407, 411. Sherry, *Preparing for the Next War*, 235.

97. See Truman, *Memoirs*, vol. 2, 41–42; *Public Papers of Harry S. Truman, 1946*, 24–86.

98. *Public Papers of Harry S. Truman, 1947*, 40–97, 279–80, 342–43; *Public Papers of Harry S. Truman, 1948*, forthcoming.

99. See Warner R. Schilling, Paul Y. Hammond, and Glenn H. Snyder, (eds.), *Strategy, Politics, and Defense Budgets* (New York, 1962), especially pages 28–47 and 273–79.

100. *Public Papers of Harry S. Truman, 1948*, forthcoming; Eisenhower notes on a conversation with Truman, December 9, 1948, *Eisenhower Papers*, vol. 10, 367.

101. Cost data from *Aviation Week* (September 6, 1948), 12, and *Aircraft of the Pima Air Museum* (Tuscon, 1987), 67. Performance data from Ray Wagner, *American Combat Planes* (3rd edn) (Garden City, 1982), 442–51.

102. The history of the B–36 is told in painful detail in 81 Cong., 1 sess., House of Representatives, Armed Services Committee, *Investigation of the B–36 Bomber Program*. It is summarized in Paul Y. Hammond, "Super Carriers and B–36 Bombers," pages 465–567 of Harold Stein (ed.), *American Civil–Military Decisions: A Book of Case Studies* (Birmingham, 1963). On the absence of operational B–36s in 1950, see *Aviation Week* (June 5, 1950), 12.

103. R. P. Hunnicutt, *Firepower, A History of the American Heavy Tank* (Novato, 1988), 111–23.

104. *Survival in the Air Age: A Report by the President's Air Policy Commission* (Washington, 1948), 23–25.

105. 80 Cong., 2 sess., Senate Report 949: Report of the Congressional Aviation Policy Board, *National Aviation Policy*.

106. Condit, *Joint Chiefs of Staff, 1947–1949*, 197. The next several paragraphs, concerning fiscal years 1949 and 1950 budgeting, draw primarily on Condit, chapters 6 and 7, Rearden's *Formative Years*, chapters 11–13, and Coletta, *United States Navy and Defense Unification*, chapters 3–6. Although not based on the documentary sources available to later writers, Schilling's "The Politics of National Defense: Fiscal 1950," pages 1–266 in Schilling, Hammond, and Snyder, *Strategy, Politics, and Defense Budgets*, remains a basic account and an important piece of analysis.

107. Condit, *Joint Chiefs of Staff, 1947–1949*, 205. Rearden, *Formative Years*, 323, has a different total for FY 1952, saying (598, n. 50) that he could not find Condit's source.

108. Pogue, *Marshall, vol. 2: Organizer of Victory, 1943–1945* (New York: Viking, 1973), 68.

109. Secretary of Defense to Secretary of State, October 31, 1948, *FRUS, 1948*, vol. 1, 644–46; Secretary of State to Secretary of Defense, November 8, 1948, ibid., 655.

110. Coletta, *United States Navy and Defense Unification*, chapter 5; Schilling, "Politics of National Defense: Fiscal 1950," 110–11.

111. *Eisenhower Papers*, vol. 10, 448–49.

112. *Aviation Week*, January 17, 1949, 11–14.

113. Survey taken July 1949, in George H. Gallup, *The Gallup Polls: Public Opinion, 1935–1971* (3 vols.) (New York, 1972), vol. 2, 858–59. The figures for college-educated respondents were 76 percent and 3 percent.

114. Huntington's seminal *Common Defense* argues that "structural" elements of defense programs—organization, pay, and so on—could continue to be handled in the old way, but "strategic" elements could not. Force characteristics were determined by a legislative process—by bargaining like that which accompanies the passage of legislation—but this process came to take place largely within the executive branch. See especially chapter 3. See also Schilling, "Politics of National Defense: Fiscal 1950," and Kolodziej, *Uncommon Defense*, chapters 8–9.

115. *Aviation Week*, January 24, 1949, 11–12.

116. *Aviation Week*, February 28, 1949, 11–14, comments on both effects.

117. *Aviation Week*, February 14, 1949, 11–12.

118. *The Gallup Polls*, vol. 1, 759, and vol. 2, 817–18.

119. Kolodziej, *Uncommon Defense*, 105–7.

120. See Donovan, *Tumultuous Years*, 60–65.

121. Kolodziej, *Uncommon Defense*, 105.

122. Eisenhower diary, February 9, 1949, *Eisenhower Papers*, vol. 10, 482–83.

123. Donovan, *Tumultuous Years*, 64–65.

124. 81 Cong., 1 sess., House of Representatives, Committee on Armed Services, *Investigation of the B–36 Bomber Program*, 32–33.

125. Hammond, "Super Carriers and B–36 Bombers," gives the best summary of the debate. Coletta, *United States Navy and Defense Unification*, chapter 8, has the most sympathetic summary of Navy arguments. Davis, *The Admirals Lobby*, gives a clinical analysis of the Navy's organization and tactics for exercising domestic influence.

126. Schilling, "Politics of National Defense: Fiscal 1950," 170.

127. 81 Cong., 1 sess., House of Representatives, Committee on Armed Services, *Unification and Strategy*, 536–37.

128. Hammond, "Super Carriers and B–36 Bombers," 549–51, reproduces the committee recommendations in full.

129. Condit, *Joint Chiefs of Staff, 1947–1949*, 262–64.

130. See Stueck, *Road to Confrontation*, chapters 3 and 5.

131. JCS comments on NSC 7, April 17, 1948, *FRUS, 1948*, vol. 1, 561–64.

132. JSPG 496/4: " 'Broiler'—Joint Outline War Plan for Fiscal Year 1949," December 18, 1947, JCS Microfilm: *The Soviet Union*, reel 4.

133. JCS 1844: " 'Frolic' [renamed 'Grabber']: Short-Range Emergency Plan," March 9, 1948, JCS Microfilm: *The Soviet Union*, reel 4; JCS 1844/2: Memorandum by the Chief of Naval Operations, April 6, 1948, JCS Microfilm: *The Soviet Union*, reel 5; JCS 1844/4: " 'Doublestar' [renamed 'Halfmoon,' then 'Fleetwood']: Short Range Emergency War Plan, May 19, 1948, JCS Microfilm: *The Soviet Union*, reel 5. See Condit, *Joint Chiefs of Staff, 1947–1949*, chapter 9; and David Alan Rosenberg, "The Origins of Overkill, Nuclear Weapons and American Strategy, 1945–1960," *International Security*, 7 (Spring 1983), 3–71.

134. *Eisenhower Papers*, vol. 8, 1585.

135. JLPG 84/5, "Quick Feasibility Test of 'Broiler'," March 19, 1948, JCS Microfilm: *The Soviet Union*, reel 4; JLPC 416/12, "The Logistical Feasibility of... 'Doublestar' [renamed 'Halfmoon']," June 15, 1948, JCS Microfilm: *The Soviet Union*, reel 5.

136. Rosenberg, "Origins of Overkill," 15; JCS 1823/14, Memorandum by the chief of staff of the air force, May 27, 1949, JCS Microfilm: *Strategic Issues: Atomic Warfare*, reel 1.

137. Curtis E. LeMay, with MacKinlay Kantor, *Mission with LeMay: My Story* (Garden City, NY: Doubleday, 1965), 481.

138. Clay Papers, vol. 2, 699–700; Memo by the director of Central Intelligence, July 28, 1948, President's Secretary's File/Intelligence File, Harry S. Truman Library, Independence, MO; Secretary of Defense to Secretary of State, July 28, 1948, *FRUS, 1948*, vol. 2, 994.

139. See the April 6, 1949, estimate by the Moscow embassy's Joint Intelligence Committee in *FRUS, 1949*, vol. 5, 603–9.

140. Memorandum by the director of the Joint Staff, July 16, 1948, *FRUS, 1948*, vol. 3, 188–93.

141. JCS to Secretary of Defense, November 24, 1948, *FRUS, 1948*, vol. 3, 289–92; Secretary of Defense to Secretary of State, September 2, 1949, *FRUS, 1949*, vol. 4, 322–23.

142. JCS 1691/7, Joint Security Control, Final Report of the JCS Evaluation Board for Operation "Crossroads," October 16, 1947, JCS Microfilm: *Strategic Issues: Atomic Warfare*, reel 2.

143. See the Air Annex to War Plan "Broiler" cited in note 142.

144. *A History of the United States Atomic Energy Commission*, vol. 2: Richard G. Hewlett and Francis Duncan, *Atomic Shield, 1947/1952* (University Park, 1969), 161–65, 175–79; JCS 1745/18, Memorandum by chairman, Armed Forces Special Weapons Project, December 2, 1948, JCS Microfilm: *Strategic Issues: Atomic Warfare*, reel 1; JCS 1745/20, JSPC Report: Atomic Bomb Assembly Teams, September 9, 1949, JCS Microfilm: *Strategic Issues: Atomic Warfare*, reel 1.

145. See, for the most recent and illuminating discussion of the "hydrogen

bomb," McGeorge Bundy, *Danger and Survival: Choices about the Bomb in the First Fifty Years* (New York, 1989), chapter 5.

146. Symington to Eisenhower, March 11, 1949, *Eisenhower Papers*, vol. 10, 534.

147. *The History of the Joint Chiefs of Staff*, vol. 4: Dewitt C. Poole, *The Joint Chiefs of Staff and National Policy, 1950–1952* (Wilmington, 1980), 29–30.

148. Secretary of State to Secretary of Defense, November 8, 1948, *FRUS, 1948*, vol. 1, 655.

149. These sentences obviously do not do justice to the complexity of Kennan's reasoning. He was particularly concerned about emphasis on nuclear weapons and was prepared to favor a higher level of military preparedness if it meant reduced reliance on those weapons; but he did not think that the effectiveness of containment or deterrence varied according to the size or character of the U.S. military establishment. See his long memorandum of January 20, 1950, in *FRUS, 1950*, vol. 1, 22–44.

150. See his report of January 31, 1949, in *FRUS, 1949*, vol. 4, 54–59.

151. See the notes in *Eisenhower Papers*, vol. 10, 515–19, for an excellent discussion of Eisenhower's role.

152. December 13, 1948, *Eisenhower Papers*, vol. 10, 365.

153. Memorandum by the director of the Joint Staff, February 25, 1949, *Eisenhower Papers*, vol. 10, 516.

154. JCS 1844/2: Memorandum by the chief of Naval Operations, April 6, 1948, JCS Microfilm: *The Soviet Union*, reel 5; JCS 1920/4: Memorandum by the chief of Naval Operations, April 4, 1949, JCS Microfilm: *The Soviet Union*, reel 6. See Poole, *The Joint Chiefs of Staff, 1950–1952*, 286–87; and *Eisenhower Papers*, vol. 10, 517.

155. Foreign Assistance Correlation Committee Policy Paper, July 1, 1949, *FRUS, 1949*, vol. 1, 347–49.

156. *Eisenhower Papers*, vol. 10, 753.

157. A summary version is in Thomas H. Etzold and John L. Gaddis (eds.), *Containment: Documents on American Policy and Strategy, 1945–1950* (New York, 1978), 360–64. See Condit, *The Joint Chiefs of Staff, 1947–1949*, 313–14, and Rosenberg, "Origins of Overkill," 15–17.

158. Eisenhower to Marshall, January 7, 1948, *Eisenhower Papers*, vol. 9, 2184.

159. See Rearden, *Formative Years*, 408–10.

160. JCS 1844/34: Memorandum by the chief of staff of the air force, January 18, 1949, JCS Microfilm: *The Soviet Union*, reel 5.

161. Futtrell, *Ideas, Concepts, Doctrine*, 142–45; John J. Midgley, Jr., *Deadly Illusions: Army Policy for the Nuclear Battlefield* (Boulder, 1986), 2–9; Coletta, *United States Navy and Defense Unification*, 220–24.

162. See, for example, JCS 1844/46, JSPC: Joint Emergency War Plan "Offtackle" [later "Shakedown," then "Crasspiece"], November 8, 1949, JCS Microfilm: *The Soviet Union*, reel 6, and JCS 1920/10, JSPG: Long-Range Plans for War with the U.S.S.R. ["Dropshot"], December 19, 1949, ibid. The latter document has been published practically in full in Anthony Cave Brown (ed.), *Dropshot: The United States Plan for War with the Soviet Union in 1957* (New York, 1978).

163. The document is in *FRUS, 1950*, vol. 1, 234–94. Earlier pages in the volume testify to Nitze's assiduity in coalition building.

164. Note by the Executive Secretary to the NSC, April 14, 1950, *FRUS, 1950*, vol. 1, 234.

165. See Niels Erik Rosenfeldt, *Knowledge and Power: The Role of Stalin's Secret Chancellory in the Soviet System of Government* (Copenhagen, 1978).

166. Edward L. Warner, III, *The Military in Contemporary Soviet Politics, An Institutional Analysis* (New York: Praeger, 1977), 22–23 summarizes earlier speculation. Scott and Scott, *The Armed Forces of the USSR* [cited in note 6 above], 105–6 details how the existence of this committee was finally officially acknowledged.

167. See Seweryn Bialer (ed.), *Stalin and His Generals: Soviet Military Memoirs of World War II* (New York, 1969), 63–88, for examples.

168. The bravest attempt to portray Soviet politics with Stalin as only one major actor is William O. McCagg, *Stalin Embattled, 1943–1948* (Detroit, 1978).

169. Vojtech Mastny, *Russia's Road to the Cold War: Stalin's War Aims, 1941–1945* (New York, 1979).

170. Alexander Boyd, *The Soviet Air Force Since 1918* (London, 1977), 215–16; William T. Lee and Richard F. Staar, *Soviet Military Policy Since World War II* (Stanford, 1986), 12. There is considerable Soviet literature on the TU–4. See particularly L. L. Kerber, *TU: chelovek i samolet* (Moscow, 1973) and M. L. Gallai, *Ispytano v nebe* (Moscow, 1963).

171. Boyd, *Soviet Air Force*, 207–11; Lee and Staar, *Soviet Military Policy*, 14; G. A. Tokaty-Tokaev, "Foundations of Soviet Cosmonautics," *Spaceflight* (October 1968), 335–46.

172. See Thomas W. Wolfe, *Soviet Power and Europe, 1945–1970* (Baltimore, 1970), 9–11; Matthew Evangelista, "Stalin's Postwar Army Reappraised," *International Security*, 7 (Winter 1982–83), 110–38. V. N. Donchenko, "Demobilizatsiya Sovetskoi armii i reshenie problemy kadrov v pervye poselevoennye gody," *Istoriya SSSR*, 3, 1970, 97–98, is, so far as I know, the only discussion of the question by a Soviet historian; he indicates that the total was probably 3–3.5 million.

173. JIC 435/12, "Soviet Intentions and Capabilities, 1948, 1952/57," November 30, 1948, JCS Microfilm: *The Soviet Union*, reel 3; Wolfe, *Soviet Power and Europe*, 46, note 42.

174. See Robert M. Slusser (ed.), *Soviet Economic Policy in Postwar Germany: A Collection of Papers by Former Soviet Officials* (New York, 1953).

175. Milovan Djilas, *Conversations with Stalin* (New York, 1962), 155ff.

176. For example, Adam B. Ulam, *The Rivals: America and Russia Since World War II* (New York, 1971), 122–23. See William Taubman, *Stalin's American Policy: From Entente to Detente to Cold War* (New York, 1982), 158–65.

177. Boyd, *Soviet Air Force*, 56–58; Wolfe, *Soviet Power and Europe*, 44–45.

178. A. A. Novikov, *V nebe Leningrada* (Moscow, 1970), 290, quoted in Timothy J. Colton, *Commissars, Commanders, and Civilian Authority: The Structure of Soviet Military Politics* (Cambridge, 1979), 158.

179. For example, Boris I. Nicolaevsky, *Power and the Soviet Elite* (New York, 1965), 120–29.

180. This was noted by the U.S. embassy in Moscow: *FRUS, 1946*, vol. 6, 768ff.

181. November 7, 1948.

182. *Izvestiya*, March 19, 1949; *Pravda*, February 8, 1949.

183. See *Current Digest of the Soviet Press* for 1949.

184. Nicolaevsky, *Power and the Soviet Elite*, 170–71, 241–52; Karel Kaplan, *Dans*

les archives du comite central: Trente ans de secrets du bloc sovietique (Paris: Michel, 1978), 164–66; Bela Kiraly, "The Aborted Soviet Military Plans Against Tito's Yugoslavia," 273–88 in *War and Society in East Central Europe*, vol. 10: Wayne S. Vucinich (ed.), *At the Brink of War and Peace: The Tito–Stalin Split in a Historic Perspective* (New York, 1982). See Vojtech Mastny, "Stalin and the Militarization of the Cold War," *International Security*, 9 (Winter 1984–85), 109–29.

2

Balances of Power: The Strategic Dimensions of the Marshall Plan

Michael Hogan

The current literature on the early Cold War in Europe focuses largely on the U.S. strategy of containment, specifically on American efforts to organize a continental correlation of forces that could deter Soviet aggression and discourage Communist subversion in areas deemed vital to the economic well-being and military security of the United States. Both the Marshall Plan and the German problem are analyzed in this context. In addition to fortifying U.S. allies, or so the argument goes, the Marshall Plan would expedite the economic reconstruction and political reintegration of the former Reich, or at least of the western occupation zones, thereby speeding recovery in Western Europe and creating a bipolar equilibrium on the continent.

This argument is sensible but inadequate. It fails to address the pivotal problem of how Germany's rehabilitation would be made acceptable to its former victims. The U.S.–Soviet alliance collapsed in part on this problem, a fact well documented in the current literature, which nonetheless slights the strain this same problem placed on the United States' relations with its European friends. Because the Western Europeans feared a resurgence of German power almost as much as an expansion of Soviet influence, assuaging this fear became one of the keys to the bipolar balance of power the Americans had in mind. Put differently, bipolar equilibrium on the continent required first and foremost the reconstruction of a viable balance of power between Germany and ancient enemies in the West.

Initially, at least, U.S. leaders wanted to achieve this balance through economic rather than military means, a fact obscured by scholars of U.S. geostrategy, who often write as if the Marshall Plan had been mere prelude to the North Atlantic Treaty. Prior to the Korean War, however, economic designs and economic tools dominated geostrategic thinking in Washington. Through the Marshall Plan, U.S. leaders used economic aid to forge an integrated single market in Western Europe, in part because such a framework would be strong enough to contain the Soviet bloc in Eastern Europe, and in part because it would be large enough to balance Germany's power against the combined power of other participants.

The U.S. task was neither easy nor fully successful, largely because of obstacles raised by key partners on the continent. The French oscillated between plans to delay Germany's recovery and proposals for a Western European union; the British wanted to protect their interests within a strictly North Atlantic system. These differences hampered progress until 1950, when the French announced the Schuman Plan for a Western European coal and steel community that would merge Franco–German interests under the guiding hand of a supranational authority. The proposed community dovetailed in key respects with U.S. efforts to build an economic counterweight to the Soviet bloc, and it came to pass just as other developments were guiding U.S. policymakers down a road that led from economic to military strategies of containment.

The geostrategic thinking behind the Marshall Plan is clear enough. Germany's expansion in the 1930s and the world war that followed had underscored in American minds the importance of European markets, workers, and industrial capacity. These were viewed as strategic as well as economic assets whose control by a hostile power would increase its warfighting capacity at the expense of U.S. security.[1] This danger appeared in the postwar period, when the Soviet Union began to consolidate its control over Eastern Europe. Developments in Western Europe added to the danger. By June 1947, when Secretary of State George C. Marshall announced his celebrated proposal for a European Recovery Program, the victorious powers had failed to agree on a German settlement, and the economic dislocations and political unrest growing out of the war had left a power vacuum that neither Britain nor France could fill. These developments raised the prospect of further Soviet expansion unless the United States assembled the components of a viable balance of power. This meant rebuilding economic and political systems strong enough to forestall aggression and defeat Communist parties, whose rise to power seemed the most likely way for the Soviets to extend their influence.

Such thinking led the War Department to press for a massive recovery program, and the same thinking was rife in other agencies as well. George F. Kennan, who headed the State Department's Policy Planning Staff, warned that continued stalemate at the negotiating table would lead to economic collapse in Western Europe and to the triumph of Communist partisans who were mere surrogates of the Soviet Union. In his view, the United States must foreclose these dangers by organizing a Western European complex strong enough to contain the Soviets.[2] The State–War–

Navy Coordinating Committee also stressed the importance of using U.S. aid to keep strategic areas and key resources in "friendly hands."[3] Marshall told the cabinet that U.S. policy should seek to restore the "balance of power" in Europe.[4] And Secretary of the Navy James Forrestal informed the Senate Foreign Relations Committee that "we are living in a world today in which there is imbalance" between the "two great superpowers." The Marshall Plan would "redress the balance" by rebuilding Western Europe and thereby creating, in Forrestal's words, the political and economic "equilibrium which is requisite to the maintenance of peace."[5]

The central problem concerned how to build a viable counterweight to the Soviet bloc. And the solution, so far as the Americans were concerned, was to be found in the economic integration of Western Europe. The State Department's economic offices thought in terms of a " 'functional' unification" of the European economies.[6] The State-War-Navy Coordinating Committee urged a "regional" trading and production system.[7] The Policy Planning Staff envisioned "intramural economic collaboration" and "regional political association."[8] All three agencies wanted the western occupation zones included in the recovery program and the integrated economic unit that resulted. So did officials in the War Department, where Colonel Charles H. Bonesteel was suggesting that international supervision of the Ruhr could lead first to integration of the French and German economies and then to a wider economic unity in Central and Western Europe.[9] Secretary Marshall and John Foster Dulles staked out a similar position at the Moscow Foreign Ministers Conference of early 1947. "As we studied the problem of Germany," Dulles reported, "we became more and more convinced that there is no economic solution along purely national lines. Increased economic unity is absolutely essential to the well-being of Europe."[10]

In the minds of these and other policymakers, integration operated as a conceptual link between the economic and strategic goals on their agenda for Western Europe. An integrated economy held together by central institutions and natural market forces would harmonize national policies and bring the gains in greater productivity and resource utilization associated with economies of scale. It would give the Marshall Plan countries, as John Foster Dulles put it, the benefits of a market "big enough to justify modern methods of cheap production for mass consumption."[11] This was the way to spur recovery, put participating countries on a self-supporting basis, and clear a path to the multilateral system of world trade envisioned in the Bretton Woods agreements of 1944.

Adding to this list were the geostrategic advantages of a Western European economic union. Besides ameliorating the economic conditions that could drive desperate governments to "accept a Soviet-dictated peace," economic integration would help to reconcile Germany's recovery with the economic and security concerns of its neighbors.[12] Bonesteel and Secretary of War Robert Patterson saw such a course as the best way to revive Germany's economy without restoring its prewar hegemony. Dulles recounted how the U.S. delegation at the Moscow Conference had suggested international supervision of the Ruhr in order to prevent its resources from again becoming "an economic club in the hands of Germany."[13] A Western European economic union, particularly if superintended by central institutions, would defuse the spirit of nationalism that had made Germany the "cockpit" of "power clashes" and the "breeder of wars."[14] It would make it possible to revive the German economy, but not the German threat to Western European security, and to integrate the former Reich into what Dulles called a "solid front" not "easily reduced even by Soviet Power."[15] "Only such a Union," Kennan elaborated, "holds out any hope of restoring the balance of power in Europe without permitting Germany to become again the dominant power."[16]

These remarks encapsulate the geostrategic design that undergirded the Marshall Plan from its inception in 1947 through the years that followed. In 1948 Marshall wrote to Ambassador Jefferson Caffery in Paris that European security and recovery ultimately depended on the formation of an integrated framework capable of controlling the Germans and containing the Soviets.[17] Dean Acheson, who succeeded Marshall as Secretary of State, made a similar point in 1949, when he wrote to Assistant Secretary of State George Perkins that integration would dampen the dangerous revival of nationalism in Germany and harness its resources "to the security and welfare of Western Europe as a whole."[18] A National Security Council (NSC) document of the same year, as well as the supporting position papers, also stressed the need to reintegrate Germany into a "strong common structure of free Europeanism." A "segmented" Germany, it warned, might again dominate the continent, "provide a fertile field for the rebirth of aggressive German nationalism," or lead to a dangerous Soviet–German rapprochement. But a Germany integrated into the framework of a "general European union" would ensure that its resources were used for Western ends and peaceful purposes.[19] A year later the State Department's Bureau of German Affairs concluded again that economic integration was the best way to forge a collective framework "into which Germany can be 'integrated,' by which Germany can be 'contained,'" [and] in which Germany can play a peaceful, constructive but not dictatorial role."[20] One of the "major preoccupations" of policymakers in the State Department, the British embassy reported from Washington, was to see "that Western Germany was brought and kept within the Western fold."[21] The only alternative, the Americans kept insisting, was a new Rapallo Pact or a neutral Germany that played West against East to the detriment of European security.

Guided by this design, the Marshall planners worked incessantly along two separate but parallel tracks. Although conceding the need for a military security board and prohibitions on war-related production, they struggled to pare down the list of German reparations, lift the restrictions on German industry, fuse the western occupation zones, and organize what became the Federal Republic.[22] At the same time, they supported a series of successful plans to liberalize intra-European trade and payments. They encouraged the Council of Europe, helped to found the European Payments Union, and tried to bestow supranational powers on the Organization for European Economic Cooperation, the European agency established to oversee the recovery program. Through these and similar initiatives, the Americans tried to utilize both market mechanisms and federal institutions to weld the Federal Republic and the Western European states into a unit of economic and political power safe from a renascent Reich and able to offset the Soviet bloc.[23] This was a coherent design and one destined to succeed. Because of obstacles raised in Paris and London, however, success would come slowly and would not square in every way with the lines first mapped out in Washington.

The French entered the postwar era assuming that France would take Germany's place as the industrial hub of the European economy and as the fulcrum in a new European balance of power. The Monnet Plan had been based on this assumption. The plan aimed to make French exports more competitive in the international economy, particularly the European economy, where the goal was to replace German with French products. Doing so was the key to French security and to a level of domestic economic growth that would ameliorate social divisions and end the redistributive battles of the interwar period. To achieve these goals, recovery in France had to precede recovery in Germany; French steel producers had to have first claim on the Ruhr's rich deposits of coal and coke, and Germany's steel output had to be limited to levels that prevented overproduction in Europe. It was this kind of thinking that led the French to claim the Saar and to demand substantial reparations, detachment of the Rhineland, and international ownership of the Ruhr coal and steel industries. Until these demands were satisfied, they refused to permit an upward revision of Germany's level of industry or to accept proposals for German unification and central administration.[24]

Under the Marshall Plan, however, the French consistently lost ground in their attempts to block the economic and political reconstruction of western Germany, which was strongly supported by their powerful ally and benefactor across the Atlantic. U.S. policymakers brought the Germans into the recovery program and rebuffed French proposals for international ownership of the Ruhr and permanent limits on German production. At the London Conference of 1948 and the Washington Foreign Ministers Conference of 1949, the Americans also succeeded in easing many of the constraints on German industry, reducing the number of plants to be removed as reparations, unifying the western zones, and replacing military government with a German administration and an Allied High Commission of civilian officials. The French, to be sure, won some concessions in return.

The United States agreed to safeguard against Germany's rearmament and remilitarization. It sanctioned an International Authority to oversee the Ruhr and retained the limits on German steel production at approximately eleven million tons per year. But these were tenuous gains at best. The Ruhr Authority was a feeble instrument of French policy. It was responsible to the Allied powers as a group, and there were no guarantees that it would retain its limited authority in the post-occupation period or inherit from the Allied steel and coal boards the right to decartelize German industry and allocate German production between internal consumption and export.[25]

Realizing that they could stall but not stop Germany's recovery, the French devised a new strategy to safeguard their military security and economic ambitions. They tried, in a fashion reminiscent of their efforts after World War I, to contain Germany's power through offsetting arrangements with its neighbors. This strategy built on initiatives dating from World War II through the first years of the recovery program. It dovetailed in key respects with U.S. strategy, and would come to fruition with the Schuman Plan of 1950.

During and after the war, General Charles de Gaulle, Georges Bidault, Jean Monnet, and a wide range of other French leaders, including Hervé Alphand and a number of officials in the Quai d'Orsay, came to believe that a European economic union might be the best way to support the French economy and tame the Germans. Policymakers in the French government and the British Foreign Office established a committee of officials to study the prospects of close Anglo-French collaboration as the cornerstone of such a union; Bidault went so far as to predict that an Anglo-Western European bloc would emerge as an independent "third force" in world affairs.[26] Nothing came of the Anglo-French committee, largely because of British concerns noted later, and notions of a European "third force" gave way as the Cold War forced the French into closer association with the United States. Nevertheless, the idea of a Western European economic union, albeit one aligned with the North American continent, remained a persistent strain in French plans to control the Germans.

In the summer of 1947, for example, the French urged the formation of a Western European customs union as part of the comprehensive recovery program that Marshall had proposed at Harvard University. A customs union, they said, would appeal to integrationist sentiment in the United States, ensure congressional support for the Marshall Plan, and bring the gains in trade and production needed to raise living standards and put Western Europe on a self-supporting basis.[27] Left unsaid were the special advantages that would accrue to the French, whose proposal for a customs union complemented their dogged support for an international authority to oversee the Ruhr. Both mechanisms aimed to contain the Germans— eventual partners in the customs union and the Ruhr authority—in part through federal regulatory instruments which the French would head, and in part by organizing a European group large enough to offset Germany's power with the combined power of other participants.

A similar strategy guided the French proposals of 1949 for a regional economic union known variously as Fritalux or Finebel.[28] Central to all of these proposals was the formation of a supranational authority through which the French could work to guarantee their security and shield their Monnet Plan against a rebirth of German power. For similar reasons, the French envisioned a European political assembly, which eventually became the Council of Europe, endowed with a strong executive and able to organize a unified European framework into which Germany could safely be integrated. They also collaborated in U.S. efforts to strengthen the Organization for European Economic Cooperation (OEEC). They proposed an "Atlantic High Council" that would centralize authority over the defense programs of member states. And, in an initiative that anticipated their subsequent scheme for a European Defense Community, they suggested that NATO's Council of Deputies, established in 1950, be equipped with an independent staff, a strong secretariat, and the power to shape national policies.[29]

These French schemes seldom dovetailed with the aspirations of the other European powers. In the Fritalux negotiations, the most thoroughgoing French proposal looked to the gradual elimination of import quotas (but not tariffs) on trade between participating countries and to an automatic system of exchange-rate adjustment, the negotiation of interindustry agreements, and the creation of collective authorities to coordinate national policies. Although the proposal left room for Germany's eventual accession to the group, the French clearly intended its provisions regarding collective coordination, interindustry agreements, and the retention of tariffs as mechanisms by which they could regulate economic developments in the former Reich and shield themselves against an invasion of German imports. As it turned out, however, the Dutch would participate only if the Germans were included from the start, if exchange controls remained intact, and if tariffs were equalized and quotas removed at a faster rate than the French envisioned. The Italians wanted provisions for the free movement of surplus labour, the Belgians objected to interindustry agreements, and neither the Belgians nor the Dutch were keen on the sort of administrative regime which the French saw, in the words of U.S. policymakers, as a "second line of defense" against the revival of Germany's economic power.[30]

Similar problems plagued and finally defeated the plans to anchor French security in a European customs union. The Italians saw this proposal, like the Fritalux scheme, as a route to Italy's political reassimilation into the Western community. But they were certain that any arrangement for liberalizing intra-European trade must not adversely affect the Italian economy, and just as convinced that Britain's membership would be needed to offset "the German menace." The Belgians preferred their own plan for integrating the European economies by liberalizing payment arrangements and eliminating quantitative import restrictions. And the Dutch would join a customs union only if the Germans were included at the start and if the British participated as well. Such a union would enable the Netherlands to reconstitute its important prewar trade with both countries and prevent France from dominating the group.[31]

For different reasons, then, both the Italians and the Dutch saw Britain's membership as a precondition to any union—as one of the keys to a rational pattern of trade and a viable balance of power in Western Europe. The same was true of policymakers in France and the United States. The French lived in fear of being left alone with the Germans in Western Europe. For them, Britain's integration would be necessary to countervail against the power of a revitalized Germany, thereby clearing a path to Germany's revival without endangering their security and the Monnet Plan. Thinking in Washington ran along parallel lines, with the result being consistent but largely unsuccessful U.S. efforts to bribe and bully the British into a European union.

Like their counterparts in Paris, Foreign Secretary Ernest Bevin and other policymakers in the British Foreign Office started the Marshall Plan years looking toward some kind of Anglo-Western European association. One line of British thinking led from wartime planning to the Treaty of Dunkirk in March 1947 and then to the Brussels Pact of the following year. It envisioned a British-led Western European security system that operated as a barrier to German or Soviet aggression, reassured the French, and gave the British defense in depth on the continent. A related line, more germane to the focus of this chapter, envisioned an economic bloc of Western European and British Commonwealth countries, an Anglo-European group allied with but not subordinate to the United States. An Anglo-European customs union would be the first step in the formation of such a bloc, and would eventually give way to a full-scale economic union and some merger of national sovereignties in strong, central institutions.[32]

For its supporters in the Foreign Office, a union of this sort would increase productivity, raise living standards to a level comparable to that in the United States, and provide a framework for controlling the Germans. There were additional political advantages as well. To be sure, Britain would have to pay for these advantages by abandoning its historic policy of playing European blocs off against one another and throwing its weight squarely into the balance. But in return it would dominate the European union, and this position would enhance the power of the British empire at a time when it was in danger of being "outclassed" by the Soviet bloc and becoming wholly dependent on the United States for the kind of economic and military support that had already seen it through two world wars. Britain, as R.M.A. Hankey noted, "cannot survive" as a world power by "hoping to sponge on American aid." Given the current direction of policy, Gladwyn Jebb agreed, "we shall eventually have to make the dismal choice between becoming a Soviet satellite state or the poor dependent of an American plutodemocracy." Through unification, however, Britain, the continental countries, and their overseas territories could forge a "completely new balance of power in Europe, and indeed the world." They could create a middle kingdom capable of playing an "important role in world affairs" and of restoring a "world equilibrium" that was "gravely imperiled," as Jebb put it, "by a 'bi-polar' system centering around what Mr. Toynbee calls the two 'semi-barbarian states on the cultural periphery.' " Any other course, according to P. M. Crosthwaite, would reduce the United Kingdom and the European countries to mere "pigmies between two giants, dependent on one for protection from the other and living in constant expectation of being trampled underfoot when they quarrel."[33]

These views formed the substance of a paper that Bevin presented to the Cabinet on January 8, 1948, when he urged an Anglo-Western European "*bloc* which, both in population and productive capacity, could stand on an equality with the western hemisphere and Soviet *blocs*." The Cabinet decided to "consolidate the forces of the Western European countries and their Colonial possessions," and this decision set the stage for Bevin's celebrated Western Union speech to the House of Commons on January 22nd.[34] "I believe," Bevin told a packed audience, "the time is ripe for a consolidation of Western Europe. . . . We are thinking now of Western Europe as a unit." This unit would include Britain, which could no longer "regard her problems as quite separate from those of her European neighbours" and which must therefore take the lead in forging a "self-reliant" union composed of the British Commonwealth, the Western European states, and their overseas territories in Africa and Asia.[35]

In framing a strategy suited to this goal, however, Bevin and his allies soon lost ground to Chancellor of the Exchequer Sir Stafford Cripps and his colleagues in the economic ministries. They had long opposed the direction of Bevin's thinking and had approved his cabinet paper of January 8th only after careful analysis led to the conclusion that Marshall's aid alone could not correct Europe's substantial payments deficit with the Western hemisphere. Europe could become self-supporting only if Britain and the other Marshall Plan countries adjusted their industrial and agricultural structures to fit a European-wide pattern. To effect this transformation, however, officials in the economic ministries favored an "empirical" approach that stopped short of the strategies envisioned by key officials in the Foreign Office. They rejected a "grandiose 'general' plan like a customs union," which would eliminate tariffs and trade preferences and expose British industry to the unbridled forces of a free market. Neither did they favour supranational institutions that would compromise Britain's sovereignty and interfere with the internal economic policies of the Labour government. They called instead for transnational economic planning on an ad hoc, project-by-project basis with a view to intergovernment and interindustry agreements aimed at maximizing dollar earnings and dollar savings across Western Europe as a whole. In theory, the empirical approach would create an integrated economic order large enough to harness the Germans, contain the Soviets, and restore equilibrium with the dollar area. But it would also permit British leaders to direct the process of integration. It would dovetail with the principles of socialist planning employed at home and enable the Labour government to limit the damage to Britain's economic structure and system of imperial preferences.[36]

Cripps and his colleagues, to put it summarily, wanted to move toward Bevin's goal of Western European integration along a path that ensured greater control than would be possible through a framework in which free-market forces and supranational regulators might override British interests. This summation foreshadows the terms of a compromise hammered out by an interdepartmental group known as the London Committee, ratified by Cripps and Bevin at a meeting of the cabinet-level Economic Policy Committee, and finally approved by the Cabinet on March 8, 1948. According to the compromise, the Marshall Plan countries could escape their dependence on U.S. aid by increasing production, liberalizing trade, improving payments arrangements, and integrating agricultural and industrial lines of production on a project-by-project basis. The last method, according to the London Committee, would be more compatible with Britain's system of imperial preferences, impose fewer restraints on the government's freedom of action, and promise greater rewards and fewer internal adjustments than would be the case with a fully "automatic policy of European cooperation" through a customs union. Neither was there any question of central direction by supranational authority; specific industrial and agricultural projects were to be arranged on an ad hoc basis through intergovernmental agreement.

If these arguments revealed the Treasury's contribution to the compromise, the final documents also displayed the unmistakable influence of the Foreign Office. The compromise called for a "modified Western European economy," a single "economic entity" to replace the "several uncoordinated economies which exist today." Pursuing this goal might entail "radical changes" in Britain's economic structure and some modification of its ties to the Commonwealth. It certainly would involve reversing Britain's traditional diplomacy with regard to the continent. The British would have to link their fate to that of a Western European group and take all of the economic and political risks that such a course entailed. But this was the only alternative to becoming "permanent pensioners" of the United States or seeking to survive alone "in a state of continuous economic uncertainty and poverty with all the disintegrating political and social results that would follow." If achieved, moreover, Anglo–Western European economic integration would guarantee strategic security within the framework of a new balance of power.

This had been Bevin's goal all along, but it would now be pursued in a way that gave the British government greater control over natural market forces and limited the scope for real supranationalism. The Cabinet captured the fusion of Treasury and Foreign Office strategies when it approved the compromise on March 8th. According to minutes of the meeting, the policy represented

an extension to western Europe of the principles of economic planning which the Government had adopted for the United Kingdom, and it was the only means by which the United Kingdom and the other participating countries could establish themselves in a position in which they were economically dependent neither on the Soviet Union nor on the United States.[37]

The differences between the British position and the one favored in Washington, with its emphasis on supranational regulators and natural market forces, became even more apparent in the months ahead. The British continued to support a "consolidation of Western Europe," although the empirical approach ruled out any arrangement that could not be reconciled with their economic policies at home or ties to the Commonwealth and empire. By mid–1948, moreover, these objections were compounded by a much greater reluctance to tie Britain to Western Europe at a time when governments there were being buffeted by forces beyond their control. The dramatic events of 1948—the Communist coup in Czechoslovakia, the Berlin blockade, the ongoing economic crisis, and the repeated eruptions of labor unrest and Communist agitation—were sour reminders of Western Europe's precarious position. Vigorous leadership was essential. But such leadership seemed impossible in countries like France, where the ruling center parties kept faltering under the weight of internecine strife and attacks from the Gaullist Right and the Communist Left. Given these circumstances, as Alan Bullock has argued, European political leaders and ordinary people alike rallied to the idea of European unity, seeking in a larger community the strength and security so sorely lacking within the framework of national politics. But the same circumstances pushed British policymakers in a different direction. Although Bevin had earlier been willing to link Britain's fate to that of a Western European group, this kind of thinking now receded into the shadows of British diplomacy.[38]

This is not to say that Bevin would disengage Britain from the continent. If anything, the events of 1948 had strengthened his belief that Western Europe needed to be reinforced lest it buckle and break under the weight of Communist subversion and Soviet intimidation. This belief led to the Brussels Pact of March and to Bevin's efforts to associate the United States with the new alliance. As these same efforts suggest, however, Bevin was more convinced than before that neither Britain nor Western Europe could save itself unless linked to the United States. He was also certain that the Commonwealth and sterling bloc, not Western Europe, now provided the most durable foundation for Britain's economic recovery and hope for survival as a great power.

This hope formed the major thread in the fabric of Bevin's thinking. Whether expressed through an Anglo-Western European union or through the Commonwealth connection and ties to the United States, the grand design of his diplomacy aimed first at restoring Britain's faded eminence as a great world power, allied with other countries to be sure, but master of its own fate nonetheless. As revised in 1948, however, this design now gave the British a role somewhat analogous to the one assigned earlier to an Anglo-Western European union. Although Britain and Western Europe could not form a "third force" between the two superpowers, Britain might at least become the pivot in a Western system of overlapping blocs, the sovereign of a middle kingdom that included the sterling area and the Commonwealth, the leader of Western Europe through the Brussels Pact and the OEEC, and the ally of both Western Europe and the United States through the European Recovery Program (ERP) and the North Atlantic Treaty being negotiated in Washington. These were three of what Bevin called "the four legs of the table," the fourth being a reorganized western Germany.[39]

The grand design, so neatly encapsulated in this homely metaphor, meant that Bevin must take great care in leading Britain into Europe. Such a leap into the dark was fraught with danger. Britain's commitments to the continent could not undermine its interests elsewhere. Neither could Britain be pushed into Europe beyond "the point of no return," which meant the point at which its economic independence and military security would be compromised if Western Europe collapsed.[40] For these reasons, Bevin now relied on the empirical approach invented by his colleagues in the economic ministries, adopting it with the zeal of a convert and applying it to both the political and economic aspects of Western European integration. In the months ahead, he and other British policymakers demanded special consideration for the sterling area in the intra-European payments agreement. They stymied U.S. efforts to give the OEEC supranational powers and undermined French plans to strengthen the Council of Europe, organize a European economic union, and endow NATO's Council of Deputies with coordinative powers, an independent staff, and a strong secretariat.[41]

Involved in all of these disputes was the old question of how to engineer a balance of power in Western Europe and a stable correlation of forces on the continent. The French and the Americans thought in terms of a North Atlantic system that linked the United States to an integrated Western Europe balanced between British and German power. Achieving this balance would satisfy France's economic and security concerns, eliminate the obstacles to Germany's full recovery and reintegration, and bring both together with Britain in a unit of power equal to the Soviet challenge. The British, on the other hand, steadfastly refused to be treated as mere Europeans, the first among equals in a strictly continental group. The British, as Bevin explained, "must have regard to the position of the United Kingdom as a power with world-wide responsibilities" to the Commonwealth and the sterling area, as well as to the United States and Western Europe.[42] Meeting these responsibilities precluded Britain's integration into Europe. It required instead a North Atlantic system in which Britain, together with the Commonwealth of course, operated as the linchpin between the continental group and the North American colossus.[43]

By mid–1949, these differences threatened to scuttle U.S. efforts to organize a Western European group that included the Germans. The Allies, to be sure, signed the North Atlantic Treaty and approved the accords that led in the fall to the formation of the Federal Republic. Policymakers in Washington thought these arrangements, together with the provision of military assistance, sufficient to reassure the French and make further progress on the German front possible. But the French thought otherwise. Neither arrangement provided specific guarantees, similar to those in the Treaty of Dunkirk, that would safeguard France against German aggression. Nor did they give France a permanent voice in the development of the German economy or bring Britain into Europe as a counterweight to the former Reich.[44] On the contrary, the drain on Britain's reserves that began earlier in the year had made policymakers in London even more leery of European financial and organizational arrangements that might jeopardize their obligations to the sterling area.[45]

Slight wonder that French leaders continued to drag their feet on German issues and made parallel efforts to create new institutions with the power to regulate national economies, including the British economy.[46] Slight wonder, too, that French leaders reacted angrily when British and U.S. negotiators met in Washington to arrange additional assistance for the flagging pound. The French were not invited to the Washington conference, which convened in September. Neither were they informed in advance of the British decision to devalue the pound, as were the Americans, or included in the continuing organization established by the Anglo-Americans to manage the crisis. These developments, together with ongoing U.S. pressure for more concessions to the Germans, sounded an alarm in Paris. They were grounds for believing that U.S. leaders had sanctioned Britain's "desolidarization" from the continent and the formation of a Western European union dominated by the Germans.[47]

Indeed, policymakers in the State Department had begun to recast their policy along lines roughly similar to what the French feared. This reformulation grew in part out of the serious drain on Britain's reserves, which raised the dreaded specter of British leaders seeking to staunch the drain through new trade and exchange restrictions that would permanently divide the non-ruble world into dollar and sterling blocs. Equally alarming was the prospect that economic dislocations in the sterling area would endanger the interests of the western alliance in parts of the world already threatened by the spread of revolutionary insurgency. Out of these concerns came a heightened appreciation of Britain's "world position" and the deep conviction, particularly in the Pentagon, "that the US needed Great Britain above everything else."[48] And out of them, too, came the understanding that British and U.S. negotiators began to hammer out at the Washington conference. The British agreed to take measures, including the devaluation of pound sterling, that would foreclose the formation of rival dollar and sterling blocs. The Americans agreed that Anglo-European collaboration must not come at the expense of Britain's commitments to the sterling area, the strategic value of which merited special organizational arrangements with the United States and additional support for pound sterling.[49]

The Americans, in a nutshell, had decided to exempt Britain from the process of European integration and to provide organizational and financial assistance outside the scope of the European Recovery Program. George Kennan and Under-Secretary of State James Webb outlined the new direction of U.S. policy in statements to the American members of the Combined Policy Committee on Atomic Energy just one day after the Washington talks on the sterling crisis. Webb gave as one of the "most important conclusions" of the talks the "mutual conviction" that the United States and Britain were "partners in the economic crisis." Part of the U.S. contribution to this partnership, he said, would be to shoulder a portion of Britain's "economic commitments in the Far East." Kennan then elaborated "current Departmental thinking." He told the committee that "it would be better if the United Kingdom were not too closely tied politically and economically to Western Europe." Britain should be aligned instead "with the United States and Canada," as this alignment would take account of its strategic commitments to the sterling area.[50]

There were dissenters, of course, but they failed to halt the reformulation of U.S. policy.[51] On the contrary, mindful of the strategic and military implications of the Communist conquest of China and the atomic capability of the Soviet Union, policymakers in the State Department became ever more reluctant to submerge Britain's sovereignty in a Western European union if this meant impairing its commitments elsewhere. By the spring of 1950, they were speaking of an Anglo-American "partnership" across the globe, the preservation of which was "essential to the security, prosperity and expansion of the free world." Dissolving this partnership, they said, would be "a disaster involving the decline and eclipse of the whole Eastern Hemisphere and a policy of isolation for the Western Hemisphere or even perhaps for North America alone."[52] Despite widespread criticism that British leaders were not doing enough to encourage a strictly continental union, geostrategic considerations led more than one U.S. official to regard Britain not "as a battered and worn out veteran" but as "the only really reliable ally of the United States and therefore a country which must be strengthened." These officials believed in "the absolute necessity of firm Anglo-American partnership," Sydney Caine of the British Treasury reported from Washington. Other Treasury officials reached the same conclusion, as did British Ambassador Oliver Franks, who formed his opinion on the basis of a dinner meeting with Acheson on March 6, 1950. Acheson spoke of the need for new U.S. initiatives in Western Europe and elsewhere, and of his conviction that these initiatives could succeed only "in partnership with Britain."[53]

Acheson's remarks came just as Anglo-American negotiators were putting the final touches on an agreement that would lead to the formation of the European Payments Union (EPU). One of the great achievements of the Marshall Plan, the EPU accord also marked a milestone on the road to greater integration of the Western European economies. The accord created a managing board to oversee arrangements that would liberalize intra-European payments and substantially reduce the quantitative restrictions on intra-European trade. It therefore embodied the U.S. faith in central institutions and free-market forces, which together could help to harmonize and integrate national economies. This explains why the Americans were willing to support the EPU through a sizeable endowment of Marshall Plan aid. It also explains why the British put one obstacle after another in the way of an agreement that might exacerbate the drain on their reserves and undermine their leadership of the sterling area. Indeed, agreement came only because the Americans had reformulated their British policy, adopting what one State Department paper termed a " 'share-the-wealth' plan," which Charles Bohlen called an Anglo-American "partnership with respect to Britain's overseas problems." Under this plan, the British "would adopt a more positive approach to the Continent," taking steps to support European integration in ways consistent with their leadership of the sterling area, in return for which the Americans would "assume unto ourselves at least the partial obligations of the sterling block [sic]." The EPU accord squared with these prescriptions. It brought the British into the payments union on terms that limited the drain on their reserves and ensured sterling's position as an international currency.[54] The reformulation of policy toward Britain did not mean a slackening support for Western European integration, which the Americans still saw as one of the keys to controlling the Germans and containing the Soviets. But it did mean that the burden of Western European integration and German reintegration would fall upon the French. According to Acheson, France and the other continental countries should push ahead with plans to liberalize intra-European trade and payments, should build "supranational institutions," and should be assured of British cooperation in ways that did not entail a merger of sovereignties. The real "key to progress" lay in "French hands." Even with the closest possible ties between the United States, the United Kingdom, and the continent, Acheson insisted, "France and France alone" could "take the decisive leadership in integrating Western Germany into Western Europe."[55]

Indeed, the reformulation of U.S. policy stemmed in part from the conviction in Washington that it would expedite, not retard, the Federal Republic's reintegration into an integrated Western European system. After all, Britain's opposition to European integration had been a persistent obstacle to progress in this direction, with results that raised the haunting specters of a resurgent German nationalism or a dangerous Soviet-German rapprochement. Although removing this obstacle would put the burden of leadership on French shoulders, it would also give the French greater incentive to harmonize their differences with the Germans and permit faster progress toward a more coherent integration than would be possible with British participation.[56] The result, in fact, was the Schuman Plan for a European coal and steel community that excluded the British.

The story of the Schuman Plan is too well known to repeat here, but it is worth noting the plan's lineal connection to such previous French initiatives as the Fritalux scheme and the proposal for a European customs union. These initiatives had also sought to control Germany's power through supranational institutions and the offsetting power of other states. The difference was to be found in the new willingness of the French to move in this direction without the active support and collaboration of the British. As the State Department had anticipated, Britain's consistent opposition to such a course, the United States' support for British desolidarization, and Anglo-American pressure to loosen the remaining restrictions on German production all combined to provoke a dramatic reassertion of French leadership on the continent. The clock was ticking for the French. They had to strike a deal with the Germans while they still had leverage, and they had to do so even if it meant risking the future of Anglo-French cooperation on which they had earlier pinned their hopes for security against the Germans.[57]

The British response was predictable. Schuman's plan envisioned agreement in advance of negotiations to a supranational system in which France would participate and through which it would share in the direction and development of German industry. Such a system did not square with Britain's "world position" or with its "settled policy" against committing itself "irrevocably to Europe." Neither did it fit with the idea of a North Atlantic community that Bevin saw as the key to Britain's security.[58] If these considerations precluded Anglo-European negotiations on the terms announced by Schuman, the general fear of playing second fiddle to a Franco-German bloc on the European continent or in the North Atlantic community made the British anxious to tailor the French initiative to their own needs. They asked for terms that ruled out agreement in principle prior to the negotiations and that looked to an intergovernmental arrangement, not a supranational system.

For the French, however, the principle had to be agreed before Germany regained the strength to resist their terms. This goal would be lost if Britain entered the negotiations in a special position. The principle of supranationalism would be compromised and the British would be in a position to replace French schemes with plans of their own. As Jean Monnet, the real author of the Schuman Plan, explained in a communication to his government: "To accept British participation on these terms—i.e., in a special capacity—would be to resign oneself in advance to the replacement of the French proposal by something that would merely travesty it. . . . There would be no common rules and no independent High Authority, but only some kind of OEEC." To avoid this danger, Monnet held to the original proposal and refused to capitulate when the British declined to participate.[59]

The U.S. response to Schuman's plan was equally predictable. Marshall planners noted that the plan dovetailed with their efforts to liberalize intra-European trade, harmonize national economic policies, and build supranational institutions of coordination and control. Policymakers in the State Department focused on the political and strategic advantages of the plan, and not simply on the prospects for relaxing industrial controls and increasing Germany's economic contribution to NATO's rearmament program. In a larger sense, the coal and steel community could help to reconcile the conflicting imperatives that had stalled a final German settlement. By providing a mechanism for harmonizing France's security with Germany's recovery, it could establish the conditions for a workable balance of power among the states of Western Europe "without full British participation as a necessary pre-condition" and create a strategic union of sufficient strength to deter Soviet expansion.[60] Small wonder that President Truman called Schuman's plan "an act of constructive statesmanship," or that Acheson termed it a "major contribution toward the resolution of the pressing political and economic problems of Europe."[61]

The Schuman Plan, together with the Council of Europe, the Organization for European Economic Cooperation, and the European Payments Union, created an institutional framework that stood in lieu of a final peace settlement in the West—an economic and political framework that no formal alliance or military guarantees could ever have replaced. Indeed, the Schuman Plan marked the high point in a U.S. strategy that relied on economic rather than military tools to achieve its objectives, a strategy geared to budgetary constraints and to the conviction in Washington that Communist subversion, not a Soviet attack, posed the gravest peril to European security. The United States, to be sure, had signed the North Atlantic Treaty in 1949. But the treaty did not give France reliable guarantees against a resurgent German threat to their economic plans and military security. Neither, for that matter, did it constitute a strong deterrent to Soviet aggression. The credibility of the United States' military commitment depended instead on its ability to forestall aggression through nuclear air attacks on the Soviet Union, and even this deterrent was partially neutralized when the Soviets exploded an atomic device in September 1949.[62]

If all of this helps to explain why the French were unimpressed when the Americans said that military assistance and the North Atlantic Treaty should expedite a final solution of the German problem, it also explains why the United States moved to strengthen Western European defenses after the Soviet Union's successful atomic test. To U.S. leaders, Moscow's atomic capability altered the strategic balance, which had to be redressed lest it encourage Soviet aggression or fuel neutralist sentiment in Western Europe. This conclusion led the Americans to develop the hydrogen bomb and to urge greater defense expenditures by the Europeans. For the first time, rearmament gained parity with recovery in U.S. policy, a balance the Truman administration might have maintained had it not been for the Korean War. With the outbreak of fighting in Korea, however, the administration approved NSC 68, which envisioned a massive expansion of U.S. defense expenditures, and escalated the pressure for European rearmament. U.S. policy would never be the same again. Economic integration gave way to military integration as the best way to contain the Soviets, with results that added a new twist to the old debates over the role that Germany should play in the Western European and North Atlantic communities.[63]

NOTES

    1. This view was embodied in U.S. war plans and National Security Council documents drafted between 1946 and 1950. See Christian Greiner, "The Defense of Western Europe and the Rearmament of West Germany, 1947–1950," in Olav Riste (ed.), *Western Security: The Formative Years: European and Atlantic Defence 1947–1953* (New York, 1985), 150–77. See also the excellent essay by John Lewis Gaddis, "The United States and the Question of a Sphere of Influence in Europe, 1945–1949," in ibid., 60–91; and Melvyn P. Leffler, "The American Conception of National Security and the Beginnings of the Cold War, 1945–1948," *American Historical Review* 89 (April 1984), 345–81.

    2. For Kennan's thinking see the essay by John Lewis Gaddis cited in note 1.

    3. See the report issued by a special subcommittee of the State-War-Navy Coordinating Committee on April 21, 1947, in the U.S. Department of State, *Foreign Relations of the United States, 1947* (Washington, 1972), 3:204–19 (hereafter *FRUS*).

    4. Walter Millis (ed.), *The Forrestal Diaries: The Inner History of the Cold War* (New York, 1951), 341.

    5. U.S. Congress, Senate Committee on Foreign Relations, *Hearings, European Recovery Program*, 80th Cong., 2nd sess., 1948, 477–80 (hereafter Senate, *ERP Hearings*, 1948).

    6. According to officials on the economic side of the State Department, the

"symbols of nationalism in France and Italy and Germany are essentially bankrupt
and in danger of being captured by reactionary and neo-fascist political elements
which we do not wish to support." The great need, they said, was for transcending
nationalism and developing "the supranational ideal of European unity," something
the United States should do by using its recovery aid to support a comprehensive
"plan which stresses the raising of European production and consumption through
the economic and 'functional' unification of Europe." Quoted in Max Beloff, *The
United States and the Unity of Europe* (Washington, 1963), 15–18. See also Joseph M.
Jones, *The Fifteen Weeks (February 21–June 5, 1947)* (New York, 1955), 243–44.

7. See the source cited in note 3.

8. Kennan memorandum, May 16, 1947, *FRUS, 1947*, 3:220–23.

9. For Bonesteel's views see Melvyn P. Leffler, "Standing Tough: The Strategic
and Diplomatic Aftermath of the Iranian Crisis of March 1946," paper presented
at the Lehrman Institute, New York, April 1985.

10. Dulles, "We Cannot Let Ourselves Be Stymied: Report on Moscow Conference," *Vital Speeches of the Day*, 13 (May 15, 1947), 450–53.

11. Dulles, "Europe Must Federate or Perish: America Must Offer Inspiration
and Guidance," *Vital Speeches of the Day*, 13 (February 1, 1947), 234–36.

12. U.S. Congress, House Committee on Foreign Affairs, *Hearings, United States
Foreign Policy for a Post-war Recovery Program*, 80th Cong., 1st and 2nd sess., 1947–
48, 73 (hereafter House, *Recovery Program Hearings, 1947–1948*).

13. See the sources cited in notes 9 and 10.

14. House, *Recovery Program Hearings, 1947–1948*, 924; and Senate, *ERP Hearings,
1948*, 549.

15. Dulles quoted in Senate, *ERP Hearings, 1948*, 588–89.

16. Kennan quoted in Gaddis, "The United States and the Question of a Sphere
of Influence in Europe," 72.

17. Marshall telegram to Caffery, February 19, 1948, *FRUS, 1949* (Washington,
1973), 2:70–71.

18. Acheson telegram to Perkins, October 19, 1949, *FRUS, 1949* (Washington,
1975), 4:469–72.

19. See the paper by Robert Murphy, March 23, 1949, *FRUS, 1949* (Washington,
1974), 3:118–27. The documents mentioned in the text were written in preparation
for a meeting of foreign ministers in Washington. The ministers were meeting to
sign the North Atlantic Treaty and discuss the German problem. In addition to
Murphy's paper noted above see Kennan paper, February 7, 1949; Beam paper,
February 24, 1949; and Kennan paper, March 8, 1949; Beam memorandum to
Murphy, March 29, 1949; Murphy paper, March 30, 1949; and Acheson memorandum to Truman, with accompanying State Department paper, March 31, 1949,
in ibid., 90–93, 94–96, 96–102, 138–40, 140–42, 142–56.

20. Memorandum prepared in the Bureau of German Affairs (February 11, 1950),
FRUS, 1950 (Washington, 1980), 4:597–602.

21. Oliver Franks, British ambassador in Washington, telegram to the Foreign
Office, November 9, 1949, Records of the British Treasury (Public Record Office,
Kew, England), Record Class T232 (Economic Co-operation Committee), 150EEC/
78/11/08A (hereafter T232, with file designations).

22. I have examined the German question in some detail in my "European Union
and German Integration: Marshall Planners and the Search for Recovery and Security

in Western Europe," in Charles S. Maier (ed.), *Germany and the Marshall Plan* (forthcoming).

23. Michael J. Hogan, "American Marshall Planners and the Search for a European Neocapitalism," *American Historical Review*, 90 (February 1985), 44–72.

24. John Gimbel, *The Origins of the Marshall Plan* (Stanford, 1976), 21–22, 38–41, 82–90, 98, 101–21, 128, 155–58, 187; Alan S. Milward, *The Reconstruction of Western Europe, 1945–1951* (London, 1984), 126–41; and Frances M. B. Lynch, "Resolving the Paradox of the Monnet Plan: National and International Planning in French Reconstruction," *Economic History Review*, 37 (May 1984), 229–43.

25. These developments are treated in detail in Michael J. Hogan, *The Marshall Plan: America, Britain, and the Reconstruction of Western Europe, 1947–1952* (New York, 1987).

26. John W. Young, *Britain, France, and the Unity of Europe, 1945–1951* (Leicester, 1984), especially 26–51.

27. British delegation to the OEEC telegram to the Foreign Office, August 4, 1947, and B.A.C. Cook minute, August 5, 1947, General Records of the British Foreign Office (Public Record Office), Record Class 371, 62552/UE6911 (hereafter FO 371, with file designations); British delegation to the OEEC telegram to the Foreign Office, August 10, 1947, FO 371, 62552/UE7116; and Caffery telegram to Marshall, August 9, 1947, General Records of the Department of State, Record Group 59 (National Archives, Washington), file, 840.50 Recovery/8–947 (hereafter RG 59, with file designation).

28. An excellent discussion of the Fritalux negotiations is scattered throughout Milward's *The Reconstruction of Western Europe*.

29. Hogan, "American Marshall Planners and the Search for a European Neocapitalism," 66–71; and Hogan, *The Marshall Plan*, 182–83, 214–16.

30. Hogan, *The Marshall Plan*, 281; Milward, *The Reconstruction of Western Europe*, 310–14; Frances Lynch, "French Reconstruction in a European Context," and Richard T. Griffiths and Frances Lynch, "The Fritalux/Finebel Negotiations, 1949–1950," European University Institute Working Papers nos. 86 and 84/117 (Florence, 1984).

31. For the Italian position see the unsigned record of conversation, February 3, 1950, FO 371, 87084/UR323. See also Hogan, *The Marshall Plan*, 66, 327, 350, 351. For the Benelux position see Caffery; telegrams to Marshall, August 9 and 14, 1947, RG 59, file, 840.50 Recovery/8–947 and /8–1447; British delegation to the Committee on European Economic Cooperation telegram to the Foreign Office, August 4, 1947, FO 371, 62552/UE6911; and British delegation telegram to the Foreign Office, FO 371, 62552/UE7194. In addition see Caffery telegram to Marshall, August 20, 1947, *FRUS, 1947*, 3:364–67.

32. Bevin's views and those of supporters and opponents in the British government are developed in the text. For background, however, see Victor Rothwell, *Britain and the Cold War, 1941–1947* (London, 1982), especially 406–56; Alan Bullock, *Ernest Bevin, Foreign Secretary, 1945–1951* (New York, 1983), 144–45, 316–18, 358; Young, *Britain, France, and the Unity of Europe*, especially 13–62; Sean Greenwood, "Ernest Bevin, France and 'Western Union': August 1945–February 1946," *European History Quarterly*, 14 (July 1984), 319–38; and John Baylis, "Britain, the Brussels Pact, and the Continental Commitment," *International Affairs*, 60 (Autumn 1984), 615–29. See also Bevin, "Proposal for a Study of the Possibilities of Close Economic

Co-operation with our Western European Neighbours," January 18, 1947, Cabinet Paper (47) 35, FO 371, 62398/UE416.

33. See the minutes by Crosthwaite of December 31, 1947, Hankey of January 3, 1947 [*sic* 1948], W. C. Hayter of January 5, 1948, F.B.A. Rundall of January 6, 1948, Jebb of January 8, 1948, and F. R. Hoyer-Millar of January 10, 1948, all in FO 371, 62555/UE12502. See also the minute by Roger Stevens, British representative on the European Customs Union Study Group, December 22, 1947, ibid.

34. Cabinet Minute (48) and Conclusion, January 8, 1948, Cabinet Minutes, Conclusions and Confidential Annexes (Public Record Office), Record Class CAB 128/12 (hereafter CAB 128, with volume number).

35. Great Britain, Parliament, *Parliamentary Debates* (Commons), 5th series, 446 (1947–48), 383–410.

36. Sir Wilfrid Eady, second secretary of the Treasury, memorandum to Cripps, February 27, 1948, Eady memorandum to Sir Edward Bridges, permanent secretary of the Treasury, and B. F. St. J. Trend, assistant secretary of the Treasury, March 1, 1948, Records of the British Treasury (Public Record Office), Record Class T236 (Overseas Finance Division), 1892/OF265/1F (hereafter T236, with file designations).

37. Cabinet Paper (48) 75, London Committee. "The Continuing Organization," undated, CAB 129 (Public Record Office), 25 (hereafter CAB 129, with volume number); Economic Policy Committee (48) 9th Meeting, March 4, 1948, Records of the Prime Ministers' Office—Clement R. Attlee Papers (Public Record Office), Record Class PREM 8/980 (hereafter PREM 8, with file designation); Cabinet Paper (48) 75, Bevin and Cripps memorandum to the Cabinet, March 6, 1948, CAB 129/25; and Cabinet Minute (48) 20th Conclusion, March 8, 1948, CAB 128/12.

38. Bullock, *Bevin*, 554, 586.

39. Record of Bevin-Attlee conversation, June 19, 1948, General Records of the British Foreign Office—Ernest Bevin Papers (Public Record Office), Record Class FO 800, 460/EUR.48/26 (hereafter FO 800 with file designations).

40. See Economic Policy Committee (49) 6, Bevin and Cripps memorandum, "Our Policy to O.E.E.C. and our Proposals for its Structure," January 25, 1949, PREM 8/980; Sir Edmund Hall-Patch letters to Eric Berthoud, April 4 and 16, 1949, FO 371, 77999/UR3483 and UR4063; and Permanent Under-Secretary's Committee (22) Final Approved, "A Third World Power or Western Consolidation?," May 9, 1949, PREM 8/1204.

41. Hogan, "American Marshall Planners and the Search for a European Neocapitalism," 51, 64–67; and Young, *Britain, France and the Unity of Europe*, 99–138.

42. Foreign Office telegram to Franks, from Bevin, October 25, 1949, T232/150/EEC78/11/08A.

43. In the words of Under-Secretary of State Roger Makins, it required an arrangement that recognized Britain's position as "the nodal point of three systems, the Commonwealth, Western Europe and the Atlantic Community." Makins, "Anglo-American-Canadian Talks: General Considerations," August 26, 1949, FO 371, 75594/UE6686.

44. Timothy P. Ireland, *Creating the Entangling Alliance: The Origins of the North Atlantic Treaty Organization* (Westport, 1981), 62–114.

45. The British position became apparent in the negotiation for a new intra-European payments agreement. See Hogan, *The Marshall Plan*, 225–35.

46. The institutions were those mentioned earlier in the text, including an Atlantic High Council and a NATO Council of Deputies equipped with a professional staff, a strong secretariat, and the power to coordinate national policies. As far as German issues were concerned, the French still refused to raise the level of German industry or further reduce reparations. They also raised strenuous objections to a substantial devaluation of the German mark and to the policy of charging a higher price for German coal exported abroad than for coal sold on the domestic market. Both policies, the French said, had U.S. support and were "unfair" to France. See David K. E. Bruce, American ambassador in Paris, telegram to Acheson, September 23, 1949, *FRUS, 1949*, 4:663–65. See also Bruce telegram to Acheson, September 22, 1949, ibid., 661–63. By the end of 1949, the French had wrestled the British and the Americans into a compromise on these issues. The Allies agreed to further curtail the dismantling of German plants as reparations and to relax other restrictions on German industry. But in return they exacted promises from the Federal Republic to join the Ruhr Authority, prohibit cartelistic business practices, cooperate with the Military Security Board, and conduct its political affairs according to democratic principles. To further appease the French, moreover, the Allies held to the current level of German production, agreed to study the dual pricing of German coal, and decided to limit the Germans to a 20 percent devaluation of the mark. This part of the story can be followed in *FRUS, 1949*, 3: 305–06, 307—08, 343–48, 448–77, 618–21, 621–25, 632–33, 633–34, 635–38.

47. Bruce telegram to Acheson, September 23, 1949, *FRUS, 1949*, 4: 663–65. See also Bruce to Acheson, September 22, 1949, ibid., 661–63; and Hogan, *The Marshall Plan*, 266–67.

48. Summary record of a meeting of United States ambassadors at Paris, October 21–22, 1949, *FRUS, 1949*, 4: 472–96.

49. Hogan, *The Marshall Plan*, especially 247–54, 257–65, 268–79.

50. Minutes of the meeting of the U.S. members of the Combined Policy Committee on Atomic Energy, Washington, September 13, 1949, *FRUS, 1949* (Washington, DC, 1976), 1: 520–26.

51. In addition to the source cited in note 45 see Bruce telegram to Acheson et al., from Perkins, October 22, 1949, *FRUS, 1949*, 4: 342–44; Bohlen letters to Kennan, October 6 and 29, 1949, RG 59, Records of Charles E. Bohlen, 1942–1952, box 3, folder: A–K Correspondence-Bohlen 1949–July 1951; and Bohlen's undated memorandum, "US Policy and Western European Integration," W. Averell Harriman Papers (Washington, folder: Ambassadors' Meeting–1st Mtg., Paris, October 21–22, 1949).

52. State Department Paper, "Essential Elements of US–UK Relations," April 19, 1950, *FRUS, 1950* (Washington, 1977), 3:869–81.

53. Caine letter to Sir Henry Wilson-Smith, February 11, 1950, FO 371, 87039/UR3113; T. L. Rowan letter to E. A. Hitchman, February 14, 1950, FO 371, 81668/AU1156/3; Franks letter to Bevin, March 8, 1950, FO 800, 517US/50/8.

54. Memorandum prepared in the Bureau of German Affairs (February 11, 1950), *FRUS, 1950*, 4:597–602; minutes of the seventh meeting of the Policy Planning Staff, January 24, 1950, ibid., 3:617–22. See also Hogan, "American Marshall Planners and the Search for a European Neocapitalism," 51–53.

55. Acheson telegram to Perkins, October 19, 1949, *FRUS, 1949* 4:469–72.

56. See, for example, Kennan's remarks to the U.S. members of the Combined

Policy Committee on Atomic Energy, September 13, 1949, *FRUS, 1949*, 1:520–26.

57. The plan was announced by French Foreign Minister Robert Schuman on May 9, 1950, and promptly reported to Washington. See U.S. chargé in France telegram to Under-Secretary of State James Webb, May 9, 1950, *FRUS, 1950*, 3: 692–94.

58. Cabinet Paper (50) 120, report by the Committee of Officials, "Integration of French and German Coal and Steel Industries," June 2, 1950, CAB 129/49. See also Cabinet Minutes (50) 34th Conclusion, June 2, 1950, CAB 128/17; and Jean Monnet, *Memoirs*, translated by Richard Mayne (Garden City, 1978), 316–17.

59. Monnet, *Memoirs*, 313; and Great Britain, Foreign Office, *Anglo-French Discussions Regarding French Proposal for the Western European Coal, Iron, and Steel Industries, May-June, 1950*, Cmnd. 7970, 1950.

60. Webb telegram to Harriman, May 13, 1950, Records of the Agency for International Development (Agency for International Development, Washington), Telegram Files of the Economic Cooperation Administration, box 65. See also Harriman telegram to Acheson, May 20, 1950; Bruce telegram to Acheson, May 23, 1950; Acheson telegram to certain diplomatic offices, June 2, 1950; and Douglas telegram to Acheson, June 6, 1950, *FRUS, 1950* 3: 702–4, 704–5, 714–15, 720–24; and undated memorandum by Wayne Jackson of the State Department, "General Comments on Certain Aspects of the Schuman Coal and Steel Proposal," Records of International Conferences, Commissions, and Expositions (National Archives), Record Group 43, box 298, folder: Schuman Plan, 1950–52.

61. Truman and Acheson quoted in Richard P. Stebbins, *The United States in World Affairs, 1950* (New York, 1951), 143.

62. See Greiner, "The Defence of Western Europe and the Rearmament of West Germany," especially 150–57; and Steven L. Reardon, *History of the Office of the Secretary of Defense, vol. 1, The Formative Years, 1947–1950* (Washington, 1984), 521–36, 545.

63. I have dealt with these issues at great length in *The Marshall Plan*, especially chapters 7, 8, and 9.

3

Britain: The Defense of Western Europe and Its Overseas Role, 1945–68

Michael L. Dockrill

From 1815 until 1914 Britain avoided too close an involvement with the affairs of Europe, in the hope that the maintenance of a balance of power between potentially hostile states would enable it to concentrate on the expansion, and later the consolidation, of its empire. Not until the early 1900s, when Germany began to construct a navy that seemed to pose a direct threat to British security, did Britain begin to shift from its so-called policy of 'splendid isolation.' While this did not lead to Britain's forming alliances with France and Russia before 1914, it did result in close diplomatic collaboration between these powers against Germany, and created the expectation, especially in France, that Britain would intervene on the side of France and Russia if they became involved in a war with Germany. This expectation was fulfilled when, after considerable heart-searching in London, Britain declared war on Germany in August 1914.[1]

After 1919 Britain sought to return to its nineteenth-century policy of concentrating on its empire and refusing to give any guarantee to France concerning French military security vis-à-vis Germany until the Locarno Pact of 1925, when Britain agreed to an extremely limited commitment. The British public and politicians alike tended to regard World War I as an aberration and they had no intention of becoming involved in any future slaughter on the western front.

As a result of its gains overseas at the expense of the former German and Turkish empires in 1919, the British empire was more extensive than ever before. London concentrated its limited financial resources on maintaining Britain's naval strength, on which the defense of its empire and trade depended, and on building up the Royal Air Force in a half-hearted attempt to 'deter' any continental aggressors. The British army came a poor third in the scramble for finance and down to 1939 it appeared unlikely that Britain would be able (or willing) to send an expeditionary force to France as it had in 1914.

When, in 1939, Britain's efforts to mediate between Germany and France had been shown to have been a dismal failure, and Nazi Germany had become even more menacing to its security in Europe, Britain reversed its policy, embarked on a full-scale rearmament program, introducing conscription and promising France that it would come to its assistance in the event of an attack by Germany. Britain was unprepared for war in September 1939, and when France was defeated in the early summer of 1940, Britain was isolated, able to defend itself against German aerial attacks, but incapable of challenging Hitler's domination of Europe.

The entry of the Soviet Union and the United States into the war in 1941 led, after a long struggle, to the final defeat of the Axis powers in 1945, but the costs of this to Britain, one of the three major victorious powers, were huge. Britain had lost almost all of its overseas investments and the bulk of its trade, while British industries were either run down or destroyed. However, as a result of its victory, London had been forced to assume onerous responsibilities, not only in reestablishing its Far Eastern possessions that had been seized by Japan, but also in providing occupation troops in Germany, Austria, and Trieste.

With the expectation that the United States would withdraw its forces from the continent of Europe in a few years, it was far from clear that Britain would be able to afford a long and costly presence on the continent. The other Western European powers, especially France, had been weakened by defeat and occupation and, until they recovered their strength, would be able to do little to defend themselves.[2]

Neither was Britain anxious to become too closely involved in the military defense of the European continent. British defense planners did not believe that the Soviet Union, however hostile it was becoming toward the West, was in any position, after its immense sacrifices during World War II, to invade Western Europe. The British government preferred to concentrate on reestablishing British power in what remained of the British empire after India, Pakistan, and Ceylon became independent in 1947. In particular, Britain wanted to reestablish hegemony in the Middle East, by organizing a coalition of Arab states against the Soviet Union and by maintaining the Suez Canal as its main military, air, and naval base in the region.[3] If war with the Soviet Union had broken out in these years, Britain would have evacuated its occupation troops from West Germany, and used its Middle East bases to bomb the Caucasus in the hope that this would force Moscow to cease hostilities.

The U.S. decision to provide Marshall Aid to Western Europe in 1947 was welcomed by the British Foreign Secretary, Ernest Bevin, as a sign that the United States was at last prepared to promote the economic recovery of Western Europe, while Washington's agreement to join the North Atlantic Treaty Organisation (NATO) in the following year meant that Britain and the other Western Europeans would receive U.S. military as well as financial aid. This would help sustain Britain's great-power status while at the same time enabling it to restore its war-torn economy. The U.S. monopoly of the atomic bomb and the stationing of nuclear-capable U.S. bombers at British bases during and after the Berlin crisis of 1948–49 gave British leaders a feeling of confidence in the future security of Western Europe vis-à-vis the Soviet Union.

This confidence was shattered by the Soviets' successful testing of an atomic bomb in August 1949 and by the Communist takeover of China during the autumn. Communism now appeared to be on the march everywhere. The outbreak of the Korean War in June 1950 injected a new urgency into the problem of the defense of the West. Military opinion in London and Washington began to consider obtaining a West German military contribution to NATO as a means of strengthening Western defenses and preventing West Germany's valuable industrial resources falling under Soviet control in the event of a Red Army invasion of Western Europe.

There were formidable obstacles to this strategy, not least that France, with its bitter experiences of defeat and occupation by Germany, would resolutely oppose measures of West German remilitarization that would enable West Germany to raise its own army. Before 1950 the Western powers had encouraged the close association of West Germany with Western Europe economically and politically, but there had been no question of their promoting its military recovery. The demilitarization and disarmament of Germany and its ultimate reunification remained the formal policy of the four occupying powers, although there appeared to be little prospect of achieving the latter on any terms that would be acceptable to both the Soviet Union and the West.

Both Britain and the United States believed that the North Korean invasion of the South was a Soviet-inspired maneuver to divert U.S. attention and resources to Asia, thus allowing the Soviet Union to settle the German question in its favor. The British government introduced a large rearmament program and increased the size of the British Army of the Rhine (BAOR) from two to four divisions. However, it would take many years before this program could be fulfilled and in the meantime the Soviet Union might seize West Berlin or invade West Germany.

The U.S. Joint Chiefs of Staff therefore demanded the immediate rearmament of West Germany. The Americans promised that if the Western Europeans agreed to this, the United States would provide NATO with additional military aid, reinforce its occupation army in West Germany by four divisions, and appoint a U.S. general as supreme commander of NATO forces in Europe. This proposal involved Britain in long drawn-out negotiations on the question of a West German military contribution. The French would not accept a West German participation in NATO even in principle, while the United States refused to send the promised additional aid to West Europe until they did. The French put forward an alternative scheme for securing West German troops which would prevent the West Germans from possessing their own national army, a general staff, or a ministry of defense. This was the so-called 'Pleven Plan' for a supranational European army in which West German effectives would be swallowed up in a European Defense Community (EDC). Britain was forced to mediate between the West Germans, who refused to accept membership of the Community except on terms of full equality with the other members, and the French, who were concerned to prevent the rise of a militaristic and revanchist Germany.[4]

After the French National Assembly finally defeated the European Defense Community Treaty in August 1954, Anthony Eden, the British Foreign Secretary in the Churchill government, took the lead in organizing a solution to the impasse by proposing the inclusion of West Germany in NATO and a revived Brussels Treaty Organization,[5] now to be renamed the West European Union. To overcome French doubts about his plan, Eden promised that Britain would indefinitely maintain its existing level of armed forces in Western Europe, that is, four divisions and a tactical air force. It was widely believed by contemporaries in Europe and in the United States that Eden's declaration marked the high point of Britain's determination to defend Western Europe. However, given that after 1950 British military planners reversed the order of its defense priorities and placed the defense of Western Europe first, and the Middle East second, Eden's promise was hardly remarkable. Moreover, since the Churchill government, in order to encourage the French to ratify the EDC Treaty, had already made a number of arrangements with the former EDC powers for close collaboration between Britain's armed forces and the EDC formations, there was little that was new in Eden's pledge.[6]

Nevertheless, Britain's willingness to maintain four divisions in Western Europe appeared to conflict with changes that were taking place in British thinking about its future global defense policy. This originated in pressure by Sir John Slessor, the chief of the Air Staff, for greater reliance by Britain in the future on nuclear deterrence, which, in his view, would enable it to reduce substantially the size of its conventional forces. This possibility had been debated in British military circles since the spring of 1952, when the British Chiefs of Staff had met at the Royal Naval College, Greenwich, to draw up a Global Strategy Paper that was intended to settle British defense policy for the remainder of the decade.

The government had been pressing the Chiefs of Staff to find ways of cutting back on Britain's defense expenditure. The rearmament program that the Attlee government had authorized in January 1951 at the height of the Korean War envisaged the expenditure of £4700 million over the next three years. By the end of 1951, however, it was clear that this burden was too much for the faltering British economy to bear. The metal-producing industries came under increasing strain as orders poured in for iron and steel for new tanks, aircraft, and other military equipment the Ministry of Defense was ordering and which competed with civil sector demands. Even before the Attlee government fell from power after the October 1951 elections it had been forced to spread the rearmament program over a longer period of time; the succeeding Churchill government continued this process.

The nuclear option, seen increasingly in the 1950s by many airmen as the solution to Britain's defense problems, originated in the decision in 1946 by a secret Cabinet Committee of senior Labour ministers to authorize the development of a British nuclear device, after the United States broke off all cooperation with Britain and Canada on exchanges of nuclear information as a consequence of the passage of the McMahon Act by Congress on August 1, 1946. Britain succeeded in testing an atomic device at Monte Bello Island in October 1952, and at about this time the British government decided to develop the hydrogen bomb. Production of Britain's long-range V-bombers was accelerated—the first Vulcan bomber squadron became operational in 1955. These developments had an important influence on British thinking about future strategy. Given Britain's increasing economic and financial difficulties after 1951 and its wide range of commitments, nuclear weapons were coming to be regarded as a less expensive, yet more effective solution than conventional forces to Britain's defense problems.

The Royal Air Force was convinced that the immense devastation it had inflicted on Germany during the latter years of World War II had made a decisive contribution to the Allied victory. The dropping of atomic bombs by the U.S. Army Air Force on Hiroshima and Nagasaki in August 1945, followed almost immediately by Japan's surrender, seemed to clinch the arguments of the air power lobby that they were now in possession of an awesome war-winning weapon that would relegate the army and the navy to the task of escorting convoys, defending air bases, and occupying territory 'liberated' by the atomic bomb. This conviction also had the advantage of giving them extra leverage in the competition between the three services for scarce defense funds, while Truman, before 1950, had made the atomic bomb the cornerstone of his containment strategy.

The Global Strategy Paper that Slessor persuaded his fellow chiefs of staff to accept in 1952 described Britain's 'three pillars of strategy' as the defense of the United Kingdom, the defense of the Suez base on the route to Australia and the Far East, and the protection of Singapore and Hong Kong. The paper suggested that the burden of these heavy responsibilities could be significantly reduced if in future more weight was given in defense planning to the deterrent effect on potential enemies of Britain's possession of the atomic, and later the hydrogen, bomb.[7]

The authors of the paper anticipated that a British decision to adopt a nuclear deterrence strategy would increase its value in U.S. eyes, so that Britain's role as the major partner of the United States could be sustained indefinitely. If, however, the United States decided to withdraw from NATO or refused to help Britain defend its vital interests, Britain would at least theoretically possess sufficient nuclear power of its own both to deter an enemy or inflict devastating blows on it without U.S. assistance. However, the British Cabinet privately believed that the United Kingdom would not be able to use the bomb except by agreement with the United States.

Slessor firmly believed that a strategy of nuclear deterrence—if allied to so-called tactical nuclear weapons that were being developed in the form of rockets and shells for the British army of the Rhine—would significantly reduce the costs of Britain's army in West Germany, since their enhanced firepower would more than compensate for staff reductions. This assumption was bitterly criticized by the army and navy, who realized that their roles would be threatened if nuclear deterrence became a major plank in British defense policy. Neither would accept that the use of nuclear weapons would be decisive in war. Both services therefore insisted on the inclusion in the Global Strategy Paper of a section which referred to a lengthy period of 'broken-backed warfare' which would follow the initial nuclear exchanges in a global conflict, and which would involve all three armed services in heavy conventional fighting before the enemy was finally overcome.

To make Britain's global strategy even more confused, at a NATO Council meeting in Lisbon in February 1952, the Allies agreed to build up their forces in Western Europe to 50 divisions by the end of 1952, with Britain supplying ten of these divisions, with a combined air force of some 4,000 planes. Further increases were also recommended for the end of 1960. Consequently, in future NATO forces could engage in the "forward defense" of Western Europe along the River Elbe. As well as protecting the territory of West Germany and its resources, this plan would give the West a greater defensive depth than hitherto. The planners based their schemes on the likelihood that a West German defense contribution would be forthcoming, but it was clear that the implementation of this plan would involve the Western Europeans in enormous sacrifices, sacrifices that in the event they were not prepared to make.[8]

During the next few years Britain expanded its overseas responsibilities. In 1951 London promoted the Central Treaty Organization, or the Baghdad Pact, including Britain, Turkey, Iraq, Iran, and Pakistan and directed against the Soviet Union. It was evident that the bulk of the land fighting would have to be undertaken by Britain's allies in the Pact, for, as the Chiefs of Staff admitted in February 1955, "We have neither the men nor the money to make the Baghdad Pact effective militarily."[9] Britain's role would be confined largely to bombing South Russia with Canberras based in Cyprus (following the Anglo-Egypt treaty of 1954 whereby Britain agreed to evacuate the Suez Canal by 1956); here the atomic bomb would make an important contribution to final victory. On September 6, 1954, Britain acceded to the South East Asia Treaty Organization, a loose alliance system comprising the United Kingdom, the United States, France, Australia, New Zealand, Thailand, the Philippines, and Pakistan.

It was one of Britain's last major overseas expeditions—the Suez War of November 1956, a desperate and last-ditch attempt by Britain and France to preserve their respective positions in the Middle East and North Africa—that impelled the British government to embark on a major effort to reduce defense expenditure. While Prime Minister from 1955 to 1956, Eden had attempted to impose cuts. Britain, he wrote later, "had attempted too much in too many spheres of influence, which had contributed to the economic crisis which every administration had suffered since 1945." His efforts were frustrated by the Suez conflict, which led to his resignation in January 1957. The humiliating circumstances under which Britain was forced to relinquish the fruits of its victory over Egypt, and the disaster that U.S. financial sanctions had inflicted on its economy, were decisive in forcing Harold Macmillan, Eden's successor in 1957, to appoint Duncan Sandys as minister of defense with a mandate to restructure fundamentally Britain's armed forces. Certainly, the long drawn-out preparations that had been required before the invasion of Egypt could be mounted, and the shortages of equipment of every kind which those preparations had revealed, led many senior ministers to question whether the heavy expenditure on conventional warfare capabilities had been money well spent.

In his white paper *Defence: Outline of Future Policy*,[10] issued in April 1957, Sandys outlined the basis for Britain's future defense policy.

It is in the true interests of defence that the claims of military expenditure should be considered in conjunction with the need to maintain the country's financial and economic strength, and that the way to reduce these claims would be for Britain to possess an appreciable element of nuclear deterrent power of her own.

In his white paper of the following year Sandys argued that there was

no military reason why a world conflagration should not be prevented for another generation or more through the balancing fears of mutual annihilation. In fact there is no reason why this should not go on indefinitely.... [W]hen fully equipped with megaton weapons, the British bomber force will itself constitute a formidable deterrent.[11]

Having based Britain's future defense policy firmly on nuclear deterrence, the 1957 white paper defined the tasks of its conventional forces as "to play their part with the forces of Allied countries in deterring and resisting aggression" and "to defend Britain's colonies . . . against local attack and undertake limited operations in overseas emergencies." While Britain will "provide her fair share of the armed forces of the free world she cannot any longer continue to make a disproportionately large contribution."[12]

The consequences of this on the size of the British army in particular were severe. Conscription was to be abolished and phased out by 1960. Total armed services personnel were to be cut from 690,000 to 375,000 by 1962. Clearly, the tests of an air-dropped British hydrogen bomb in May 1957, the coming into squadron service of the Victor bombers, capable of hitting Moscow, and the decision to develop a British Blue Streak long-range ground-to-ground ballistic missile enabled Sandys to emphasize the nuclear deterrent with greater confidence than his predecessors.

There was nothing new in this white paper. It was the culmination of thinking about nuclear deterrence in British defense policy making circles since the early 1950s. Ending conscription was electorally popular; it had not been a very efficient way of securing skilled personnel for the increasingly technologically complex weapons systems that were being developed.

While the cuts that Sandys imposed were considered drastic at the time, no thought had been given to reducing the considerable array of overseas commitments with which Britain had encumbered itself since 1945 and which had necessitated the reintroduction of national service in the first place. The white paper in fact insisted that there was no question of Britain abandoning its world role—merely the reduction in the size of a few overseas garrisons. Nuclear deterrence was regarded as a way of preserving Britain's role as a great power on the cheap and compensated to some extent for the loss of its *amour propre* at Suez. With the relaxation of U.S. restrictions on the exchange of nuclear information between the two countries after 1957, Britain believed that it could look forward to close cooperation with the United States in the future.

In the event, few of Sandys's calculations were fulfilled. Nuclear deterrence was destined to become an increasingly expensive burden as new and more sophisticated missile systems were developed, which meant that Britain's nuclear "independence" turned out to be illusory in the long run. London was eventually forced to purchase U.S. missiles since they were cheaper than it could produce itself.

Sandys intended that the BAOR should bear the main share of the cuts in army personnel. Thus, Eden's decision in 1954 to maintain Britain's forces in West Germany for an unspecified period was not as "historic" as he had claimed at that time. Britain had then assured its continental neighbours that it "would maintain the present fighting capacity" of its forces in Europe, an escape clause that allowed the Cabinet to reason later that if British troops were provided with tactical nuclear weapons their "fighting capacity" would be enhanced, thus permitting a reduction in the number of troops in the British Army of the Rhine. This was the excuse made when in 1957

Sandys cut the size of the BAOR from the 1954 figure of 77,000 men to 64,000 and halved the size of the Second Tactical Air Force in West Germany. Two years later, Britain announced that it was further reducing the size of the BAOR to 55,000 men. This decision was justified not only by reference to the growing arsenal of tactical nuclear weapons, but also to the increasing expenses of maintaining British forces in West Germany. Since West Germany had ceased to be an occupied power in 1955 Britain could no longer charge the costs of its occupation forces to the German exchequer; these costs were running some £50 million per year in 1957 and would increase to £75 million annually in 1960. After prolonged bickering the West Germans agreed to contribute toward the support costs of the British Army of the Rhine by £12 million a year between 1958 and 1962, although the British complained that this met only a fraction of the total costs.[13]

In 1960 Britain advised its allies that it was cutting the size of the BAOR again, this time to 49,000 men. This caused consternation in Western Europe. Fears were expressed that this would become a continuing process, with Britain's contingent on the continent eventually reduced to a battalion. Others feared that Britain's actions would encourage West Germany to demand the right to acquire nuclear weapons for itself on the grounds that Britain's failure to live up to its 1954 promise had deprived Germany of adequate defenses, especially as it would encourage other NATO members to follow the British example. Few took Britain's excuse about the provision of tactical nuclear weapons seriously, and indeed the West Germans feared that the use of such devices would turn their country into a wasteland. In the event, the Berlin Crisis of 1960 and West Germany's agreement to increase its support costs persuaded the British government to abandon the proposed reductions and maintain its force level in West Germany at the figures of 55,000.

Thus Britain's efforts to cut conventional British personnel levels in West Germany came to a grief when the West Europeans finally managed to turn Eden's promise of 1954 against his successors. A pledge made in 1954 to maintain British forces in Europe at a level of four divisions did not seem a major sacrifice when Britain's total armed forces, swollen by national service, numbered 900,000. However, after 1957 it seemed to be an intolerable burden when conscription was abolished and the size of the British army was cut to the bone.

Neither would this have seemed an excessive commitment if the Sandys white paper had suggested anything other than marginal cuts in Britain's overseas role. After 1960 Britain clung to its East of Suez role with the same determination as before. To Harold Wilson, the Labour Prime Minister after 1964, this became an article of faith. He informed Parliament in December, "I want to make it clear that we cannot relinquish our world role."[14] The Secretary of State for Defense, Denis Healey, told an audience in Canberra, Australia two years later that "we have no intention of ratting on any of our commitments."[15] As a result Britain's forces in NATO suffered from increasing neglect in terms of weapons and other military equipment. In 1965 Harold Wilson suggested that, given the reduced threat from the Soviet Union, Britain could withdraw troops from Western Europe for East of Suez purposes, although this came to nothing.

However, increasing dissatisfaction in Whitehall with the diplomatic and economic advantages of the Commonwealth, the growing realization that the "special relationship" with the United States had little meaning in President Lyndon Johnson's eyes, and the inability of Britain, despite its East of Suez presence, to influence events either in the Middle East or in South Vietnam, finally led the British government to reexamine its priorities. Nevertheless, the decisive factor in causing Britain to abandon the bulk of its extra-European responsibilities in 1968 was a series of economic and balance-of-payments crises, each one more serious than the last.

In 1967 Harold Wilson turned reluctantly to Europe as the means of securing Britain's economic salvation. France, West Germany, and the other Western European powers had formed the European Economic Community in 1958 from which Britain, more concerned with its global status, the Commonwealth, and its special relationship with the United States, had stood aside. France vetoed Britain's application in 1967.[16] After 1968 Britain, free of its main overseas commitments, now concentrated its military efforts on trying to rejuvenate the NATO alliance. In 1973 Britain finally joined the European Economic Community. Thereafter London devoted its major military resources to the defense of Western Europe.

It can hardly be maintained that there was widespread enthusiasm in British political circles in the 1970s for the abandonment of Britain's overseas role and its concentration in future on Europe. While in opposition in the late 1960s and 1970s, the Conservative Party promised that it would revive some of the extra-European defense commitments the Labour governments had abandoned. However, once returned to office, the Conservative governments of Edward Heath (1970–74) and Margaret Thatcher (1979 to the present) discovered that continuing financial pressures made it impossible for them to do much to redeem their election pledges. After 1970, therefore, Britain's defense efforts were orientated almost entirely to Western Europe, the Falklands War of 1982 being the only exception to this.

It has not been an easy transition to make. Britain had regarded its close military involvement in Europe between 1914 and 1918 and between 1939 and 1940 as exceptional: the preservation of the British empire was seen as its preeminent concern. After 1943 and 1945, when the defeat of Germany and Italy compelled London to maintain large occupation forces in Germany, Austria, and Italy, it continued to regard Western European defense as an unwelcome distraction from its task of reestablishing its authority in the Middle East and in its Far Eastern possessions. Indeed, until 1950 the

Middle East ranked above Western Europe in the order of its defense priorities.

It was only from 1949 to 1951, a period of heightened East–West tension primarily resulting from the Communist takeover of China and the ensuing Korean War, that Britain was forced to take a closer interest in Western European defense, causing it to increase its occupation forces in West Germany. However, Britain's major preoccupation in these years was to encourage the Western Europeans to make more strenuous efforts to defend themselves and to persuade France to accept a West German military contribution to Western defense. The successful outcome of Britain's efforts would enable it to turn its attention once again to its global role, and this process was assisted by the improvement in East–West relations after 1953.

Anthony Eden's promise in 1954 to retain British armed forces in West Germany indefinitely enabled him to overcome France's opposition to a West German defense contribution to NATO. This was as far as the British government was prepared to go toward bolstering Western European defenses and, indeed, after 1957 London attempted, with partial success, to reduce the commitment Eden had made. The Suez fiasco of 1956 did not cause Britain to abandon its overseas pretensions in 1957. It placed much greater reliance on nuclear deterrence, hoping that this would enable it to maintain its global status with fewer conventional forces than hitherto. London attempted to recover its lost prestige and position in the Middle East from new bases in Cyprus and later in Aden, with Kenya as another possible base in the area before it gained its independence in the early 1960s.

While it was clear that Britain was even more reluctant after 1956 than it had been before to contemplate major overseas expeditions without the assistance of allies, the number of low-intensity operations in which it became involved during the late 1950s and early 1960s in the Middle East, the Persian Gulf, and the Far East increased in number, culminating in the sustained campaign between 1963 and 1965 in which Britain's ground, air, and naval forces were all involved, to thwart Indonesia's efforts to undermine the Federation of Malaysia, to which Britain was tied by defense agreements. The "confrontation" with Indonesia was a severe strain on Britain's armed forces which, coupled with the abandonment of Aden, amidst considerable bloodshed, led to growing doubts inside Britain about the advantages of its overseas role. Was the East of Suez posture essential to the protection of Britain's overseas investments and trade, as the Wilson government claimed? Did it help uphold Britain's standing in the world and in the eyes of the United States, as Denis Healey insisted? Was the Commonwealth of such value to Britain that it required the maintenance of substantial British army, navy, and air forces across the globe to sustain it?

The increasing feeling in Whitehall during the 1960s was that the answer to all these questions was in the negative. This consensus was as important to the Wilson government's decision in 1967 and 1968 to abandon the bulk of Britain's overseas commitments as was its accelerating financial and economic difficulties, although the concatenation of all these circumstances was crucial. After all, Britain could have kept its overseas role if it had been prepared to make greater sacrifices and if it had thought that it was worthwhile: the fact was that many politicians now doubted that it was. The outcome was therefore a reluctant and halting decision to concentrate British energies in the future on Western Europe and its defense, a prospect that leading British politicians, civil servants, and senior army, navy, and air force officers had spurned between 1945 and 1967.

NOTES

1. See C. J. Lowe and M. L. Dockrill, *The Mirage of Power: British Foreign Policy 1902–1922* (London, 1972), vol. 1.

2. John W. Young, *Britain, France and the Unity of Western Europe 1945–1951* (Leicester, 1984), 129–30.

3. William Roger Louis, *The British Empire in the Middle East 1945–1951* (Oxford, 1984), 105ff.

4. For the general account of the EDC negotiations, see Major-General Edward Fursdon, *The European Defence Community: A History* (London, 1980).

5. Formed in 1948 as a mutual security organization of Britain, France, Belgium, Luxembourg, and Holland and a precursor of the enlarged NATO organization.

6. For the British approach to the question of West German rearmament between 1945–55, see the forthcoming book by Saki Dockrill, *Britain and a West German Contribution to NATO*.

7. The paper is still closed to researchers. For Slessor's ideas see Sir John Slessor, *Strategy for the West* (London, 1954).

8. I am grateful to Mr. Martin Navias of King's College London for allowing me to use this quotation, which he found in the COS files at the Public Record Office, Kew.

9. Quoted in Stephen Kirby, "Britain, NATO and European Security," in John Baylis (ed.), *British Defence Policy in a Changing World* (London, 1979), 104.

10. London, HMSO, Cmd 124, April 1957.

11. Quoted in A.J.R. Groom, "The British Deterrent," in Baylis (ed.), *British Defence Policy*, 130.

12. Quoted in Sir Richard Powell, "The Evolution of British Defence Policy," in *Perspectives upon British Defence Policy 1945–1970*, collected papers of a Ministry of Defence Conference at Winchester, April 1974, 44–45 and 51.

13. F. W. Mulley, *The Politics of Western Defence* (London: Thames and Hudson, 1962), 132–33; Hugh Beach, "British Forces in Germany 1945–1985," in Martin Edmonds (ed.), *The Defence Equation* (London: Brassey's, 1986), 164.

14. Quoted in Philip Darby, *British Defence Policy: East of Suez 1947–1968* (Oxford, 1973), 284.

15. Darby, ibid., 296.

16. An earlier application in 1963 had also been rejected by France.

4

Rings and Flanks: The Defense of the Middle East in the Early Cold War

Bruce R. Kuniholm

This chapter is concerned in general with Anglo-American efforts to defend the Middle East during the Truman administration and in particular with U.S. policies toward what came to be known as the Middle East's northern tier. The focus of the chapter in no way implies that the United States was a more important factor than Britain in this joint endeavor, or that Greece, Turkey, and Iran were of greater significance in the larger scheme of things than Egypt or Palestine—both of which were of central concern to Britain and occasionally the subject of vehement discussion between the two Western allies. Neither does it suggest that the geopolitical role played by the northern tier states in great-power politics deserves greater attention than the internal forces that were operative in those countries in the early postwar years. However, it does recognize that the countries that bordered the Soviet Union's southern flank—Turkey in particular—were central to the policy of containment, and that it was this policy that undergirded Anglo-American attempts to coordinate their defense policies in the Middle East during the early postwar years. In the course of containing Soviet influence in the region, officials came to see countries previously characterized as parts of larger "problems" and "questions" as part of the outer "ring" of concentric circles whose locus was at Suez and, subsequently, as perceptions changed, as the southern "flank" of a front whose center was in Western Europe. The changing nature of these conceptions and the evolution in thinking that contributed to them constitute the focus of this chapter.

The Western Allies' defense of the Middle East in the Cold War builds on a long history of competition between East and West that dates back at least to the nineteenth-century rivalry between Russia and Britain. The competition for influence in the region that separated those expanding imperial rivals was characterized in different ways—the "Balkan Problem," the "Eastern Question," the "Persian Problem," and the "Great Game." However it was characterized in its various components, it provided the dynamic for a struggle that took place across a broad area that stretched from the Balkans to British India, and manifested itself during this century in various attempts both to protect and to advance great-power interests. These concerns, at once offensive and defensive, led Britain and Russia to reach a series of *modi vivendi*, in the course of which both great powers attempted to carve out spheres of influence in the region.[1]

The countries that were subject to these understandings, meanwhile, did what they could to survive. In the period between World War I and World War II, for example, they allied among themselves against threats from without. The alternative to forming alliances was playing one great power off against the other or looking to third powers, such as Germany, for assistance. After World War II, however, the survival of these countries was threatened by the relative disparity between Soviet and British power. Only five of thirteen non-Communist states that bordered the Soviet Union before the war were independent when it was over. In the Near East, Afghanistan retained its traditional role of a buffer state; Turkey and Iran, however, were subject to Soviet pressures and were in serious jeopardy of being drawn into the Soviet fold.

The British empire, meanwhile, was disintegrating. Within three years of the end of World War II, British forces would withdraw from Greece, Turkey, India, and Palestine. While the states of the Middle East welcomed the decline of British influence, Turkey and Iran, because they bordered the Soviet Union, were directly threatened by the Soviets, who appeared to be following traditional guidelines. During this time Stalin attempted to carve out a sphere of influence in the Balkans, supported Bulgarian irredentism in Macedonia and Thrace, asked for a port on the Aegean, and put pressure on the Turks to control the Turkish Straits. He sought Turkey's eastern provinces (through Georgian and Armenian irredentist pressures), as well as a sphere of influence in Iranian Azerbaijan (where he supported Kurdish and Azeri separatist movements). Every action, one should note, had a precedent in tsarist policies.

Stalin himself, one should also note, had assured Secretary of State Byrnes that he had no designs, territorial or otherwise, on Iran and no intention of infringing upon Iran's sovereignty. On March 2, 1946, however, in spite of an agreement that Allied forces would withdraw from Iran six months after the end of World War II, the Soviets put heavy political pressures on the Iranians and moved at least 200 tanks into northern Iran in an apparent attempt to intimidate and ultimately control the Iranian government.

Profound anxieties caused Iran to do what it had always done: seek a countervailing force to balance Soviet influence. Given Britain's postwar difficulties, not to mention its imperialist legacy in the region, the obvious choice was the United States. The protracted and complicated Iranian case before the United Nations was central to the hardening of U.S. attitudes toward the Soviet Union in the early years of the Cold War. When differences between the Soviet Union and Iran were referred to bilateral discussions, the result was to subject the Iranians to heavy-handed Soviet intimidation and to suggest to U.S. officials the value of anticipating rather than reacting to Soviet initiatives. The Soviets withdrew from Iran in May 1946 and the situation was resolved later in December only because of a combination of firm U.S. policies, skillful Iranian diplomacy, and the possibility that Stalin saw further confrontation as undermining Soviet interests in Turkey.

Stalin himself had negotiated the Soviet border with Turkey in 1921. His antipathy for the Turks, encouraged by the head of his secret police, Lavrenti Beria (who, like Stalin, was a Georgian), resulted in pressures on Turkey, which was thought to be diplomatically vulnerable because of its neutral role in World War II. The catalyst, as far as U.S. policy was concerned, was a Soviet request in August 1946 that Turkey agree to a joint defense of the Straits. In and of itself, the request might have seemed almost routine, but in the broader context of Stalin's policies toward the region, it was more ominous and prodded the Truman administration, on August 15, 1946, to take a stand.

Six months earlier, the Joint Chiefs of Staff (JCS) had rejected a military commitment in the Middle East because of problems posed by long lines of communication.[2] By August 1946, however, their views had changed. Events in the region had schooled the administration in balance-of-power politics and educated it in the fundamentals of containment, even before the containment thesis was consciously propounded. In what President Truman considered to be his most important decision since the bombing of Hiroshima,[3] he concluded that Soviet control over Turkey would make it virtually impossible to prevent the loss of the Near and Middle East. Given the strategic importance of the region, the President decided that it was in the vital interests of the United States that the Soviet Union not obtain control over Turkey—either by force or the threat of force. Believing that only a threat of U.S. force could deter the Russians, Truman decided that he would resist with all means at his disposal, including the force of U.S. arms, any Soviet aggressions against Turkey. This decision was a significant departure from previous U.S. policies toward the region and reflected a fundamental change in attitude toward the Near East.

The President's decision on August 15, 1946, supported by the Secretaries of State, War, and the Navy,[4] must be seen not (as one scholar would have us see it) as an unwarranted overreaction to a legitimate Soviet request, but rather as a reasonable and prudent response to a number of developments in the region: a growing awareness of Soviet political pressures on Turkey; a hardening perception of Soviet policy, derived from Stalin's calculated diplomatic maneuvering during the crisis in Iran; concern over the deteriorating situation in Iran and the Balkans; and apprehension about the weakened position of the British, who were gradually withdrawing their troops from the region.[5]

Following the President's decision, diplomatic and military policies in Iran, Turkey, and Greece were formulated. In the Mediterranean, the United States formally established a Mediterranean force: its declared purpose was to support the Allies in occupied Europe, to protect U.S. interests, support U.S. policies, and create good will. By year's end, the Mediterranean command included one aircraft carrier, three cruisers, and eight destroyers, and the United States was recognized as the dominant sea power in the Mediterranean, where naval air power combined with the potential of nuclear weapons to create a new strategic environment.[6]

In the wake of changes in U.S. naval policy in the Mediterranean, the Department of State sought to define policies toward Greece, Turkey, and Iran. While these policies were grounded in the special needs of each country, they were closely related. They all placed symbolic value on the principle of support for the independence and territorial integrity of small countries. Underlying the question of principle was the usual complex of economic and strategic interests. The strategic situation of each country was related to that of the other. Turkey was viewed as the most important strategic factor in the Eastern Mediterranean and the Middle East. Recent events clearly indicated Soviet intentions to weaken Turkey, with the object of bringing it under the Soviet Union's direct influence. Were the Soviets to obtain their objectives in Turkey even partially, Greece and Iran would be dangerously exposed. Greece was the only country in the Balkans not yet subject to Soviet hegemony; with Turkey, it formed the only obstacle to Soviet domination of the Eastern Mediterranean. Iran was seen as a "cushion" to Soviet advances in the Middle East, which would threaten access to the Persian Gulf's oil; it was also one of the few favorable areas for counter-offensive action against the Soviets. Together, Iran, Turkey, and Greece constituted a bulwark that protected U.S. interests in the Near and Middle East as a whole, the focal point of which was Middle East oil.[7]

The first public postwar commitment by the United States to the defense of the Near East was articulated by President Truman on March 12, 1947, in what has become known as the Truman Doctrine. This unprecedented commitment was sharpened by the President's decision on Turkey seven months before. It was precipitated when the British, who had been apprised of that decision toward the end of 1946, informed the United States in February 1947 that their strained resources made further assistance to Greece and Turkey impossible. In the mind of Under-Secretary of State Dean Acheson, who was a key figure in the decision, this was the most important decision with which the United States had been faced since the war; the choice was clear and there could be only one decision.[8]

It should be emphasized that the President's commitment to the defense of the Near East was not one to send U.S. armed forces to the regions. U.S. armed forces had been reduced from 12,000,000 in June 1945 to 3,000,000 in June 1946, and by June 1947 would be at 1,600,000. Defense expenditures, at $81.6 billion in fiscal year 1945, had been reduced to $44.7 billion in fiscal year 1946, and $13.1 billion in fiscal year 1947. Neither of these trends suggested that the United States had much with which to undertake global responsibilities. Nonetheless, the administration's decision constituted a qualified acceptance of the general responsibility of maintaining the balance of power in the Near East, and was voiced in the Truman Doctrine, which called for a $400 million appropriation to aid Greece and Turkey.[9]

Up until this time, the balance of power in the region had traditionally been maintained by Britain. Now Britain could no longer fulfill this role— at least not alone. The problem that confronted the administration was whether or not the United States, which had previously had no role in regional great-power politics, should take on at least a part of that responsibility. Confronted with this problem, and the prospect of Britain's imminent withdrawal from Greece and Turkey, the President chose to pursue what became known as the policy of containment, with its implicit notion of an equilibrium of forces. It had been a cornerstone of British policy in the region for over a century, and would come to play the same role for U.S. policy in the postwar era.

The necessity of Anglo-American cooperation in pursuing this policy in the Middle East, however, would soon pose additional difficulties. How firm were U.S. commitments? What priority would they have once other priorities developed? To what extent were British and U.S. interests compatible? To what extent could responsibilities be shared? Although Iran's independence was clearly central to the balance of power between East and West that was undergirded by the Truman Doctrine, Iran had not been included in the discussion of aid to Greece and Turkey. This was because Britain, which had important oil interests in Iran, had not requested that the United States include Iran in its new responsibilities. Given the emerging nationalist sentiments within the region, and Britain's determination to hold on to what influence it continued to exercise in Iran and Egypt, to what extent would Anglo-American cooperation undermine rather than facilitate the defense of Western interests against Soviet influence in the region? These were some of the questions that would soon be raised by the situation developing in Europe—questions that would complicate Anglo-American defense of the Middle East in the early Cold War.

In the two years that followed the enunciation of the Truman Doctrine, the administration's attention focused on problems in Europe, and subsequently on the Far East. The object of U.S. policy during this time was to restore the balance of power in Europe and Asia.[10] As a result, when Europe, too, began reconstruction and rearmament, the United States was forced to reassess the value of assistance to the Near East and to give careful thought to the region's role in its overall strategic interests. As these conceptions evolved, they were tugged first one way and then another by the changing assumptions that supported U.S. policies.

Turkey's problems require brief explanation. The Turks had escaped the ravages of war and consequently did not have Greece's problems of reconstruction, but recent Soviet policies had forced the Turks to maintain a large army. The primary mission of the Turkish armed forces was to deter Soviet aggression. Deterrence was based on a standing army of 485,000, supported by outmoded equipment (80 percent of which was of German design), and capable of being augmented within a month by approximately one million reserves. Turkey's mobilization plan, according to General Omar Bradley, was not complicated: "Everyone turns out to fight and that is all the plan amounts to." But Turkey's determination to deploy this army if necessary suggested that its defeat could be realized only through a costly war. As the early postwar years had made clear to the Turks, however, the Soviets had other means short of war by which they could achieve their ends. Because approximately 50 percent of Turkey's budget went to national defense, funds that otherwise would have been used for economic development went elsewhere. Curtailment of essential governmental services, reduction of economic productivity, and a diminished potential for necessary capital development constituted a fundamental threat to the government's long-term viability.[11]

The Joint Chiefs of Staff did not believe that the Soviet Union would attempt to impose its will in the Near East by direct military measures; in Turkey, they envisioned the Soviets' using political pressures and subversive tactics to achieve their ends. As a result, the objective of assistance to Turkey was to stiffen the Turks' will and ability to resist Soviet pressure, and to improve their military potential so that, should it become necessary, they could resist Soviet aggression and conduct a holding action in Turkey. Effective assistance to Turkey, General Eisenhower noted, involved political, economic, and psychological factors that were even more important than military ones; they were so intertwined that they could not be separated.[12]

Greece's problems were more complex and less susceptible of solution than those of Turkey. Serious economic dislocations had been created by the ravages of war. If World War II had ended, the civil war went on. Albania, Yugoslavia, and Bulgaria supported Greek guerrillas in their attacks across 600 miles of Greece's 723-mile border, contributing to a massive refugee problem, and compounding a chronic lack of stability in Greek politics. Limitations of space preclude examination here of Greece's internal difficulties and allow only brief mention of U.S. efforts to address them. Suffice it to observe that the third round of the civil war, which began in the spring of 1946, would continue into the fall of 1949. It would end not because of U.S. assistance, which was significant, but primarily because of Marshal Tito's defection from the Soviet camp and his subsequent decision to cease aiding the Communist guerrillas.

On a more general level, U.S. perceptions of Greece and Turkey focused on the symbolic role they played in the conflict between the Soviet and Western systems, and on their function as a bastion of Middle East resistance to potential Soviet aggression. As a result, Foreign Minister Bevin's decision in July 1947 to withdraw Britain's remaining 5,000 troops from Greece (9,000 had been withdrawn since March) alarmed the JCS and elicited an angry response from U.S. Secretary of State Marshall. Marshall saw British forces as symbolic of both Western determination and joint Anglo-American responsibility, and he was concerned that British withdrawal would be interpreted as an abandonment of that responsibility at a very critical time, with probable repercussions throughout Europe. Regardless of the President's determination to resist Soviet aggression in the region with all means at his disposal, and in spite of the aid program that had been initiated earlier in the year, what these commitments meant in practice had yet to be spelled out. Until that time, the cornerstone of Marshall's and U.S. thinking continued to be the maintenance of Britain's position in the Middle East to the greatest extent possible.[13]

Bevin's response to Marshall suggested a joint review of the entire situation in the Middle East for the purpose of arriving at a "gentlemen's understanding" on a common policy and joint responsibility throughout the area.[14] The "Pentagon Talks" on the Middle East and the Eastern Mediterranean between Britain and the United States in the fall of 1947 revealed that in the event of war, the British Chiefs of Staff saw the Middle East as a strategic theater second in importance only to Europe. Reasons for their assessment included lines of communications, oil, and strategic bases for launching a counteroffensive against the Soviet Union. The British acknowledged the importance of Greece, Turkey, Iran, and Afghanistan as a line of defense, but underscored what had been increasingly evident: they regarded recent U.S. actions as relieving Britain of its burden in Greece and Turkey and as transferring to the United States responsibility for the rehabilitation and defense of those two countries. The British were especially concerned about Iran, where they clearly intended to maintain their special position if possible, and were less interested in Afghanistan, whose strategic importance was not comparable to that of Iran, Turkey, and Greece.[15] These and subsequent discussions would reveal that the British were more interested in the area centered around Suez. Except for Iran, they hoped that the United States would take the lead in assisting the Middle East's northern tier countries.

State and Defense officials participating in the Pentagon talks operated on the assumption that the August 1946 decision to resist Soviet aggression against Turkey should apply with equal force to Italy, Greece, and Iran, as well as Turkey. Such a policy, however, would be unrealistic unless the British maintained their position in the region, and unless Britain and the United States followed parallel policies.[16]

Their recommendations that the United States should make full use of its power and resources to assist the northern tier countries in maintaining their territorial integrity and political independence were embodied in an "American Paper" approved by the National Security Council on November 21, 1947, and by President Truman three days later. A similar document was approved by the British Cabinet at about the same time. While there was no ironclad agreement, both countries agreed to work on a cooperative basis, to exchange views, and to pursue parallel policies.[17]

As Anglo-American discussions proceeded throughout 1948 and early 1949, a variety of different mechanisms for ensuring Greece's and Turkey's security were considered. These included an extension of the North Atlantic Treaty to cover Greece and Turkey, a pact that would initially exclude but eventually provide for their association with the original signatories, a North Atlantic-Mediterranean regional defense arrangement; a separate Mediterranean security system with which the United States would be associated, a treaty of reciprocal military assistance; unilateral declarations of assurances; and a protocol attached to the treaty to cover the two Near East countries and Iran.[18]

The problems that the North Atlantic Treaty posed for Greece and Turkey were serious. As long as no commitment had been made by the United States to any country, there was no apparent difference between intentions to ensure the security of one country or another. Once the United States had concluded a close defensive arrangement with Western Europe, however, what was one to do about countries such as Greece and Turkey— equally threatened, less able to defend themselves, but not similarly protected? Failure to give them a guarantee similar to that given the countries of Western Europe could give the Soviet Union the impression that it could commit aggression against Turkey in comparative safety. The possibility existed that the foundations of resistance would be eroded and the Soviet Union tempted to increase its pressures on them.

The United States, for its part, did not want to spread its sphere of activity too widely. Government officials thought the United States was doing a great deal already, and felt that little more was needed to indicate a continuing interest. Limits, many believed, had to be drawn somewhere. If Italy were admitted to the North Atlantic Treaty, for example, Greece would want to be included; if Greece were admitted, Turkey would want in; and if Turkey were admitted, Iran too would seek admission.

The regional bureaus in the Department of State recognized these problems. They sought public assurances that the defense of friendly nations was as important to the United States as that of Western Europe—that an attack on them would be an attack on the security of the United States and would produce a corresponding reaction.[19] In the case of Turkey and Greece, concerns would continue until the two countries had become members of the North Atlantic Treaty Organization (NATO).

Throughout this period, U.S. assistance to Greece and Turkey was only temporarily funded by yearly appropriations. As a result, when the possibility of future military support for Western Europe created competing priorities, assistance to Greece and Turkey was threatened with reduction, and the United States was faced with a choice of expanding its means to fit its interests or contracting its interests to fit its means. The result was a review of long-range U.S. interests.[20]

In late November 1948 the JCS provided their views. The security of Greece and Turkey were of critical importance to the United States. While both countries offered bases for operations in the Eastern Mediterranean, Turkey was strategically more important because it dominated the major air, land, and sea routes from the Soviet Union to the Eastern Mediterranean and Persian Gulf. While Greece could probably never resist an attack in force, Turkey could impose an appreciable delay on attacking forces and, supported by the United States, offer strong resistance. Based on these considerations, the JCS defined the following long-range U.S. strategic interests:

- a Greek military establishment capable of maintaining internal security in order to avoid Communist domination
- a Turkish military establishment sufficient to ensure continued resistance to Soviet pressure, and able to delay Soviet aggressions long enough to permit U.S. and allied forces to deny certain portions of Turkey to the Soviet Union[21]

By March 1949, the National Security Council (NSC) had approved this redefinition of U.S. strategic interests in Greece and Turkey as a basis for planning military assistance to those countries, and the State-Army-Navy-Air Force Coordinating Committee had given priority for military aid in Europe and the Near and Middle East above all other regions. In the Mutual Defense Assistance Act, signed by the President in October 1949, the North Atlantic Treaty states were allocated $1 billion in military assistance; Greece and Turkey were allocated $211 million.[22]

In spite of increasing commitments in U.S. military assistance to Turkey and Greece, however, strategic thinking about them continued to be rooted in the defense of the Eastern Mediterranean and the Persian Gulf. By 1949 the JCS and Secretary of Defense Forrestal had approved short-range emergency plans that envisioned, as a minimum goal in the Eastern Mediterranean, holding the Cairo-Suez-Khartoum area as a base for air offensives, and, subsequently, as a base for further operations to regain Middle East oil resources in the Persian Gulf.

An NSC report on Iran illustrated the necessity of such plans, estimating that in its last years the European Recovery Program would depend on the Middle East for 80 percent of its oil; denial of Middle East oil, it asserted, would seriously jeopardize the ERP. In view of the need for oil, the U.S. government was also considering other bases—in Turkey among other countries—although such plans were complicated by political questions and the lack of forces to ensure their retention after the initial stages of a war. From a strategic point of view, however, both Britain and the United States still saw Turkey, Greece, and Iran as they had since 1946: an area in which to conduct holding actions in a retreat to more tenable positions along Britain's line of communications. The JCS saw Turkey's main strategic role as that of a buffer against Soviet expansion into the Eastern Mediterranean and Middle East.[23]

Between the signing of the North Atlantic Treaty in early April 1949 and the beginning of the Korean War in June 1950, the urgency of U.S. support for Greece and Turkey was increasingly challenged by competing priorities. Attempts to restore the balance of power in Europe, first economically, and then militarily, continued to call into question the relative importance of the Near East and led the Turks to seek a security commitment or association within the security framework being established in Europe.

In the fall of 1949, moreover, the Soviet testing of an atomic weapon and the collapse of Chiang Kai-shek's regime together focused the attention of government officials on broader issues: development of a thermonuclear bomb, the use of atomic weapons, national objectives, and strategic programs. By January 1950 reassessments of the international situation had seriously diminished the *relative* importance of U.S. military strategic interests in the Middle East. As a result, while previous statements and policy objectives continued to be reaffirmed throughout the first half of 1950, what those policies were in fact was far from clear.

Turkish concerns about being abandoned by the West, meanwhile, caused the Turkish government to press repeatedly for the inclusion of Turkey in the Atlantic Pact. Athens, perhaps because it did not border the Soviet Union, was less anxious about the problem than Ankara; it was also far more preoccupied with immediate internal problems. The United States, for its part, was consistent in refusing to consider a security pact with Turkey, Greece, or Iran until U.S. capabilities were judged as adequate to defend its vital interests. The strengthening of Western Europe, it was argued, was the first order of business; it was a prerequisite to restoration of the balance of power in Europe and would help to deter Soviet aggression elsewhere. Congress and the U.S. public, moreover, had to assimilate the new departure in U.S. foreign policy.[24]

The "loss of China," meanwhile, particularly after the Sino-Soviet Treaty of February 14, 1950, precipitated a concern about U.S. commitments outside the North Atlantic area, including the Near East. Some officials, such as Army Chief of Staff General Lawton Collins, worried that Iran—which the British, too, acknowledged to be a "soft spot"—would develop into a "second China."[25] The process of formulating national security problems clearly required more coherence, and eventually would result in NSC 68.[26]

In the interim, subtle changes became apparent in U.S. policy toward Turkey. Because Turkey could not be included in the Atlantic Pact, the United States earlier in 1949 had decided that it would be unwise to construct forward air bases or stockpile aviation gas in Turkey. It had also chosen not to expose Turkey to increased pressures from the Soviet Union. In October 1949 this policy was reversed. The United States and Turkey reached agreement in principle on the reconstruction of military airfields in Turkey, some as far east as Diyarbakir. While keeping the lid on publicity and information about the details, the United States intended to build airfields designed for use by bombers and jet aircraft. By June 1950 it had also decided to give Turkey jet aircraft—in part, apparently, to justify the fact that larger airfields were being built in Turkey. The airfields appear to have been intended for use in support of the tremendous strategic air offensive that the United States planned to launch against Russia in the event of war—a plan about which General Collins apprised President Inonu in late March.[27]

The pervading problem for the United States during this time was how far to go in accepting its new responsibilities in the Middle East. While the JCS saw no change in the importance of the area, higher priorities in other areas made it impossible to devote any substantial portion of the United States' limited resources to the Middle East. This line of thinking was reflected in Title II of the Mutual Defense Assistance Act, under which Turkey was allocated only $67.4 million, or 73 percent of the $91.8 million allocated in fiscal year 1950.[28]

The North Korean invasion of South Korea in late June 1950 raised anew the question of Turkey's strategic importance. It confronted decision-makers once again with the question of how far the United States should go in accepting its responsibilities in the Near and Middle East. Discussing the breaking crisis with his assistant, George Elsey, on the day after the war began, Truman bent over a globe and put a finger on Iran. He told Elsey:

Korea is the Greece of the Far East. If we are tough enough now, if we stand up to them like we did in Greece three years ago, they won't take any next steps. But if we just stand by, they will move into Iran and they will take over the whole Middle East. There is no telling what they will do, if we don't put up a fight now.

Once the tide was turned in Korea, a short-term solution in the Near East circumvented fundamental issues; the United States and its NATO allies decided to offer Turkey and Greece the opportunity to associate themselves with NATO's military planning for the Mediterranean. Objectives and programs embodied in NSC 68, meanwhile, whose adoption was made virtually certain by the Korean War, were approved by the President on September 30, 1950. As the implications of this document were being absorbed by the foreign policy bureaucracy, the intervention by the People's Republic of China in Korea in late November ended hopes of separating Moscow and Peking; it also shook the confidence of public officials and intensified discussions over Turkey and Greece, which now took place at the highest levels of the government.

The outcome of these deliberations was the President's decision of May 24, 1951, that the United States should press immediately for the inclusion of Greece and Turkey in NATO.[29] In order to illuminate the strategic conceptions that informed these discussions, it will be useful to examine some of the factors that were instrumental in the decision. Three days after the beginning of the Korean War, President Truman directed that the NSC survey its policies affecting the entire perimeter of the Soviet Union. An initial assessment, NSC 73, ruled out the likelihood of overt Soviet aggressions against Iran, Turkey, or Greece. Such an attack, it was believed, because it could provoke a general war and lose the Soviets the advantage of surprise, would have to be part of simultaneous attacks elsewhere; it would indicate, in other words, that a general war was at hand. Soviet intimidation and testing of U.S. firmness, however, was regarded as a real possibility.[30]

British plans during this time were to concentrate on the defense of what they called the Middle East's inner core, or "inner ring," centered in and about the 38,000-man British garrison at Suez (which included 34 military stations and ten airfields). Available forces made it extremely difficult to defend the "outer ring"—a line running from the Mediterranean coast above Silifke in Turkey, along the Taurus Mountains and the rim of the Turkish Plateau to Lake Van, and then along the arc of the Zagros Mountains to Bandar Abbas at the Strait of Hormuz. British assistance there would be limited to air support. The British had agreed to take the initiative in any action in the region, but had expressed the hope that the United States could help.[31]

A subsequent assessment by the United States, NSC 73/4, in late August recommended that if Soviet forces attacked Greece or Turkey, the United States should supply military assistance and deploy those forces that could be made available without jeopardizing U.S. national security. In Iran, the United States intended initially to rely on Britain for principal responsibility, and then, as in the case of Greece and Turkey, deploy forces that could be made available without jeopardizing U.S. national security. Earlier in the month, as part of a supplemental appropriation of $4 billion for military assistance, the President had asked for $193 million for Greece, Turkey, and Iran. As a result, the guidelines agreed to by NSC 73/4 could be seen as recognition of British weakness in Greece and Turkey, and constituted an attempt to shore up an area in which the United States and Britain were each looking to the other for help.[32]

Following a formal Turkish request in August 1950 that it be admitted to NATO, Acheson asked for the views of the Defense Department on a range of alternatives. The principal reasons for Turkey's request, he explained, appeared to be the hope of obtaining additional arms and an allied commitment in the event of war, as well as the conviction that Turkey's adherence to the pact would deter Soviet aggression. Acheson noted that the inclusion of Turkey would, for political reasons, require the inclusion of Greece, although Iran might be excluded on the grounds that it was not a European country. Acheson was concerned that if the United States decided to enter into some arrangement with the Turks, it be in a position to provide sufficient military support to justify the arrangement.[33]

The JCS, to whom Acheson's memo was referred, believed that the defense of the North Atlantic Treaty area was a primary commitment and that the admission of Turkey and Greece might adversely affect its development. They ruled out a regional pact because, with the exception of Turkey, the nations of the region were too weak to defend themselves. Admission of Turkey, on the other hand, would allow for the concert of plans and actions in the region.

As a result, the JCS recommended associate status for Greece and Turkey; this would allow NATO's members to obtain the benefits of Greek and Turkish participation in a coordinated defense of Western Europe, the Mediterranean, and to some extent the Middle East. At the same time, such status would minimize the disadvantages of granting the two countries full membership because it would not impede progress now evident in the integration of NATO forces. The JCS also recommended that the question of full membership for Greece and Turkey be raised as soon as NATO's defense was reasonably assured, but that Iran's association with NATO not be given serious consideration.[34] In light of these considerations, Acheson proposed, and the foreign ministers of France and Britain agreed, that Turkey and Greece associate themselves with NATO planning on the defense of the Mediterranean.[35]

Among the factors that underscored the increasing importance of the Middle East to the West at this time was the fact that Middle East oil was supplying 75 percent of all European requirements. The region's proven reserves—estimated in 1950 to be approximately 40 billion barrels—were equal to those of the rest of the world, and were almost double those of the United States. If probable or possible reserves were taken into account, estimates approached 150 million barrels. While these reserves obviously were important, their vulnerability to attack appeared to preclude an effective defense: both U.S. and British officials believed that the Gulf's refineries would be destroyed by bombing early in the war regardless of who possessed them.[36]

By adopting a lower profile for the Middle East than had the British, the Joint Chiefs of Staff hoped to urge their Commonwealth friends to do more for the Middle East than they would have otherwise; as a result, because of this tactical consideration and because General Collins, Chief of Staff of the army, was concerned primarily with Western Europe, the U.S. chiefs assessed differently from their British counterparts the strategic importance of the Middle East. They planned no military sacrifices in the region and opposed any measures that, in the event of global war, would even tend to commit U.S. forces to the Middle East. As one U.S. official explained to the British Chiefs in October, the word "vital" was applied freely to the Middle East in planning, but in practice the United States seemed to question whether a large part of the Middle East could be held.[37]

One of Britain's aims in planning talks between the British and U.S. Chiefs in late October 1950 was to persuade the United States to give the Middle East a higher priority—possibly to station forces in the region in order to facilitate their augmentation should that become necessary, and through such preparation to deter an attack similar to that which had taken place in Korea. The Americans were unreceptive. In the event of war, General Collins told the British Chiefs, the Middle East was a British responsibility. While agreeing that the Middle East in war was of importance second only to Western Europe, the JSC would not commit forces to the area during the first two years of war.[38]

The British understood the limitations of U.S. support but nonetheless managed to get a promise of some assistance from the United States. The JCS agreed that Strategic Air Command strikes would assist in the area's defense. In the event of a crisis in Iran, the United States promised to consider sending an aircraft carrier to the Persian Gulf as a show of force. The JCS also agreed to examine the feasibility of successful operations in the area and to undertake with the British a joint review of present and projected capabilities for the defense of the so-called "outer ring." Defense of the region anchored on Turkey in the West and running southeastward along the Zagros Mountains of Iran, the Chiefs believed, would provide some protection for the oil fields in southern Iran and the Arabian Peninsula. Although the British, in the event of a war, did not believe they could defend even the inner ring centered on Suez, growing evidence pointed to the need for at least some Middle East oil throughout the war. In their judgment, such a requirement would make defense of the outer ring essential.[39]

One of the objectives sought by the United States in joint defense planning with Turkey, meanwhile, was the capacity to deny the Soviet Union an exit from the Black Sea through the straits. The prospects for controlled mining of the straits appeared to be increasingly feasible. Another U.S. objective, coordination between the Greeks and Turks, was realized in staff talks that were both cordial and productive.[40] What the Turks wanted from the United States was clear: a guarantee. What they could offer in return was a strategic role in the defense of Europe that was only gradually coming to be appreciated.

Meanwhile, plans for Turkey's armed forces were made to conform with JCS recommendations; these recommendations envisioned a delaying action in Thrace, withdrawal to Anatolia, and successive delaying actions in the mountains back behind the inner ring to Iskenderun in the southeast. If the Soviets attacked from the east, the Turks planned to withdraw and delay back to the same area.

The Turks were striving for maximum readiness by May 1, 1951, when, intelligence suggested, there was a possibility that the Soviet Union might attack.[41] Because of Turkey's preparations, the Soviets would have to use sizeable forces to achieve a quick victory over the Turks; they would also be forced to deploy far greater forces than they would have earlier if they were to attack south toward the oil fields. The deterrent value of these preparedness measures was clear; their implications for NATO were gradually being absorbed by officers who were new to their responsibilities in this area. General Yamut, chief of the Turkish General Staff, discussed these matters with Ambassador Wadsworth in December. Yamut argued that what was needed was an integrated defense plan. If Yugoslavia were secured, Greece, Turkey, and Yugoslavia could provide a force of 50 to 60 divisions— more than all NATO countries could produce at the moment. Along with a German army, he asserted, Western forces could establish a real balance of power in Europe.[42]

The Greeks, it was clear from staff talks, believed that a pact with Turkey was desirable. Greece was vulnerable to a Bulgarian attack, and a pact with Turkey would deter the Bulgarians. The Turks agreed that a pact would deter Bulgaria, but they did not see it as practicable unless it were part of a broader treaty embracing the Mediterranean.[43] By itself, Greece was of less strategic importance than Turkey and could offer the Turks little support. When the Greek chief of staff visited Turkey, General Yamut had told him that Turkey and Greece should be considered as a whole from geographical and historical points of view. This perception had growing support within the U.S. government as well. The Balkans as a whole had the capacity to pose serious problems for the Soviets should they choose to attack Europe.[44]

By the end of the year, George McGhee had come to see the October 1950 agreement on Anglo-American responsibilities in the Middle East as implying abandonment of the region in the event of a global war. Since October, major changes had occurred in the world arena: there had been progress in Western Europe's organization, and the rate of the U.S. buildup had increased. In fact, the final defense authorization for fiscal year 1951 came to $48.2 billion, an increase of 25 percent over the initial request of $13.5 billion. Clearly, the implication of this buildup was that NATO might acquire sufficient strength sooner than initially expected. In the Middle East, however, the situation had deteriorated. Plans there should be based not on Soviet capabilities, McGhee believed, but on estimates of the *probable* effort the Soviets were likely to exert, and on judgments about the extent to which U.S. interests justified commitments that were necessary to deter it. If the Middle East were to be defended, he wrote Acheson, if the West were to make wartime use of Middle East oil, bases, and personnel, positive political and military action was required.[45]

Access to Middle East oil was essential to Europe. Britain, meanwhile, could not defend the region, and U.S. actions did not reflect NSC findings that the Middle East was "vital" to the defense of the United States. What McGhee wanted was a commitment to the defense of the Middle East against aggression, and an agreement with Britain and Turkey to plan and to attempt to hold the outer ring. Discussion between McGhee and the JCS revealed the extent to which U.S. conceptions of the Middle East in general, and Greece and Turkey in particular, were beginning to reflect but had not yet reached any consensus on emerging realities. The United States was the only country doing much about Greece and Turkey; it had not yet incorporated those two countries in anything ressembling a coherent view of the Eastern Mediterranean. Coordination between the United States and Britain, meanwhile, was lacking.

Admiral Sherman, chief of naval operations, felt that the question of Anglo-American responsibility was complicated and could not be compartmentalized by arbitrary lines on a map. Greece and Turkey were not only the northern flank of the Mediterranean as a theater and a line of communications, but were tied into the problems of Western Europe as well. Previously, they had been thought of in a Middle Eastern context; the current situation required that they be regrouped. The Balkans needed to be thought of as an entity and not always linked up with the Middle East. Italy, Yugoslavia, Greece, and Turkey, he suggested, might be usefully grouped together for planning purposes. General Collins, however, saw the Middle East as a British responsibility pure and simple. The United States was kidding itself, he asserted, if it did anything that indicated that it was going to put forces in the area. He was unalterably opposed to the idea. He was interested, however, in the idea of Balkan forces, particularly from Yugoslavia, together with Italian and U.S. forces, holding a short line in northern Italy. Exactly how Turkey fit into Collins's picture was not clear. From the standpoint of the Turkish army, he noted, Turkey was a part of the Middle East. In the event of trouble, it would have to pull out of European Turkey almost at once, falling back to southeastern Turkey.

He acknowledged that the Turks could fight and be of considerable help, but his focus was on Western Europe—"first, last, and always."[46] If the United States could hold onto Western Europe, he believed, it could absorb the loss of the Middle East and go down there later to clean up whatever problems it had.

McGhee, trying to steer between the army and the navy, understood that the priority assigned to the Middle East affected to some extent the allocation of military appropriations. If ground forces were committed to the Middle East, the navy would require considerable equipment and facilities to support and defend the lines of communication on which ground forces were dependent. In this debate, aside from the merits of the argument, his bureaucratic allies were in the air force (which needed bases in the Near East) and the navy: Admiral Sherman, the chief of naval operations, and Admiral Carney, commander in chief of U.S. naval forces in the Eastern Atlantic and Mediterranean, whose mission was the strategic coordination of military missions in Greece and Turkey.[47]

How the issues being discussed would be resolved was uncertain. Whether Turkey should be viewed in a Middle Eastern context, or in a European context, or both, presented serious command problems; that issue would be the subject of extended debate both within the U.S. government and between the Americans, British, French, and Turks. Whether, in the event of war, Turkey and Greece were a U.S. or British responsibility was also unclear; the problem would continue until Greece and Turkey entered NATO. In the State-JCS discussion, General Bradley was unable to recall the October agreement with the British (which had been vague on Greece and Turkey). The truth of the matter, he observed, was that there was a lack of organization in the Mediterranean area. General Eisenhower, who in the previous month had been appointed Supreme Allied Commander of Europe (SACEUR), would have to study the problem. It was he who should determine the relationship between the Middle East and Europe.[48]

The short-term plans prepared by the relevant regional planning groups in NATO at this time, and accepted as a basis for initiating operations in the event of an emergency, were relatively straightforward. The Western region was to hold the enemy as far to the east as possible. The EMMO region (Europe Meridonale-Mediterranean Occidental) was to defend the area under its responsibility, including air and sea lines of communication, as far north and east as possible.[49] Where Greece and Turkey fit in was unclear.

While Eisenhower's developing conception of the relationship between the Middle East and Europe would take time, and would be complicated by bureaucratic and political problems,[50] his strategic conception of the defense of Europe, outlined for President Truman on the day after McGhee's discussions with the JCS, gave some indication of the role he envisaged for Turkey and Greece. Europe, Eisenhower told Truman, was shaped like a long bottleneck with Russia the wide part of the bottle, Western Europe the neck, and Spain the end of the bottle. The West controlled bodies of water (the North Sea and the Mediterranean) on either side of the bottle, and had land on the far side of the water (England and North Africa) good for bases. The West had to rely on land forces in the center, and apply great air and sea power on both flanks. As far as the Mediterranean was concerned, this meant giving arms to Turkey and Yugoslavia, and supporting them with a great fleet of air and sea power. If the Russians tried to move ahead in the center, he would hit them hard from both flanks, allowing the center to hold and forcing the Russians to pull back.[51]

Turkey's potential role in the security of Europe was clearly being perceived as increasingly significant, and was evident in George McGhee's conversation with President Bayar in Turkey two weeks later. In that conversation, Bayar dwelt at some length on Turkey's desire for a security guarantee and noted that Turkey could provide 25 divisions under arms in short order. McGhee promised that he would convey to President Truman Bayar's deep concern over a security commitment, and said that he would do everything that he could to accelerate consideration in Washington on the question. Leaving Ankara, he went to Istanbul in February 1951 where he presided over a week-long conference of Middle East Chiefs of Mission. One of the major results of that conference, which appears to have been a substitute for the joint review contemplated earlier, was a strong recommendation to the Department of State that the United States enter at the earliest possible moment into reciprocal security arrangements with Turkey and Greece. Admiral Carney, who attended the conference, sent a similar recommendation to the JCS.[52]

Using McGhee's conversation with Bayar and the recommendations of the Istanbul Conference to legitimate reconsideration of a security commitment to Turkey, Secretary of State Acheson in late March 1951 raised the issue with General Marshall. Acheson's memo initiated a process which, in May, resulted in a presidential decision: the United States should press immediately for the inclusion of Turkey and Greece as full members of NATO—that being the most desirable form of reciprocal security arrangement.[53]

The rationale behind the decision was interesting for what it revealed about U.S. perceptions of the defense of the Near East in general, the role of Turkey in particular, and how those perceptions had changed since the Truman Doctrine was enunciated four years before. Turkey was still seen as the strongest anti-Communist country on the periphery of the Soviet Union, and the only country in the eastern Mediterranean capable of substantial resistance to the Soviets. It constituted a deterrent to Soviet aggression and provided something of a protective screen for the region. Loss of Turkey to the Soviet Union would give the Soviets a valuable strategic position in the region. If the Soviets attacked Iran, and Turkey remained neutral, the Soviet right flank would be protected. If Bulgaria attacked Greece, Turkey would not oppose Bulgaria unless intervention were dictated by the requirements of a larger security framework that included the United States. Oil interests in the Gulf, meanwhile, would be vulnerable, and European economic viability would be threatened. None of this was new.

What was new was the conviction of a mutuality of benefits: Turkey and Greece on the one hand, and Europe and the United States on the other, all stood to benefit. Turkey was already linked by a treaty of mutual assistance with Britain and France; the treaty had last been reaffirmed in 1949, although no one was sure how much emphasis to place on it. Since the United States believed that the Soviets would attack Turkey only if they were prepared to face the likelihood of global war, and since the United States had important political and strategic interest in Turkey, as well as a profound moral commitment to it, many officials believed that Washington would assist the Turks whether or not it had a reciprocal treaty arrangement with them. The United States was, in effect, already committed to support for the security of Turkey; however, it may have been reluctant to extend that commitment to the rest of the region. That was the import of virtually every major decision on Turkey since August 1946. For the United States to obtain Turkey's full cooperation—to "maximize its contribution"—in international security issues, or to ensure its co-belligerency in the event of an attack on Europe, a U.S. security commitment was required. A security commitment was also necessary to secure access to its valuable bases and to close the straits.[54]

Without a security commitment from the United States, there was concern that Turkey would drift toward neutrality, as it had in World War II, and as Iran appeared to be doing at the time under Prime Minister Mosadeq.[55] If this happened, officials reasoned, the United States and Europe would lose the assistance of a powerful ally. Greece and Iran, if they were to be protected, required mutual defense arrangements with Turkey; this was only possible under a broader security arrangement of which the United States was a part. As members of NATO, however, Turkey and Greece would be important to SACEUR (Supreme Allied Command Europe), both as a deterrent to a Soviet attack and as a threat to the Soviet's southern flank. If the region's military potential were integrated in a security framework, the Soviet Union would have to commit significant forces to protect its southern flank and its vital oil fields around Baku.[56] A security commitment to Turkey, therefore, would constitute a far more effective deterrent than previous arrangements for resisting a Soviet attack, not only along the Middle East's entire northern tier—which provided a buffer for European and U.S. oil interests in the Persian Gulf—but in Europe as well.

The Turks felt they badly needed this commitment. Experience had taught them the value of a credible deterrent. Their leadership saw itself as

European and their country as constituting Eisenhower's strong right flank. They had, moreover, something to contribute. As President Celal Bayar told McGhee, Turkey "wants to give a guarantee, and it would like to receive a guarantee." The exchange was perceived to be to Europe's advantage: Turkey would be giving more than it received.

The U.S. government, in assessing the merits of the problem, decided that admission to NATO was a quick and easy way of bringing Turkey and Greece into the overall defense picture. The Turks were already associated with NATO for planning purposes; they wanted in, they wanted to be an integral part of the West, they had something to contribute, and their prestige was involved. These factors led the United States to press immediately for the inclusion of Turkey and Greece as full members of NATO.[57]

The French initially rejected the idea of a Middle East Command. They wanted Greece and Turkey under Supreme Headquarters Allied Powers in Europe, serving as the right flank of SACEUR. They conditioned their approval of Turkey's admission to NATO on the promise that France would have a senior officer in the Middle East Command and a substantial naval command in the Western Mediterranean. The United States, sensitive to some of Turkey's priorities, opposed separate NATO and Middle East Commands; it supported, however, the appointment of a British officer who would control a British Eastern Command under SACEUR. The United States refused, on the other hand, to condition Turkey's admission to NATO on any formula, although it exerted its best efforts to get Turkey to agree to participation in a unified command in the Middle East under NATO. According to General Bradley, all the NATO countries agreed that a unified command in the Middle East was the best way to protect NATO's right flank.[58]

The Turks, while prepared to some extent to go along with the British, insisted on being under the command of SACEUR, and preferred to place their forces under Admiral Carney's Southern Command rather than under the British. The Turks saw themselves not as a Middle Eastern nation but as a European nation facing Russia, and as an important factor in Europe's defense against the Soviet Union. They agreed to the creation of a Middle East Command—a notion that was stillborn because of Egypt's refusal to accept it—but placed emphasis on their first priority: Turkey's integration into NATO.

Since none of the arguments that were made in these negotiations called into question the basic assumptions of the initial U.S. decision, it suffices to note that in September 1951, the NATO Council unanimously voted to extend invitations to Greece and Turkey, and that in February 1952 the two countries were formally admitted to full membership in NATO.

With the admission of Turkey and Greece to NATO, Anglo-American defense of the Middle East was integrated at least in part with the defense of Europe. Subsequent conceptions of Middle East Command—the Middle

East Defense Organization, the Baghdad Pact and the Central Treaty Organization—changed, but the basic conception of the northern tier established during the Truman years would continue to dominate and the role of Turkey would continue to be pivotal. Turkey's defense, at least since 1946, had been vital to the security of the United States, although arguments had been raised about how vital it was and whether it was only peripherally vital. Those who gave priority to the balance of power in Western Europe had done so because they believed that difficult choices had to be made. Those who argued that the balance of power in the Near East was almost if not equally as important had done so from the conviction that the two were inseparably linked. The fact that proponents of one or the other argument often reflected a bureaucratic perspective in no way diminished the sincerity of their convictions. When difficult choices between these two groups were no longer required, categorical conceptions of Turkey as a Near Eastern country no longer were necessary or useful. Turkey's unique geopolitical position clearly made it both a European and a Near Eastern country, with an important role to play in the defense of both regions. By the early 1950s, defense of the Middle East interlocked with the defense of Europe and the postwar policy of containment in the region was firmly established.

NOTES

1. For more detailed documentation of the discussion that immediately follows, see Bruce R. Kuniholm, *The Origins of the Cold War in the Near East: Great Power Conflict and Diplomacy in Iran, Turkey, and Greece* (Princeton, 1980); portions of the subsequent discussion are also drawn from an essay originally prepared for the Harry S. Truman Centennial Symposium at the Woodrow Wilson International Center for Scholars, Washington, DC, September 7–8, 1984, which will be published in somewhat different form in a forthcoming volume containing the proceedings of the conference.

2. United States Army, Operations Division, Modern Military Records Branch, National Archives, Washington, DC, CCS 092 United States 12–21–45, February 10, 1946 Report by Joint Strategic Survey Committee.

3. *Foreign Relations of the United States* (hereafter *FR*), *1949*, vol. 6, 1649.

4. *FR, 1946*, vol. 7, 840–42.

5. See Melvyn Leffler, "The American Conception of National Security and the Beginnings of the Cold War, 1945–48," *American Historical Review*, 89:2 (April 1984), 346–81, as well as the comments by Bruce Kuniholm and John Gaddis, and the references cited therein; and his equally problematical "Strategy, Diplomacy, and the Cold War: the United States, Turkey, and NATO, 1945–1952," *The Journal of American History*, 71:4 (March 1985), 807–25.

6. See Walter Millis (ed.), *The Forrestal Diaries* (New York, 1951), 211; Robert Albion and Robert Connery, *Forrestal and the Navy* (New York, 1962), 187; *New York Times*, October 1, 1946; Stephen Xydis, *Greece and the Great Powers, 1944–1947: Prelude to the Truman Doctrine* (Thessaloniki, 1963), 357–359, 644, 715–716;

Arnold Ragow, *James Forrestal: A Study of Personality, Politics, and Policy* (New York, 1963), 179–80; Jonathon Knight, "American Statecraft and the 1946 Black Sea Straits Controversy," *Political Science Quarterly*, 90 (Fall 1975), 453–55.

7. *FR, 1946*, vol. 7, 240–45, 894–97.

8. *FR, 1947*, vol. 5, 53; interview with Loy Henderson; Dean Acheson, *Present at the Creation: My Years in the State Department* (New York, 1969), 218.

9. *FR, 1947*, vol. 5, 47–58, 94; *Legislative Origins of the Truman Doctrine: Hearings Held in Executive Session Before the Committee on Foreign Relations*, United States Senate, Eightieth Congress, First Session on S. 938, Washington, DC, 1973. For elaboration of the process by which the Truman Doctrine was written and for an assessment of its implication, see Kuniholm, 410–25. For the statistics cited, see John Gaddis, *Strategies of Containment: A Critical Assessment of Postwar American National Security Policy* (New York, 1982), 23.

10. John Gaddis, *Strategies of Containment*, 57; Walter Millis (ed.), *The Forrestal Diaries*, 341, 349–51, 366–67. *FR, 1947*, vol. 1, 579–80, 770–71.

11. *FR, 1947*, vol. 5, 113, 233–36, 400–1. *FR, 1951*, vol. 5, 31.

12. *FR, 1947*, vol. 5, 110–14, 297–98, 309, 969.

13. *FR, 1947*, vol. 5, 268, 274–78, 290, 301–2, 308, 313, 322, 327–29, 330–32.

14. *FR, 1947*, vol. 5, 321–23, 330–32, 488–96, 511—13.

15. *FR, 1947*, vol. 5, 532–33, 566–80, 592–93, 607–8. The Afghans were interested in abandoning their traditional neutrality in return for military aid. *FR, 1948*, vol. 5 (Part 1), 491–94; *FR, 1949*, vol. 6, 46.

16. *FR, 1947*, vol. 5, 561, 575–76.

17. *FR, 1947*, vol. 5, 580–85, 623–25, 1289.

18. *FR, 1948*, vol. 3, 41, 47, 59, 63–67, 85–88, 92, 97, 225, 331–32, 342; *FR, 1949*, vol. 4, 13–14; *FR, 1949*, vol. 6, 31–45.

19. *FR, 1948*, vol. 4, 172–76.

20. *FR, 1948*, vol. 4, 144–45, 158–60, 191–92; Gaddis, 23.

21. *FR, 1948*, vol. 4, 191–92.

22. In December 1948, the JCS approved $100 million in military assistance to Turkey and $200 million to Greece. *FR, 1949*, vol. 6, 42, 269–79; *FR, 1949*, vol. 1, 259–67, 277, 317–18, 398.

23. *FR, 1949*, vol. 6, 32, 42, 549, 1644–45, 1654–55, 1681–82; *FR, 1948*, vol. 5 (Part 1), 2–3, 244–46; *FR, 1948*, vol. 3, 933–34. The importance of Middle East oil to the implementation of the Marshall Plan was recognized almost immediately; *FR, 1947*, vol. 5, 665–66. Concern in 1948 that available forces could not retain major portions of the oil producing areas from the outset of a war was mitigated somewhat by the knowledge that allied forces could deny use of oil producing facilities in the Middle East to the Russians; *FR, 1948*, vol. 5 (Part 1), 2–3. In the event of a Soviet occupation of Turkey, the British apparently contemplated denial operations through aerial bombing; *FR, 1949*, vol. 6, 1681–82. In the event of a Soviet occupation of Iran, the Shah anticipated withdrawing to the mountain areas in the west and southwest of Iran in order to attempt a defense of the oil fields; *FR, 1949*, vol. 6, 471–72. In November 1949, during a visit to the United States, the Shah discussed this plan with the Joint Chiefs and was told by General Bradley that it was probably the best that could be devised under the circumstances; *FR, 1949*, vol. 6, 581–82. See also *FR, 1950*, vol. 5, 508.

24. *FR, 1949*, vol. 6, 62, 117–20, 141–45, 175, 243–44, 270, 359–60, 1642, 1647–

53, 1662, 1669–70, 1682, 1685; *FR, 1950*, vol. 3, 79; *FR, 1950*, vol. 5, 152–58, 1231–32, 1252, 1264, 1273.

25. *FR, 1950*, vol. 1, 314–15; *FR, 1950, vol. 5, 523*. See also the memo by John Foster Dulles, *FR, 1950*, vol. 1, 314–16.

26. *FR, 1950*, vol. 1, 234–92. For discussion of NSC 68, see Samuel Wells, Jr., "Sounding the Tocsin: NSC 68 and the Soviet Threat," *International Security*, Fall 1979, 116–58; John Gaddis, "NSC 68 and the Problem of Ends and Means," and Paul Nitze, "The Development of NSC 68," *International Security*, Spring 1980, 164–70 and 170–76; and Gaddis, *Strategies of Containment*, 89–126.

27. *FR, 1950*, vol. 5, 1234, 1241–47, 1250, 1256, 1270–71, and 1350. See also *FR, 1946*, vol. 7, 561. See also George Kennan, *Memoirs: 1925–1950*, 411.

28. *FR, 1949*, vol. 6, 55, 58, 63; *FR, 1950*, vol. 3, 975–76; *FR, 1950*, vol. 5, 122–23, 153–54, 157. Turkey's armed forces were now under 300,000; *FR, 1950*, vol. 5, 1236.

29. The quote from Truman is cited in Robert Donovan, *Tumultuous Years: The Presidency of Harry S. Truman, 1949–1953* (New York, 1982), 204–5, 420. *FR, 1950*, vol. 1, 400; Wells, 157. See also John Gaddis, *Strategies of Containment*, 89–126.

30. *FR, 1950*, vol. 1, 331–38.

31. *FR, 1950*, vol. 1, 188–91, 352–53; *FR, 1950*, vol. 3, 1664–65; *FR, 1950*, vol. 5, 195, 218.

32. *FR, 1950*, vol. 1, 338–41, 375–89; *FR, 1950*, vol. 5, 382–86, 572–74, 1289–92. In late July, General Bradley, chairman of the Joint Chiefs of Staff, and General Tedder, marshal of the Royal Air Force and British Permanent Representative at the NATO Standing Group, agreed that in the Middle East the British would take the initiative in regard to any steps that needed to be carried out; *FR, 1950*, vol. 5, 188–89.

33. *FR, 1950*, vol. 3, 257–61.

34. *FR, 1950*, vol. 5, 1306–9.

35. Acting on the advice of the JCS, Acheson also told the Turkish Foreign Minister that it was difficult to conceive of a Soviet attack on Turkey under conditions that would not bring on a general war. To ensure surprise, an attack, if it came, would be against the United States, Western Europe, and Turkey all together; *FR, 1950*, vol. 5, 1321. That Acheson believed this is evident not only from earlier NSC judgments, but by his remarks in conversation with the British and French foreign ministers; *FR, 1950*, vol. 3, 1218. For concern about assurances that would have to be given to Iran, see *FR, 1950*, vol. 5, 600–1.

36. In 1950 the Middle East produced 1,800,000 barrels of oil per day (bpd), with U.S. companies producing 45 percent, British (and Dutch) companies 50 percent, and French and other companies 5 percent of the total. The breakdown by country was:

Iran	700,000 bpd
Saudi Arabia	555,000 bpd
Kuwait	350,000 bpd
Iraq	125,000 bpd

Qatar   40,000 bpd

Bahrain   30,000 bpd

FR, 1950, vol. 5, 72–73, 76–77. For a detailed discussion of the significance of Middle East oil, see *FR, 1950*, vol. 5, 76–96, 233. For an examination of the importance of oil in Western Europe under peacetime conditions, see NIE–14, *FR, 1951*, vol. 5, 268–76, which asserts that Western Europe would not be able to compensate for the loss of Middle East oil.

37. *FR, 1950*, vol. 5, 217–39, 610–11; *FR, 1950*, vol. 3, 1686–89; *FR, 1951*, vol. 5, 9–11. The British, of course, frequently tried to get the United States to do more—an effort which, given past performances, generated some terse comments. See, for example, *FR, 1948*, vol. 4, 147.

38. *FR, 1950*, vol. 5, 232, 236, 611.

39. *FR, 1950*, vol. 3, 1691–95; *FR, 1950*, vol. 5, 233, 611; *FR, 1951*, vol. 5, 7.

40. *FR, 1950*, vol. 5, 439–40, 1293–96, 1332–25, 1328–35, 1338–45, 1350–51; *FR, 1950*, vol. 1, 352; *FR, 1950*, vol. 2, 89–90, 110–12.

41. See note 40. For earlier assessments that the Turks were capable of fighting for only three months with existing stocks, see *FR, 1950*, vol. 5, 1323.

42. *FR, 1950*, vol. 5, 1241–47, 1344–53; *FR, 1951*, vol. 3, 470–73; *FR, 1951*, vol. 5, 42.

43. *FR, 1950*, vol. 5, 1338, 1340–41.

44. *FR, 1950*, vol. 5, 382–85, 398, 1348–49.

45. *FR, 1951*, vol. 5, 4–11; Gaddis, 113.

46. *FR, 1951*, vol. 5, 27–42.

47. *FR, 1951*, vol. 5, 10–11, 27–42; and Walter Waggoner, "Turkish-Greek Bid for Full Tie Gains," *New York Times*, March 18, 1951.

48. *FR, 1951*, vol. 5, 27–42, 108, 115; *FR, 1951*, vol. 3, 490–91.

49. *FR, 1951*, vol. 3, 460–61.

50. *FR, 1951*, vol. 5, 108, 115; *FR, 1951*, vol. 3, 479–85, 488–97, 523.

51. *FR, 1951*, vol. 3, 454.

52. For the conversation with Bayar, see *FR, 1951*, vol. 3, 466–73; for the allocation of military aid ($1.4 billion over five years) to Greece, Turkey, and Iran—resulting from the guidelines of NSC 68 and made available under Title II of the Mutual Defense Assistance Act—see *FR, 1950*, vol. 1, 437–38, 466; for the Istanbul Conference, see *FR, 1951*, vol. 5, 50–76; for the reports by McGhee and Carney, see *FR, 1951*, vol. 5, 102–4; *FR, 1951*, vol. 3, 505.

53. For some of the key documents in the decision, the substance of which is discussed in the paragraphs that follow, see *FR, 1951*, vol. 5, 50–76, 102–4, 113–20, 1117–26, 1148–62; *FR, 1951*, vol. 3, 501–5, 511–15, 520–22, 575.

54. See Kenneth Condit, *The History of the Joint Chiefs of Staff and National Policy, vol. 2, 1947–1949* (Wilmington, 1979), 288–302; Gaddis, 94; *FR, 1951*, vol. 2, 12; *FR, 1951*, vol. 3, 540, 569, 662; Hamilton Fish Armstrong, "Eisenhower's Right Flank," *Foreign Affairs*, July 1951, 651–63; and C. L. Sulzberger, "Atlantic Parley Will Strive to Bolster Europe's Flank," *New York Times*, September 2, 1951.

55. Serious attention has continued to be given to Iran since 1945. For examples of such concern in 1951, see *FR, 1951*, vol. 5, 103, 106, 264; *FR, 1951*, vol. 3, 526. See also the testimony of George McGhee and Dean Acheson *The Middle East,*

Africa, and Inter-American Affairs (Historical Series), vol. 16; Selected Executive Session Hearings of the Committee on Foreign Affairs, 1951–56, U.S. House of Representatives, Washington, DC, 1980, 33, 50.

56. See the comments, by Prime Minister Menderes; *FR, 1951*, vol. 5, 220.

57. *FR, 1951*, vol. 3, 470, 516; Kilic, 150–58; for Celal Bayar's diplomacy and its contrast with the cautious diplomacy of Inonu, see Metin Tamkoc, *The Warrior Diplomats: Guardians of the National Security and Modernization of Turkey* (Salt Lake City, 1976), 228–47. The relative strategic importance assigned to Turkey over Greece is evidenced by NSC 109 (on Turkey), *FR, 1951*, vol. 5, 1148–62, and NSC 103/1 (on Greece), *FR, 1951*, vol. 5, 451–66, which shows that in February, U.S. policy toward Greece did not include support for Greek membership in NATO; this policy was amended in May in light of the decision to press for Turkish membership in NATO.

58. For the various positions, see *FR, 1951*, vol. 5, 155, 162–63, 173–75, 185–87, 193–95, 212–18, 220, 265–67; *FR, 1951*, vol. 3, 520ff., 551–56, 568–74, 597–99, 670–71, 713–14, 743–44, 1262–68. See also Walter Poole, *The History of the Joint Chiefs of Staff, The Joint Chiefs of Staff and National Policy, Vol. 6, 1950–1952* (Wilmington, 1980), 310–18; the testimony of Dean Acheson, *Executive Sessions of the Senate Foreign Relations Committee* (Historical Series), Committee on Foreign Relations, vol. 3, Part 2, 82nd Congress, 1st Session, 1951 (Washington, 1976), 449–62, and vol. 4, 82nd Congress, 2nd Session, 1952 (Washington, 1976), 137–59. Peter Calvocoressi, *Survey of International Affairs, 1951* (London, 1954), 288ff.; Armstrong, 660–63; Acheson, 569–70, notes 45 and 54.

5

Major and Minor: The Defense of Southeast Asia and the Cold War

Peter Dennis

Five years ago, speaking at a meeting of the Organization of American Historians, John Lewis Gaddis suggested that after a decade of impassioned academic controversy, a postrevisionist synthesis was emerging to explain the origins of the Cold War. He went on to suggest that postrevisionist scholars had overturned the New Left assertion that the United States had forced itself on other countries, and that, in his words, "the American sphere of influence arose as much by invitation as by imposition."[1] His observation was directed toward Scandinavia and the Middle East but could apply, at least in part, to southeast Asia, which of all the areas of Cold War confrontation was the only one apart from Korea where the war became "hot." U.S. involvement was reluctant and, in the eyes of other regional powers, alarmingly belated. That reluctance grew out of a deliberate decision at the end of the war with Japan to draw the line on U.S. involvement at the shores of what by 1945 had become an American lake.

During World War II, President Roosevelt had taken a keen interest in the postwar futures of the European empires there, especially the French in Indochina and the Dutch in the Netherlands East Indies. He seemed determined to use U.S. power to force changes in the political, economic, and social structures of those territories. The Dutch and the French lacked the means to deflect Roosevelt, but they had a ready ally in the British, who saw that their own position in southeast (and indeed south) Asia was equally threatened by the U.S. stance. The Permanent Under-Secretary at the Foreign Office, Sir Alexander Cadogan, wrote darkly of "the President's sinister intentions with regards to Indo-China,"[2] but when it came to the test, U.S. attempts to pursue Roosevelt's anticolonial policies amounted to very little. In the case of the Netherlands East Indies, Roosevelt seemed satisfied by the vague and general speech broadcast by Queen Wilhelmina on December 7, 1942, and thereafter paid little attention to the Dutch.[3] His previously staunch opposition to French participation in the reconquest of Indochina weakened following the Japanese coup against the Vichy government in Saigon in early March 1945. Within ten days he had ordered U.S. air forces to assist the French resistance in Indochina if that could be done without weakening the main drive against the Japanese. Furthermore, he accepted the postwar resumption of imperial control if the French agreed that the ultimate goal of their policy was independence for Indochina.[4] So complete was the abandonment of U.S. claims to direct the postwar future of Indochina that at the United Nations conference in San Francisco in May 1945, Secretary of State Edward Stettinius, Jr. could blithely assure the French that "the record is entirely innocent of any official statement of this government questioning, even by implication, French sovereignty over Indochina."[5]

The withdrawal of the United States from almost all of southeast Asia was decided at the Potsdam conference in July 1945, when at U.S. insistence the boundaries between MacArthur's southwest Pacific area and Mountbatten's South East Asia Command (SEAC) were redrawn (without reference to Mountbatten). To the original SEAC area of Burma, Siam, and the Malay peninsula were added Java, Borneo, Dutch West New Guinea, and the vast island archipelago making up the East Indies, and the southern part of Indochina below the 16° parallel north. Only the Philippines remained in the U.S. sphere. Even before the British became responsible for this territory, U.S. indifference to what was clearly seen as the peripheral areas of southeast Asia had become apparent. Through a Civil Affairs Agreement concluded in December 1944, MacArthur had handed over to the Dutch complete control of and responsibility for all civil affairs behind the advancing battle front, which itself bypassed mainland southeast Asia and island-hopped to the Philippines in fulfillment of MacArthur's promise to return. Thereafter the United States showed little active interest in southeast Asia for several years. The enormous problems of bringing the war to an end against an enemy that had not only been defeated in battle in the respective territories of the former imperial powers; the repatriation of over a million Japanese soldiers (let alone Allied servicemen) in a situation where all shipping was controlled by an inter-Allied shipping pool, and where there was good evidence to suggest that MacArthur was deliberately obstructing the return of disarmed Japanese troops to Japan; the protection of civilian populations—both European and indigenous—against increasingly murderous attacks by local forces (whether genuine political revolutionaries or simply bandits operating in the wake of the breakdown of law and order and in many cases armed with weapons supplied by the Japanese in direct contravention of the terms of the surrender)—involvement in all of this mess was neatly sidestepped by the United States with the change of boundaries. Indeed, even before the thrust of military operations rendered southeast Asia of less concern in the prosecution of the war against Japan, the United States had avoided entanglement. In February 1944, British suggestions that U.S. Civil Affairs Officers be attached to SEAC were rejected on the grounds that to do so would strengthen the belief in India and throughout Asia that Britain and the United States were pursuing a common policy.[6]

It was not quite so easy, however, to pursue a policy of withdrawal. Within southeast Asia there were practical considerations that worked against U.S. reluctance to become involved. SEAC remained an Allied command, even though the last U.S. military personnel (mainly in Mountbatten's headquarters) were withdrawn in October 1945. Large amounts of U.S. equipment, originally supplied through Lend-Lease, remained in southeast Asia and were used by the British, French, and Dutch to reimpose European control. This dismayed the United States, and gave rise to widespread criticism from U.S. correspondents in Saigon, who wrote that the white U.S. Army star was barely concealed on trucks used by French troops and that French officers swaggered around carrying U.S. 45-caliber automatic pistols. President Truman nonetheless agreed to a British request to turn 800 jeeps and trucks over to the French on the grounds that it would be impracticable to remove U.S. materiel already on the ground.[7] Despite an avowed policy of "strict neutrality" over the Netherlands East Indies, the United States continued to provide training facilities at Quantico for the Dutch Marine Brigade and eventually made available shipping to move it to the East Indies, even though the Dutch complained that the move was far too late. British policy in the Netherlands East Indies sought to restore Dutch rule while forcing the Dutch to make substantial concessions to the Indonesian nationalists, and to get both sides to hammer out their differences around the conference table. The need for a negotiated settlement was accepted by the United States in what one U.S. historian of the Cold War has called a "diplomatic triumph," an assessment that can be sustained only by exclusive reference to the twists and turns of U.S. policy.[8] It was a "triumph" only in that it marked the first stage in a long U.S. process of coming to terms with the world as it was, rather than as it ought to have been. Furthermore, while the British Foreign Office and, to a lesser extent, the British Chiefs of Staff acknowledged some debt to the Dutch and (rather more reluctantly) to the French, the United States felt no such obligation. Neither country in U.S. eyes had played any noteworthy part in the war against Japan, and France was doubly disgraced by the Japanese maintenance of the Vichy government in Indochina until March 1945. Nor did de Gaulle's insistence on the dignity and grandeur of France endear him to the Americans. Truman for one could not abide de Gaulle, remarking that he "took himself and his ideas of French prestige altogether too seriously," and adding that "to use a saying we have away back in Missouri, he was something of a pinhead."[9]

This is not to suggest that the United States had no interest in the outcome of events in southeast Asia. It kept a close watch on the widening nationalist struggles in Indochina and the Netherlands East Indies, and within the State Department an intense and at times bitter struggle developed between the Offices of European and Far Eastern Affairs, the former insisting that America's primary interests were with Europe (if not necessarily *in* Europe) and could not be jeopardized by taking an anticolonialist stance. Within the overall sphere of Asia, U.S. energies were concentrated first on Japan, where MacArthur directed the Allied occupation with complete autocratic control, and the Philippines, toward which the United States felt a special responsibility. China too was of particular interest, but there U.S. influence was limited and marginal. Southeast Asia was no more than another region, although some U.S. officials early drew attention to its economic importance, not least to Britain which, without the dollar earnings that Malayan rubber and tin brought, would be unable to pay off its war debts to the United States.

This policy of noninvolvement in southeast Asia changed with the outbreak of the Cold War. In 1948 the British declared a state of emergency in Malaya as much more than a local struggle against colonial rule. The deterioration of the French position in Indochina, with continued fighting following the Viet Minh's rejection of the March 1949 proposals for the former emperor, Bao Dai, to become president of an "associated state" with the French union, gave rise to alarmist predictions in British circles and to pressure on the United States to help defend southeast Asia against the communist advance. The communist success in China raised the specter of the absorption of southeast Asia into a sphere hostile to U.S. and Western influence. Truman's decision on May 1, 1950, to allocate $10 million in military aid to the French-sponsored governments of Indochina was at least in part a response to the British pleas for the United States to reactivate its interest and involvement in an area from which it had virtually withdrawn in 1945.[10]

In one sense, then, the U.S. decision to extend financial aid for military purposes to Indochina might be seen as an example of the "invitation not imposition" thesis, but there are, of course, objections to this. It could equally be seen as an extension of the great-power (as opposed to superpower) struggle to maintain empire and hence positioning the wider contest for supremacy between U.S. capitalism and Russian-Chinese communism. A more convincing example can be found in the case of Australian policy from World War II on. Lest it be thought that this is merely a chauvinistic choice, and a bizarre one to boot, let me remind you that together with New Zealand, Australia was the only Western country continuously engaged in combat in southeast Asia from mid–1950 until December 1971. This 21-year period began with the commitment of Australian air forces to the Malayan Emergency in mid–1950 (plus the commitment of Australian land, sea, and air forces to the Korean War), continued with the extension of that commitment with the despatch of Australian land forces to Malaya in 1955 and their subsequent involvement in the Malaysian-Indonesian "confrontation" of 1962-66, dramatically widened with the sending of Australian Army advisers to South Vietnam in 1962, and culminated in the introduction of conscription for overseas service and the commitment of some 50,000 Australian troops to the Vietnam War. This record of fighting in the wars of "great and powerful friends" earned Australia the unflattering sobriquet of being the "white Gurkhas" of the modern world.[11] While it is not coincidence that Australia's active involvement in the defense of southeast Asia began with the fall of the Labor government of J. B. Chifley and the election of a coalition Liberal-Country Party government under R. G. Menzies, and ended with the fall of Sir William MacMahon's coalition government and the election of a Labor government led by Gough Whitlam, here was an underlying continuity in defense and foreign policy between the two sides of the Australian political forum, more so than either side, and particularly the Left, would care to admit.

From the foundation of the various Australian colonies until the establishment of the Federation and beyond, the defense of Australia had always been placed firmly within the context of an imperial defense policy. When Britain went to war against Germany in 1914, Australia automatically followed suit, and hardly a voice was raised against the pledge of the Labor leader and soon-to-be Prime Minister, Andrew Fisher, that Australia would "stand beside our own to help and defend her to our last man and our last shilling."[12] That promise was fulfilled at a frightful cost (Australian casualties were, with New Zealand's, proportionately the highest of any combatant nation), which made Fisher's successor as Prime Minister, W. M. Hughes, determined that Australia's special interests, as opposed to those of the empire as a whole or to those of the great powers individually or in concert, should not be ignored in the peace treaty negotiations. Those special interests centered on the disposition of German colonial territories in the Pacific and on the role of Japan, which was viewed with suspicion and distrust in Australia, notwithstanding the Anglo-Japanese Naval Agreement of 1902. Throughout the 1920s and 1930s, Australian planners looked to the construction of the vast base at Singapore to tie Britain materially and psychologically to the active defense of Australia, while whatever land forces Australia was likely to have in a future war would be committed to the Middle East to secure communications through the Suez Canal. Whatever else it held for Australia, imperial defense meant defense on the cheap.

The assumptions and security of imperial protection disappeared with the Japanese attack on Pearl Harbor. While Australian Prime Minister John

Curtin did not immediately call for the return of Australian forces from the Middle East, he nevertheless quickly appreciated that the United States had to become for Australia the "great and powerful friend" that Britain had hitherto been but could no longer be, at least for the time being. "Without any inhibitions of any kind," he wrote in a Melbourne newspaper in late December 1941, "I make it quite clear that Australia looks to America, free of any pangs as to our traditional links or kinship with the United Kingdom."[13] Churchill was far from happy, not least because at the time of Curtin's appeal he (Churchill) was in Washington, and he feared that just when he was negotiating a grand alliance and a common strategy with the United States, Curtin's message might destroy the appearance of imperial unity that Churchill was anxious to present to the Americans. (Neither, I should add, was Roosevelt impressed.) Yet Churchill himself, during the subsequent bitter exchanges with Curtin over the return of Australian troops from the Middle East, had advised Curtin that the diversion of one of the divisions to Burma would assist Roosevelt in his desire to maintain access to China. The Americans, Churchill emphasized, "alone can bring into Australia the necessary troops and air forces, and they appear ready to do so." If Australia refused to help stem the Japanese advance by agreeing to the proposed diversion, Churchill warned, "a very grave effect will be produced upon the President and the Washington circle, on whom you are so largely dependent."[14]

Curtin's appeal to the United States was answered insofar as following the collapse of the Philippines, Australia became the land base for the U.S. effort in the southwest Pacific, and the site of MacArthur's headquarters. But Curtin's hopes that Australia would be taken into the planning process for the overall war effort were never realized. Rather than the executive body that he wanted, he had to settle for Australian membership of Roosevelt's suggested Pacific War Council, which met in Washington with decreasing frequency throughout 1942 and 1943. The best that a recent Australian assessment has been able to say about the Council was that "it apparently did no harm . . . and there is no sign that it influenced Allied strategy." The same historian has also suggested that "a more courageous and skilled Australian war leader might have decided . . . to opt for cooperation with, rather than subservience to, America."[15] The sentiment is no doubt appealing, but misplaced: at that time Australia never had the sort of military or industrial strength that would have given it any special leverage with the United States, or enabled its relationship to be other than one between a global power and a minor regional one. Furthermore, for all its professions of goodwill toward Australia, the United States never placed the defense of Australia among its "mandatory" objectives; once the drive against Japan had begun in earnest with the offensives in central and southwest Pacific, Australia had even less claim to special U.S. consideration.

The attitude of the Australian government toward the United States was ambivalent. On the one hand, it viewed with some alarm the gradual U.S. retreat from Australia's sphere of interests; on the other, it insisted on an Australian voice being heard in the highest circles, even at the risk of offending and alienating the United States. That Australian voice tended to be H. V. Evatt, the Minister for External Affairs, whose pursuit of what he saw as Australian interests aroused strong feelings of antipathy in Allied circles. After listening to Evatt's interminable lobbying efforts at the United Nations conference at San Francisco in May 1945, Sir Alexander Cadogan of the British delegation had had enough. Evatt, he wrote in his diary, is "the most frightful man in the world."[16] Three years later, while Evatt gloried in being what he liked to call "president of the world" (i.e., president of the UN General Assembly, 1948-49), the U.S. ambassador to Australia complained that he was a "completely untrustworthy and unscrupulous egomaniac."[17] Evatt's abrasive personality and his determination to have Australia's voice heard seems to have achieved little, other than to alienate those whose support he was ultimately seeking. Thus his sponsorship of the January 1944 Australian and New Zealand Army Corps agreement with New Zealand, with its rejection of any potential U.S. claims to the retention of Pacific islands taken in the course of the campaigns against Japan, aroused enormous anger in the United States, which had paid so dearly for virtually every island that it captured.

What made Evatt's position ultimately so untenable was his subsequent attempts to use Manus Island as a means of fixing a postwar U.S. presence in the western Pacific in order to provide for the defense of Australia by its great and powerful friend at little cost to itself. Manus Island, part of the Admiralty group just north of Papua New Guinea, had been placed under Australian control as part of a League of Nations mandate after World War I. Following its recapture from the Japanese, the Americans had spent millions of dollars transforming its natural harbor into a major naval base and expressed interest in maintaining its facilities there after the war. Evatt tried to use that interest to force the United States to enter into a western Pacific pact and to allow Australia reciprocal rights in U.S. bases. He vastly overplayed his hand. The United States faced much more burning issues elsewhere, especially in Europe, and was not interested in becoming embroiled in the defense of so peripheral an area as the western Pacific or its southeast Asian littoral. Far from being an offer too good to refuse, the invitation to Manus Island and all that it stood for in U.S. eyes could readily be turned down, and was. This first postwar Australian attempt to get the United States involved in the western Pacific was a fiasco, and to add insult to injury, the Americans sold off much of the equipment on Manus to the nationalist Chinese, whom the Australian government rightly regarded as hopelessly corrupt and unreliable.[18]

Evatt's efforts to tie the United States to the western Pacific and ultimately to the defense of Australia were fruitless. His failure stemmed mainly from the fact that during the postwar years of the Labor government, the Pacific and southeast Asia were not seen as primary areas of U.S. interest. There was as well a growing suspicion in Washington circles that at different levels of the government and bureaucracy in Canberra, there was a disturbing leftward tilt. Thus Prime Minister Chifley rejected strong British hints that a commitment of Australian forces to the Malayan Emergency would be welcomed by London, and also advised the British government that Australia would not follow the British example and send forces to strengthen the Hong Kong garrison in the face of communist advances on the mainland. In the prevailing atmosphere of increasingly strident Cold War rhetoric, Chifley consistently maintained that economic deprivation and nationalist aspirations, rather than communism, were at the root of many of the troubles in Asia. Evatt had long since failed to endear himself to the Americans, and some of his senior staff, including the youthful Secretary of the Department of External Affairs, Dr. John Burton, were tagged by U.S. embassy reports as "fellow travellers."[19]

With the outbreak of the Korean War in mid–1950, seven months after the defeat of the Labor government in Australia and its replacement by a Liberal-Country Party conservative coalition, the strategic and political scene was dramatically changed. Although the new Prime Minister, Robert Menzies, was an ardent but not uncritical anglophile, his foreign minister, P. C. (Percy) Spender, was determined to achieve what had eluded Evatt: a U.S. defense guarantee to Australia. The Korean War provided the circumstances to bring that about. Menzies consulted with the British government and on being told that London did not intend to commit forces to Korea, instructed his cabinet likewise, and left for Washington on the *Queen Mary*. While he was at sea, the British government changed its mind, whereupon Spender, determined that Australia should not be seen as slavishly following a British lead, persuaded the cabinet to overturn Menzies' instruction, and then used international time differences to beat the British announcement. With the outbreak of the Korean War, the United States was fully committed to securing a liberal peace treaty with Japan in order to bind the Japanese to the U.S. side of the Cold War. Such a lenient peace was bitterly opposed by Australia, which argued that only a harsh settlement that broke up Japan's industrial might could prevent the resurgence of Japanese aggressive imperialism. For the United States, an appropriate settlement with Japan overrode its previous reluctance to extend guarantees to Australia and New Zealand, and when in February 1951 Spender bluntly told John Foster Dulles that without a tripartite pact Australia would not be a party to the lenient peace treaty with Japan that Washington wanted, the United States gave way. The ANZUS Treaty of September 1951, concluded in the same month as Australia ratified the peace treaty with Japan, was much less than the close diplomatic and military relationship that Spender wanted. It provided only for the parties to "act to meet the common danger," and established no central planning staff or secretariat, or any combined force dedicated to the implementation of the treaty. Thus it fell far short of Spender's hope that it would become a Pacific version of NATO, and Australian attempts to invite the United States to adopt a greater presence in the southwest Pacific met with only very limited response.[20]

Furthermore, it put strains on Australia's relations with its traditional "great and powerful friend," Britain. There was evidence that when U.S. desires to have Britain excluded from a Pacific pact had become known, the British had tried to prevent any pact from being formed, fearing that Commonwealth solidarity might be threatened and that Britain's preeminent role in the defense of Malaya and Singapore would be undermined by the redirection of Australian interest toward the United States. This rift largely disappeared with the defeat of the Attlee government in 1951, and had in any case been offset by Menzies' decision in mid–1950 to send transport and bomber aircraft to assist the British in the Malayan Emergency.[21]

U.S. reluctance to become directly involved in the defense of southeast Asia meant that it maintained an arm's-length attitude to the British struggle in Malaya against the communist uprising, and refused to give official recognition to the Australia, New Zealand, and Malaya defense arrangement, whereby Australia and New Zealand, in conjunction with Britain, undertook to coordinate strategic planning for the regional defense of the southwest Pacific, including the general Malayan area.[22] (It should be noted that British sensitivities over the nature of the problem in Malaya and the status of the colony meant that at British insistence "strategic planning" dealt only with external questions, which boiled down to an agreement that Australia could prepare steps to protect the sea communications between Australia and Malaya—and nothing more.) As well as its unwillingness to relinquish its sovereignty over Malaya in any way, however implicitly, Britain also hoped to persuade the Australian government to make its major commitment to an area that Britain saw as potentially much more dangerous in Cold War terms, the Middle East. When British Foreign Secretary Ernest Bevin put this proposal to the Australian government in January 1950, Spender had replied that Australia's attitude would necessarily be conditioned by the firmness of U.S. commitments to the Pacific. Bevin's counterargument—that the United States would be much more inclined to assume Pacific defense burdens if countries such as Australia showed their willingness to assist in the global struggle against Soviet aggression by sending troops to the Middle East—failed to convince the Australian government and, as the subsequent history of the ANZUS treaty showed, rested on the too-convenient belief that in the context of the Cold War the interests of major and minor powers would coincide.[23]

One example of that difference in interests was in U.S. and Australian attitudes to Indonesia. Australian support for the nationalist movement from

1945 had been equivocal, Australia arguing for a devolution of power rather than for total independence.[24] Nevertheless, Australia had basically sided with the nationalists against the Dutch, and at the United Nations in December 1948 the Australian spokesman had called for the expulsion of the Netherlands from the world body following the launching of the second "police action." The Australian attitude was conditioned partly by Labor's hostility to colonialism, and also by the fear that the Dutch would prove incapable of defending Australia's most vital area against external attack. However, the United States, while sympathetic to the nationalist cause, was not prepared to endanger the willingness of the Dutch (and the French vis-à-vis Indochina) to contribute to the defense of Western Europe by pressing them to grant full independence. By 1947-48, those positions had changed. The communist uprising in eastern Java in September 1948 caused considerable alarm in Australian circles, where there were fears that an independent Indonesia might fall prey to forces hostile to Australian interests. In the United States, however, the fact that the revolt was successfully suppressed by the nationalist government at a time when elsewhere in Asia— in Indochina and on the Chinese mainland—the communists were moving from strength to strength, made a strong impression on U.S. policymakers, and within several months Washington had sent its first CIA agent to the nationalist capital, Jogjarkarta.[25]

Thereafter, fears that Dutch intransigence might push some of the nationalists into the communist camp impelled the United States to support Indonesian claims for independence, and more. Acheson's warning to Truman in December 1949 that the "loss of Indonesia to the Communists would deprive the United States of the highest political, economic and strategic importance" still held force ten years later when Sukarno attempted unilaterally to settle the dispute over the status of West New Guinea, which had remained under Dutch control after the establishment of the totally independent Indonesian Republic in December 1949. Indonesian claims to the area, which shared a border with the Australian protectorate of New Guinea and the colony of Papua, were based on the assertion that the whole of the former Dutch empire in the East Indies should pass to Indonesian control, despite the obvious racial differences between West New Guinea and the rest of the archipelago. Walt Rostow advised President Kennedy that the dispute had to be settled in a way that would not risk losing Indonesia to communism, a fear that stemmed from recent signs of strengthening ties between Indonesia, the Soviet Union, and China. In January 1961, for example, Indonesia had signed a pact with Moscow for US$400 million in arms credits; two months later, Chou En-Lai visited Indonesia and signed a friendship agreement that expressly supported Sukarno's stand over West New Guinea. Kennedy had just taken the decision to make a substantial increase in the U.S. effort in Vietnam and was understandably loathe to involve the United States in another military confrontation. Were the United States to be forced to side with the Dutch in an outright rejection of Indonesian claims, Dean Rusk warned Kennedy, "such hostilities would be a catastrophe for the Free World." Robert H. Johnson, a senior staff member of the National Security Council, added that "the loss of Indonesia could be as significant as the loss of mainland Southeast Asia and would make defense of the latter considerably more difficult."[26]

Clearly, the United States was prepared to go to almost any lengths to settle the West New Guinea dispute to the satisfaction of the Indonesians, and bowing to the inevitable, the Australian government backed down and accepted an Indonesian takeover. In explaining to a hostile public why Australia had reversed its position, External Affairs Minister Sir Garfield Barwick put the issue as bluntly as had ever been stated: "In terms of the 'hard facts' of international life . . . the actions of this Government must at the critical time take full account of the attitudes of our great allies."[27] Prime Minister Menzies went even further:

Thank God, we have a power bloc in the world! It will be a poor day for Australia if, in the name of some theoretical idea about the United Nations, we abandon our lines of communication with, to repeat my own phrase, our great and powerful friends. No country in the world more than ours needs great and powerful friends. I am all for them. I believe that the people of Australia are all for them, and I believe that any policy pursued by us which would put at risk our friendship with those countries would be rejected by every sensible person in the country.[28]

The best that Australia could salvage from this rebuff was to arrange for the communique issued following the May 1962 ANZUS meeting in Canberra to reiterate that the terms of the treaty covered not only the three states themselves but "any island territory under the jurisdiction of any of the three governments in the Pacific," that is, to Papua and New Guinea.[29] That presumably was of some comfort to the Australian public, but it did nothing to align Australian and U.S. interests in the region, which again were at odds during the period of Indonesian "confrontation" with Malaysia from 1962 to 1966. Only the Indonesian army's suppression of an internal communist coup in September 1965 prevented the conflict developing into outright war which, at a time when both the United States and Australia were already involved in Vietnam, would have placed dangerous strains on U.S.-Australian relations. At least part of the credit for the fact that this situation did not develop rests with the Australian government, which bent over backwards to maintain diplomatic relations with Djakarta even while Australian troops were fighting Indonesian forces in Borneo and pursuing them across the border into Indonesian territory.

I should briefly mention one last attempt to tie the United States to the active defense of southeast Asia. Following the Geneva conference in 1954 on the future of Indochina, Australian policymakers widened their approach

and tried to involve the United States through a regional security pact that
would not suffer from one evident weakness of the ANZUS Treaty: the
fact that the latter was a "white man's pact." The Australian aims in participation in the Manila conference that led to the South-East Asia Treaty
Organization (SEATO) pact of September 1954 were to gain access to U.S.
military thinking through the institution of joint planning procedures,
something that was denied them under ANZUS; to have used in the treaty
a form of words that would enable the President to respond to a military
threat in the SEATO region without reference to Congress; and, despite
the obvious reason for having a treaty, to keep the word "communist" out
of the treaty for fear of provoking China or lest other independent Asian
states such as Indonesia would refuse to join (which in any case they did).
The resultant treaty was a very mixed success for Australia in terms of these
aims: it failed to achieve the first two, and on the third had to be content
with agreeing that the United States could in an appendix restrict its obligations to responding to a threat from communist sources. In the long
term, SEATO contributed almost nothing to the defense of southeast Asia.
Its membership was too disparate; it had no forces of its own least of all
from U.S. sources; and even though Menzies claimed in 1955 when committing an Australian battalion to the Emergency in Malaya that the Australian action was in fulfillment of its SEATO obligations, this was only
technically true, since Malaya was covered by SEATO only by virtue of
being a British colony, and after its independence in 1957 did not rush to
join the organization.[30]

    The inequality of obligation thus enshrined in SEATO reinforced Aus-
tralian insecurity. In theory at least, the United States could choose whether
or not to define a threat to the region as emanating from a communist
source, whereas territorially based members such as Australia had to respond
to every threat. The Menzies government believed in the communist threat,
and its foreign affairs spokesmen frequently alluded to the dangers of a
downward thrust of communism even before the collapse of the French in
Vietnam. Domestically, Menzies played the communist bogey to the hilt,
and the 1955 split in the Labor Party, with a basically Catholic right wing
breaking away to form the Democratic Labor Party and henceforth directing
its election preferences to the conservative coalition, provided an added
incentive to maintain a hard anticommunist line. Disappointments over the
utility of SEATO and the realization that despite ANZUS Australia could
not rely on automatic U.S. support combined with a long-standing acceptance of what later became known as the "domino" theory. For Australia,
this meant that notwithstanding ANZUS, or perhaps because under AN-
ZUS there had been some criticism that Australia was unwilling to pay the
price in defense terms of a cooperative relationship with the United States,
the Australian government readily involved Australian forces in the U.S.
war in Vietnam. One does not have to subscribe to conspiracy theories to

accept that Australia's commitment to Vietnam sprang from an Australian wish to support U.S. commitment for longer-term purposes, rather than from any irresistible U.S. pressure. That Australian support was always limited, despite Prime Minister Harold Holt's public assurances that Australia was "all the way with LBJ," and it abruptly ended with the defeat of the conservative coalition in 1972. By then President Nixon's Guam Doctrine was already four years old, and the domino theory, which rested on a misreading of southeast Asian history and an outmoded Cold War view of the region, was discredited. Few mourned Australia's withdrawal, and its consequences, in terms of the potential harm it might have done to Australia's relations with the United States, were minimal.[31]

I conclude by suggesting that when looking at the question of the Cold War and the defense of southeast Asia, we need to remember that the late 1940s and 1950s were a period of enormous upheaval in this area. The circumstances of the end of the war against Japan; the gradual retreat of the European colonial powers; the confusion between nationalist and communist movements; and the overshadowing of the region by the apparently much more serious threat in Europe and the Middle East all reinforced U.S. reluctance to become involved. When Cold War superpower rivalries and perspectives imposed themselves on southeast Asia, they fed on conditions that dated back well before the defeat of Japan and flourished in the interregnum between the Japanese surrender and the halting return of the metropolitan imperial powers. Without suggesting that the United States ultimately did so for other than its own reasons, misguided or otherwise, there can be little doubt that its commitment to the defense of South Vietnam answered a long-standing, if sometimes only implicit, Australian invitation for it to become the leader in the defense of southeast Asia. Of course, critics of the Vietnam War, both in the United States and in Australia, might reply that in this case Australia was merely a stalking horse for U.S. interests. They would be wrong.

NOTES

1. John Lewis Gaddis, "The Emerging Post-Revisionist Synthesis on the Origins of the Cold War," *Diplomatic History*, 7:3 (Summer 1983), 171-90 at 177.

2. Cadogan, minute, 27 February 1945, FO 371/46304 F127/11/G61, Public Record Office (PRO), London.

3. For the text of the Queen's speech, see Yong Mun Cheong, *H. J. van Mook and Indonesian Independence: A Study of His Role in Dutch-Indonesian Relations: 1945-1948* (The Hague, 1982), 200-2.

4. Walter La Feber, "Roosevelt, Churchill, and Indochina: 1942-1945," *American Historical Review*, 80 (December 1975), 1292-94. See also Christopher Thorne, *Allies of a Kind: The United States, Britain and the War against Japan, 1941-1945* (London, 1978), *passim*; and John J. Sbrega, *Anglo-American Relations and Colonialism in East Asia: 1941-1945* (New York, 1983), chapter 5.

5. Stettinius to Joseph Grew, May 8, 1945, DSR 851 G.01/5 845, RG 59, National Archives and Record Service (NARS), Washington.

6. James C. Dunn (director, Office of European Affairs) to J. C. Hilldring (director of Civil Affairs Division, War Office), February 24, 1944, *Foreign Relations of the United States, 1944*, vol. 5 (Washington, 1965), 1195.

7. Dean Acheson, minute, January 18, 1946, DSR 851G.00/1–1846, RG 59, NARS.

8. Robert J. McMahon, *Colonialism and Cold War: The United States and the Struggle for Indonesian Independence, 1945-1949* (Ithaca, 1981), 111.

9. J. Balfour (British embassy, Washington) to FO, 16 August 1945, FO 800/464, PRO.

10. A very useful recent discussion of the importance of Malaya in this context is Andrew J. Rotter, "The Triangular Route to Vietnam: The United States, Great Britain, and Southeast Asia, 1945-1950," *The International History Review*, 6:3 (August 1984), 404-23.

11. Gerald Stone, Vietnam correspondent for the *Australian* and the Sydney *Daily Mirror* in 1966, quotes a U.S. sergeant watching the return of men from the 1st Battalion, Royal Australian Regiment, from one of their first combat missions: "The British have their Gurkhas, now we got ours"; *War without Honour* (Brisbane, 1966), 50. The term was first applied to Australian soldiers in the Gallipoli campaign in 1915. Then meant as a compliment, by the time of the Vietnam War it had acquired a double meaning, until by the 1980s it was used to denote the subservient role of Australia generally. See Donald Denoon, "The Isolation of Australian History," *Historical Studies*, 22:87 (October 1986), 252-60 at 255.

12. *The Argus* (Melbourne), August 1, 1914.

13. *The Herald* (Melbourne), December 27, 1941.

14. Churchill to Curtin, February 20, 1942, in Lionel Wigmore, *The Japanese Thrust* (Canberra, 1957), 450-51.

15. John Robertson, *Australia at War 1939-1945* (Melbourne, 1981), 113.

16. David Dilks (ed.), *The Diaries of Sir Alexander Cadogan, O.M., 1938-1945* (London, 1971), 745.

17. Quoted in Gregory Pemberton, *All the Way: Australia's Road to Vietnam* (Sydney, 1987), 5. See also P. G. Edwards, "Evatt and the Americans," *Historical Studies*, 18:73 (1979), 546-60, and "On Assessing H. V. Evatt," *Historical Studies*, 21:83 (October 1984), 258-69.

18. Roger Bell, "Australian-American Discord: Negotiations for Post-War Bases and Security Arrangements in the Pacific 1944-1946," *Australian Outlook*, 27:1 (1973), 12-33; E. M. Andrews, *Australia and China: The Ambiguous Relationship* (Carlton, 1985), 128.

19. Peter Edwards, "The Australian Commitment to the Malayan Emergency, 1948-1950," *Historical Studies*, 22:89 (October 1987), 608-9; chargé d'affaires, U.S. embassy, Canberra, to State Department, April 15, 1948, cited in Neville Meaney (ed.), *Australia and the World: A Documentary History From the 1870s to the 1970s* (Melbourne, 1985), 544-45.

20. The best account of the establishment of ANZUS is by Robert O'Neill, *Australia in the Korean War 1950-1953*, vol. 1: *Strategy and Diplomacy* (Canberra, 1981), chapter 13.

21. T. B. Millar, *Australia in Peace and War: External Relations 1788-1977* (Canberra, 1978), chapter 13.

22. O'Neill, *Strategy and Diplomacy*, 39-40.

23. See Margaret George, *Australia and the Indonesian Revolution* (Carleton, 1980). I have offered a more critical account of the early Australian position in Peter Dennis, *Troubled Days of Peace: Mountbatten and South East Asia Command, 1945-1946* (Manchester, 1987), 215-24.

24. George M. Kahin, "The United States and the Anticolonial Revolutions in Southeast Asia, 1945-1950," in Yonosuke Nagai and Akira Iriye (eds.), *The Origins of the Cold War in Asia* (New York and Tokyo, 1977), 338-61 at 350.

25. Memorandum, Acheson to Truman, December 14, 1949, cited in Pemberton, *All the Way*, 73.

26. Memorandum, Rusk to Kennedy, April 3, 1961; memorandum, Johnson to McGeorge Bundy, December 18, 1961: cited in ibid., 87, 97.

27. *Commonwealth Parliamentary Debates (House of Representatives)*, vol. 34, 907, March 25, 1962.

28. Ibid., 1164, March 29, 1962.

29. J. A. C. Mackie, *Konfrontasi: The Indonesia-Malaysia Dispute 1963-1966* (Kuala Lumpur, 1974) does not deal with the international diplomacy of the dispute. For reasons that have not been publicly stated, it appears that the forthcoming official history of Australian involvement in the Malayan Emergency and the Vietnam War will not include the intervening confrontation episode.

30. See Millar, *Australia in Peace and War*, chapter 11; W. J. Hudson, *Casey* (Melbourne, 1986), 266-67.

31. Pemberton, *All the Way*, is currently the best guide to Australia's entry into the Vietnam War. Michael Sexton, *War for the Asking* (Ringwood, 1981), was the first extended attempt to suggest that the Australian government eagerly sought an invitation to join in the Vietnam War. A multivolume official history, directed by Dr. P. G. Edwards of the Australian War Memorial, is currently underway, and will include two substantial volumes on strategy and diplomacy.

6

Continental Defense and Arctic Sovereignty, 1945-50: Solving the Canadian Dilemma

David Bercuson

On August 8, 1953, Soviet leader Georgi Malenkov told the Supreme Soviet in Moscow that "the United States has no monopoly in the production of the hydrogen bomb"; four days later, the Soviet Union detonated its first thermonuclear device, a version more advanced than that possessed by the United States.[1] This single event led to an immediate shuffling of defense priorities in both Canada and the United States and to the construction of the Mid-Canada Line in 1956 and the Distant Early Warning or DEW Line the following year.[2] The former was a relatively cheap detection system largely designed, and wholly built, paid for, and staffed by Canada. The latter was a far more sophisticated and expensive system built, paid for, and staffed by the United States. Its construction brought about a major invasion of Canada by U.S. service and service-related personnel,[3] certainly the largest in the north since the construction of the Alaska Highway and the North West Staging Route during World War II.

The building of the Alaska Highway and the North West Staging Route had posed a major threat to Canada's de facto control of the northwest even though those activities were carried out in an area that was clearly sovereign Canadian territory. According to British High Commissioner Malcolm MacDonald, U.S. influence there had grown so pervasive by 1943 that the U.S. forces referred to themselves as "the army of occupation."[4] The building of the DEW Line posed no such problem even though it was located in a region where Canada's claims to sovereignty were much weaker; when construction ended, most of the Americans went home and Canadian sovereignty over the north was preserved.

In his essay "The Strategic Significance of the Canadian Arctic," published in 1966, R. J. Sutherland argued that the 1955 DEW Line agreement between Canada and the United States secured for Canada "what the United States had up to that time assiduously endeavoured to avoid, namely, an explicit recognition of Canadian claims to the exercise of sovereignty in the far north."[5] In fact, however, the United States had clearly and unmistakably recognized Canadian sovereignty over the far north many years before. From 1946 on, agreements between Canada and the United States covering arctic weather stations, cold weather test facilities, naval maneuvers, radar installations, and overflights for mapping, surveying, and training purposes established the fact of Canadian sovereignty in the north on both de jure and de facto grounds. The DEW Line agreement gave both countries what they were primarily concerned with: the United States built the radar system it believed necessary for continental defense while Canada's ultimate sovereignty was protected.[6] It was a good compromise, but it was only the latest in a long series of such compromises worked out over the previous nine years.

Canada faced a major defense and foreign policy dilemma at the close of World War II. The Canadian Arctic was obviously to be a front line in any future war. Did Canada have the resources to guard that front line to the satisfaction of its superpower ally, the United States? It was obvious, almost from the start, that it did not. But could Canada allow the United States to mount that "long polar watch" alone, from Canadian territory? Would this not be an admission that whatever sovereignty Canada claimed in the polar regions was weak at best and nonexistent at worst?

Canada's claims to sovereignty over the high Arctic, especially the archipelago, were not particularly strong in 1945. They rested primarily on Britain's transfer of this area to Canada in 1880. British claims had not been based on occupation or use, but on the tenuous rights of discovery and the sector principle.[7] Although Canada did begin to assert some degree of control over the region as early as the turn of the century, its presence there was almost nonexistent up to the post–World War II era, and its claims to the region were based both on the transfer from Britain and on the sector principle. Both were weak. According to Gordon W. Smith, the transfer of 1880 was "certainly binding upon British subjects, but not necessarily upon foreign states, which conceivably could have raised some awkward questions about them."[8] The United States, for example, never recognized the sector principle as a basis for sovereignty when used by other countries in Antarctica, and never advanced its own claims based upon it.[9]

Despite Ottawa's postwar nervousness about the strength of Canadian claims to the Arctic, keeping the United States out was not an option. First, Canada shared basic assumptions with the United States both about the political nature of the Soviet Union and about its military capabilities and intentions. High-level meetings between Canadian and U.S. diplomats, politicians, and military personnel throughout the late 1940s confirmed and reconfirmed the fundamental similarity of Canadian and U.S. views about the Cold War and the Soviet Union.[10]

It was also totally unrealistic for Ottawa to consider denying the United States access to the Arctic when the U.S. thought of Canada's arctic frontier as a continental front line and when the two countries had been so closely tied together in continental defense matters since 1940. As Minister of National Defence Brooke Claxton put it just after taking office: "Self-interest and our good relations with the United States should lead Canada to play an adequate part. . . . [That] part . . . should be especially related to the defence of Canada and to doing the things that we can and should do in preference to the United States, particularly in the North."[11] The dilemma, then, was this: how could Canada help protect the continent against the Soviet Union—a job Ottawa agreed needed doing—while, at the same time, it protected the Canadian north against the United States?

The initial basis for postwar Canadian defense cooperation with the United States was laid by the Advisory Committee on Post-Hostility Problems. On February 28, 1945, this committee recommended a series of broad principles that were adopted by the Cabinet on December 19, 1945. The recommendations specified the agencies that would represent Canada in joint defense planning with the United States and laid out the broad objectives at which Canada should aim. One of those objectives directly concerned sovereignty in the north: "Canada should accept full responsibility for all such defence measures within Canadian territory as the moderate risk to which we are exposed may indicate to be necessary."[12]

It was one thing for the Cabinet to settle on a set of Canadian objectives, but another to get both countries to agree to those aims. The job was undertaken by the Permanent Joint Board on Defence (PJBD) which met several times from November 7, 1945 to April 29, 1946, to formulate principles for a revision of ABC–22, the Basic Canada-United States Defence Plan which had governed defense cooperation during World War II. The result was Recommendation 35 of the PJBD, which went before the Cabinet on May 9, 1946.

Recommendation 35 called for close collaboration between the two countries in defense planning, the sharing of intelligence, the interchange of personnel as required, standardization of equipment, joint maneuvers and testing, and the right of transit. There was little said about sovereignty[13] or how it was to be protected while all these joint measures were being undertaken. Prime Minister William Lyon Mackenzie King would have none of it: "I said I believed the long range policy of the Americans was to absorb Canada," he wrote in his diary, "[the Americans] would seek to get this hemisphere [as] completely one as possible."[14] Taking King's lead, the Cabinet deferred action on Recommendation 35, ostensibly to await the outcome of "current defence discussions with other Commonwealth coun-

tries."[15] Nervous of America's growing power, King's fanciful solution was
to throw a lifeline to Britain.[16]

The Cabinet's refusal to act on Recommendation 35 left a major hole in
continental defense planning; aside from the outmoded ABC–22, there was
no overall framework for Canadian-American defense cooperation. That refusal came as U.S. requests for access to the Canadian north for new operational purposes (it was, at the time, still operating the North West Staging
Route)[17] were beginning to mount. At the end of April 1946, the U.S. army
air force sought permission to begin regular training and weather survey
flights by B–29 aircraft over the Canadian arctic from Alaska to Iceland (Operation Polaris). The Cabinet Defense Committee agreed on condition that
publicity about the flights was kept to a minimum and that Canadian observers be allowed to participate.[18] Similar conditions were set when permission
was granted for Operation Nanook, a joint U.S. navy/marines landing exercise carried out in the Viscount Melville Sound/Lancaster Sound (Northwest Passage) area in the late summer of 1946.[19] These requests were easy to
deal with—they involved only a temporary U.S. presence in the air or on the
sea. But a request to establish a chain of arctic weather stations, first advanced in early May 1946, was another matter.

Reliable weather information is vital to air operations; in 1946 there was
virtually none available for the polar basin. The United States hoped to
rectify this through the establishment of a chain of weather stations (by
1950 five were established) in the central and western regions of the arctic
archipelago. The first, planned for Melville Island, was to be set up in 1946.

On May 4, 1946, the U.S. embassy in Ottawa raised the subject of the
arctic weather stations with the Department of External Affairs. The Americans offered to "establish, maintain and operate" the stations—which would
be staffed by civilians employed by the U.S. Weather Bureau—but would
be glad to accept Canadian participation in view of the Canadian government's "general policy of maintaining control of establishments in Canadian
territory." If Canada was reluctant to allow the United States to go it alone,
Washington suggested either that both countries jointly establish the stations
under ultimate Canadian control or that Canada carry the whole project by
itself.[20] In conveying the request from the embassy, U.S. Counselor Lewis
Clark stressed to Under-Secretary of State for External Affairs Norman A.
Robertson that the United States "had no thought of interfering in any way
with Canadian sovereignty."[21]

Robertson favored a compromise; he wanted Canada to contribute to the
project and retain operational control over it. Before discussion could even
begin, however, the atmosphere in External Affairs grew noticeably more
chilly when a report by a subcommittee of the Air Coordinating Committee
in Washington came into the possession of the Canadian embassy there.
The report raised the question of which country would own newly discovered islands that might be found in the Arctic Ocean in the area between

the known islands of the arctic archipelago and meridian 141—the western "boundary" of the Canadian sector. This followed from Washington's traditional refusal to recognize sovereignty claims based on the sector principle. The report contained an implicit questioning of Canada's claim to any undiscovered lands that might exist within the sector, although not to the land masses Canada already claimed. It recommended that if the United States did not accept Canadian claims to the uncharted area, then reconnaissance flights should be initiated to see if any new lands could be found.[22]

The Air Coordinating Committee report set off alarm bells in Ottawa. Ronald M. Macdonnell, head of External's Third Political Division, noted that Canada would have to "examine carefully the whole question of Arctic sovereignty," especially in light of recent U.S. requests.[23] In the next few weeks the Americans pressed for quick action on the weather stations so that the first one could be set up before the short arctic summer waned.[24] But the Canadians refused to be rushed as the Department of External Affairs, the Cabinet Defence Committee, and the military studied the implications the U.S. request had for Canadian sovereignty. In an extraordinary lapse of judgment, Canada's ambassador to the United States, Lester B. Pearson, even considered an informal approach to the State Department to plant the suggestion that the United States declare its intentions to honor Canada's claims to the Arctic.[25] Acting Under-Secretary of State Hume Wrong quashed the idea.[26]

It was obvious that some general principles were needed before the weather station project could go ahead if Canadian sovereignty were to be safeguarded. One of the most thoughtful documents to emerge during this period, prepared under the auspices of the Chief of the General Staff by Major General D. C. Spry, pointed the way. Spry addressed the question of how U.S. requirements could "best be met without [the] infringement of [Canadian] sovereignty." He believed Canadian claims to the Arctic were "at best somewhat tenuous and weak" because there was little effective Canadian occupation, settlement, or development there.[27] Canada therefore would have to be very careful to safeguard her sovereignty "at all points and at all times . . . lest the acceptance of an initial infringement of her sovereignty invalidate her entire claim." Since the Arctic was now front and center in strategic considerations, Canada had three choices: provide the necessary services and facilities itself; cooperate with the Americans; or "abandon almost all substantial basis to her claims."[28] Spry recommended Canada follow a set of joint participation guidelines that were partially based on World War II precedents since it was unlikely that Canada had the resources to go it alone. He suggested that full title and control of all military installations be vested in Canada; that a majority of the personnel on any project be Canadian; that the United States be required to obtain permission for any use of Canadian territory for maneuvers or exercises; that Canadian participation in all U.S. exercises or maneuvers be ensured beforehand, even when it was "in token form"; and that publicity relating to joint programs always stress their "joint" nature.[29]

When the Cabinet Defence Committee met on June 6, 1946, to study the weather station question and formulate proposals to the Cabinet, it recommended approval if Spry's suggestions were followed. The committee stipulated that Canadians be allowed to participate in, and if possible operate, the weather stations; that Canada exercise ultimate ownership over all permanent structures to be built as part of the program; that U.S. personnel stationed in Canada as part of the project be subject to Canadian law; and that the undertaking be considered "joint," even if the United States paid the lion's share of the costs.[30]

The conditions were workable and nothing the United States could not agree to if its intentions were honorable. But the Cabinet, meeting on June 12, was nervous. U.S. requests to fly over, march over, or sail through Canadian territory seemed to be coming thick and fast, especially through military channels. Most disturbing was the work of the Canada-United States Military Cooperation Committee. In the summer of 1946 the MCC produced initial drafts of an "Appreciation of the Requirements for Canadian-United States Security" and a "Joint Canadian-United States Basic Security Plan." The documents asserted that the next war would begin with a Soviet air-atomic offensive against North America and called for the construction of a vast and expensive air defense network to meet that threat. If implemented, the scheme would have meant a tremendous increase in the resources Canada would have had to devote to national defense.[31]

King was out of the country when the Cabinet met on June 12, and the ministers decided to defer the weather station request until his return;[32] the Americans could wait a little longer. King arrived back in Canada three days later and on June 27 the Cabinet took up the weather station request once again. King was annoyed that the question had been brought back to Cabinet so soon after it had been deferred.[33] He made it clear he wanted all projects relating to the defense of the north to be dealt with together, and insisted that the "general problem [of North American defense] should not be tackled until the end of the current parliamentary session." The Cabinet agreed.[34] The United States was informed there would be no arctic weather stations established in 1946; the Americans were "considerably upset."[35]

Mackenzie King was fearful to the point of paranoia on the matter of postwar U.S.-Canadian defense cooperation. But those fears were, in part, based on very real considerations. At the best of times, King was a cautious man who did all he could to avoid controversy. If he had any doubts that U.S. troops in Canada could cause such controversy, the press was there to remind him.

It was impossible to keep all the secret U.S.-Canadian discussions from the Washington and Ottawa press; stories about the defense negotiations began to leak out in mid-May. Writing in *The New York Times*, James Reston mistook the PJBD's draft Recommendation 35 for a "united Arctic defence plan" proposed by the United States to Canada.[36] Appearing at a time when the Canadian Cabinet was still wrestling with the PJBD's recommendations, the story was, at worst, inconvenient. It paled beside a front-page *Financial Post* story by Kenneth B. Wilson which appeared in late June with the headline "Canada 'Another Belgium' In U.S. Air Bases Proposal?" Wilson claimed that the United States had handed Canada "a virtual ultimatum . . . to fortify her northern frontier."[37] Nothing of the sort had happened, of course, and King was so furious that he denounced the story in the House of Commons.[38]

King's fury notwithstanding, stories about joint exercises and projects continued to appear in both countries throughout the balance of 1946 and into 1947. Some of the publicity was favorable to joint arctic defense,[39] but just as much was based on misinformation and appeared designed more to inflame Canadian nationalist passion than to inform. One article by Canadian Leslie Roberts, which appeared in a U.S. newspaper at the end of 1946, claimed that "U.S. militarism" alarmed Canada "more than Soviet expansionism."[40]

Canada's refusal to act on the U.S. request to establish weather stations in 1946 did not, of course, put an end to U.S. requests. In March 1946, the two countries had started to explore the future of the U.S. base at Goose Bay, Labrador through low-level diplomatic contacts and under the auspices of the PJBD. The U.S. military made clear that it considered the base at Goose Bay important to the defense of North America; in July 1946, it asked the State Department to step up negotiations with Canada over the future of the base. The State Department wanted to hold off until the Military Control Committee (MCC) could complete its work on the joint plan and appreciation, but it relented in September and approached Canada to "permit . . . tactical air units to use and be stationed at Goose Bay for a fixed period of years."[41] This came shortly after other requests to reopen a chain of weather stations in northern Quebec and Baffin Island that had been operated by the U.S. military during the war,[42] and to allow approximately 100 U.S. service personnel to participate in cold weather tests at Churchill, Manitoba over the coming winter.[43] In the latter two cases Ottawa gave its approval on a temporary basis only; in Cabinet King again stressed the importance of "relating all projects for military undertakings in northern Canada to an over-all plan for continental defence which would have the approval of the government after full cabinet consideration."[44]

On September 19, 1946, the PJBD met to reconsider the 35th Recommendation which the Canadian Cabinet had refused to approve in May. Amendments were proposed designed to "safeguard the sovereignty and protect the interests of the country in whose territory joint exercises [were] undertaken." The new principles established that defense projects would be under the supervision of the host country, that no permanent rights or status would accrue to the forces of the visting country, that temporary rights and status were to be decided upon for each particular project, and that public statements regarding joint defense projects should be made by mutual agreement between the two countries.[45]

These changes went far toward meeting Canadian concerns, but not far enough. King still refused to make specific long-term commitments until the Canadian government had a far more complete picture of U.S. defense plans in the Arctic. The Americans were beginning to worry. Acting Secretary of State Dean Acheson urged President Harry S. Truman to bring the Canadians into line on continental defense[46] and Truman made a special point of raising the issue with King when both men met at the White House on October 28. He told King there was a need for the two countries to cooperate in defense and specifically mentioned the U.S. desire to set up arctic weather stations and expand its facilities at Goose Bay. The following day the United States delivered an "oral message" summarizing the President's views and urging action on three matters: Canadian endorsement of the MCC joint planning process; approval of the PJBD's Recommendation 35; and expansion of the U.S. presence at Goose Bay.[47] Little came of this initiative, however, except a commitment by Truman and King to have the State Department and the Department of External Affairs discuss the full picture and "work toward an agreement" sometime soon.[48]

When the MCC issued its final report on North American air defense in early November matters got worse. The Canadian Chiefs of Staff agreed with much of the reasoning behind the MCC documents, but disagreed sharply with the notion that the main Soviet effort would be launched against North America. When the Cabinet met on November 14 and 15 for its first major postwar review of defense policy, Chief of the Air Staff Robert Leckie told the ministers that the Canadian chiefs believed an attack on North America would be "diversionary." Claxton, for one, was struck by the "fundamental difference" that appeared to exist between the Canadian and the U.S. Chiefs of Staff.[49] The Cabinet therefore approved the PJBD's proposed amendments to Recommendation 35, but refused to take any further action on joint defense until it was perfectly clear what the Americans had in mind.[50]

The impasse was broken in Ottawa on December 16 and 17 when a broad-ranging review of defense and foreign policy questions was conducted by military and diplomatic representatives of Canada and the United States. At these meetings the Canadians discovered that the Americans were really not interested in implementing the MCC's air defense schemes because high-level U.S. views on Soviet military intentions and capabilities were not very different from those held in Ottawa. Major General G. V. Henry, chairman of the U.S. Section of the PJBD, told the Canadians that "in any war which might develop in five or six years, the threat to the physical security of North America would be . . . slight."[51] In the all-important area of joint defense planning, both sides agreed that all defense plans were "somewhat utopian" and that their implementation had to be "decided step by step" with the rate of implementation "under constant review." In future, therefore, a distinction was to be made between "governmental acceptance . . . as a goal towards which to work" and the "governmental decisions" that were necessary to actually put such plans into operation. This gave each government "complete freedom to say at what rate the plan should be translated into action."[52]

Canada now had its escape hatch. State Department Soviet expert George F. Kennan, one of the U.S. delegation, later remembered the discussions as having been "helpful in persuading the Canadians to agree to further development of . . . defense arrangements . . . and in making them feel that we were taking them into our confidence generally."[53] On January 16, 1947, the Cabinet approved a final version of Recommendation 35 of the PJBD, which had, in the meantime, been relabeled Recommendation 36.[54] Presidential approval followed on February 4 and the two governments announced the "joint statement," as they referred to it, on February 12, 1947.[55]

The 36th Recommendation was an explicit U.S. assurance to Canada that the United States had no wish to violate the de jure sovereignty Canada claimed over the north. Indeed, there had been no such violations. Canadian preservation of its de facto sovereignty, however, was something Canada alone could accomplish and major problems remained. For example, it was well and good to claim that each country should remain sovereign over, and should control, joint defense projects on its soil, but Canada did not have the resources to completely pay for the continental defense projects in Canada. Neither would this have been fair since many, if not most, of these projects were needed by the United States far more than Canada in any case. But if the United States ended up paying most or all of the costs of those projects, Canadian sovereignty existed only in theory, not in substance.[56] It was a vexing problem.

The bilateral discussions in Ottawa in December 1946 touched on this issue. A suggestion was made that a joint U.S.-Canadian financial committee be established to work on the problem, but nothing ever came of it.[57] Canada was reluctant to explore the idea of a specific cost-sharing formula based, for example, on a ratio of national incomes or populations because of the inflexibilities that would have introduced. One memo prepared for King suggested it was best to share costs on a project-by-project basis with Canada supplying sites, buildings, administration, and housekeeping, and some or all of the operating personnel. The United States could supply technical equipment, personnel, and the bulk of the transport services.[58]

This approach was in line with the suggestions first made by Major General Spry in May 1946, and followed the conditions set by the Cabinet

Defence Committee for the establishment of the arctic weather stations in June 1946. It quickly became standard operating procedure in Ottawa even though the Canadians recognized that the United States would not be happy about spending money for military installations in Canada when it did not enjoy long-term military rights.[59]

Although it derived as much from ad hoc decisions as from careful planning, the policy served Canada well. No blanket approvals were given Washington. The details of each operation were worked out separately. Canadian participation was ensured, even if token, and each agreement brought another U.S. recognition of Canadian claims to the Arctic. No country as unwilling as Canada was in the late 1940s to spend money on its own defense could have done better to defend itself against a superpower neighbor.

In early 1947, Canadian consideration of U.S. requests for joint defense-related projects in the Arctic resumed. The Cabinet approved the arctic weather installations and three low-frequency Loran stations (action on Goose Bay was deferred until the final political status of Newfoundland was determined).[60] In each case similar conditions were laid out: at least half the personnel staffing these facilities were to be Canadian; Canadians were to be in overall charge of the operations; Canada would retain title to all lands and permanent installations built and would, wherever possible, pay for the construction of permanent structures. Other costs were to be borne by the United States. Washington was also to provide transportation and supply services.[61] The expectation in Ottawa was that Canadian participation in these projects would increase as soon as more Canadians became technically qualified.[62]

By the spring of 1947 defense-related projects in the north were moving ahead on several fronts. Preparations were being completed for the establishment of the new weather and Loran stations. The older USAF-operated weather stations in the northeast were reopened. The cold weather testing facilities at Churchill were being expanded. Aerial mapping and photography were being carried out by the Royal Canadian Air Force while hydrographic surveys were being conducted by the U.S. navy.[63] Ottawa remained extraordinarily sensitive about the U.S. presence in the Canadian north. Minister of National Defence Brooke Claxton insisted that the United States limit the number of C–54s flying into the north on supply operations in order to "avoid unnecessary public notice."[64] When asked by reporters to comment on northern developments while on a visit to Winnipeg in mid-April, Claxton would say only that Canada was continuing northern development "both for military as well as civilian uses."[65]

Given the government's secrecy policy, it should not have been surprising that the introduction of a bill into the Commons on May 23, 1947, to define the jurisdiction of Canadian courts over U.S. service personnel created an uproar among the opposition. The bill was innocuous enough. It established that Canadian courts would have complete jurisdiction over U.S. troops for all matters that were offenses under Canadian law. U.S. service courts would only have jurisdiction over U.S. personnel for crimes committed under U.S. military law that were not also covered by Canadian statute.[66] But many members of the opposition took the occasion to demand how many U.S. troops were in Canada, what they were doing, and why they were there at all. There were heated claims that the government was surrendering Canadian sovereignty to the United States. "Where will it end?" one opposition member demanded to know, "What will happen when the Chinese are here? What will happen if the Russians come here?"[67] The bill was extensively debated for most of three days and, given the government's majority, it passed without much difficulty. But the length and tone of the debate clearly disturbed the government.

On August 12, 1947, the Cabinet Defence Committee and the Canadian members of the Permanent Joint Board on Defence met for an extensive review of the state of defense collaboration with the United States. The meeting was in part prompted by the Commons debate and in part by the growing realization that U.S. requests and requirements were going to be far more extensive than had been foreseen. Since the PJBD was the key agency in coordinating the joint defense relationship, it was important to ensure that its Canadian members fully understood the Cabinet's views. The protection of Canadian sovereignty was the chief concern. Areas such as the operation and financing of facilities, command relationships, and publicity were given close attention, and each joint operation was examined in detail. General A. G. L. McNaughton, chairman of the Canadian Section of the PJBD, assured those present that "there had been an attitude of complete propriety regarding Canadian rights" at Board discussions and that while the United States did not recognize the sector principle, Canadian "claims in the Arctic Archipelago were being progressively strengthened."[68]

By the end of 1947, Canada had effectively established the principle of its sovereignty in the arctic, a principle that the United States agreed with each time another joint defense-related project was embarked upon. The United States was, for the most part, scrupulous in seeking permission for operations in Canada on a case-by-case basis. When minor transgressions came to light—as, for example, when U.S. aircraft carried out photographic missions over the arctic archipelago without permission[69]—the United States was quick to apologize and set matters right.[70] But major problems remained. No policy for the sharing of costs had been agreed upon,[71] while the lion's share of the supply operations for northern installations was still being carried out by the United States.

In early 1948, concerns about Canada's inability to contribute substantially to the northern supply effort came to a head following U.S. requests to upgrade the landing strip at Resolute, on the southern shore of Cornwallis Island, where the main facility of the weather station chain had been established. It was a somewhat strange request because the United States asked that a "security classification" be placed on the project and wanted to know if Canada had any objections to the work being done entirely at U.S. expense.[72]

The U.S. request raised an important policy question. Canada considered it "of great importance" that any U.S. activities in Canada be within the limits "of a programme previously approved by the Canadian government."[73] Was this true of U.S. plans for Resolute? The air strip there had been built the previous September to allow supplies to be flown in during the winter months when the weather station was inaccessible by sea. The strip was a primitive dirt affair usable only when the ground was frozen. Now the United States wanted to lengthen it, hard-pack it for year-round use, and build "ancillary facilities on a substantial scale." The Chiefs of Staff Committee (COSC) told the Cabinet Defence Committee that the improvements could be "justified on supply grounds alone" but also that the U.S. Strategic Air Command had "evinced a particular interest in the base."[74]

The COSC believed that Canada's decision on Resolute would have important implications for the future; if Resolute could be turned into a bomber base, any air strip in the north could also be converted. Canada could agree to the U.S. request and place the usual stipulations on the project, but that would mean a Canadian control that was at best "nominal."[75] In the case of facilities such as weather stations, that was not too important. But if Resolute was to be converted into a bomber base, Canada had to know beforehand and had to have ultimate control. As matters stood, the COSC believed, Canada's inability to supply Resolute and other far northern points was allowing control over those bases to pass into the hands of the United States. The committee recommended, therefore, that the Americans be allowed to go ahead with the air strip improvement subject to the usual conditions, but also that Canada undertake immediate construction of a "suitable ice breaker." They concluded that in the long run, "the only way in which Canada can eventually exercise effective control over the Canadian Arctic is to provide and operate the sea and air transport and other facilities required to supply the bases and support other activities in the area." This would mean substantially increased financial commitments.[76]

The U.S. request moved the Cabinet to action. It was clear that more money was needed, and soon. In early March 1948, the Cabinet authorized construction of an ice breaker and a supply vessel capable of operating in arctic waters.[77] Steel for the ships was given top priority.[78] In late June, the Cabinet also authorized the immediate establishment of an additional Royal Canadian Air Force (RCAF) air photography squadron equipped with Lancaster aircraft. Although not directly connected to the Resolute request, the move was an indication of the increased urgency being felt in Ottawa to devote more resources to the north.[79]

Canada could not hope to assume the major role in aerial or seaborne supply during the construction phase of northern facilities. When the weather station at Isachsen, on Ellef Ringnes Island, was established in April 1948, 84 tons of supplies were flown in by U.S. air force (USAF) transports in ten days.[80] The RCAF could not hope to match this type of performance with its small number of four-engine transports—it had but ten of the new Canadair North Stars on strength that spring.[81] But after construction was completed, the demand for air and sea lift capacity dropped off sharply. Once a suitable number of RCAF squadrons had been equipped with the North Star, the air force inaugurated a regular northern supply service out of Montreal, and Canada assumed a fairer share of the transport burden.[82] As for Resolute, Washington dropped its plans due to budgetary constraints. Although in 1950 the USAF briefly considered using Resolute as an emergency strip for crippled bombers, the air strip never became a Strategic Air Command (SAC) base.[83]

From August 15 to August 18, 1948, U.S. Secretary of Defense James V. Forrestal visited Ottawa for wide-ranging discussions of joint defense questions with Claxton and the Cabinet Defence Committee. The talks touched on issues from the far north to the U.S.-leased bases in Newfoundland. The Americans were somewhat concerned about the low level of Canadian defense spending, and about the failure of Canada and the United States to find an overall cost-sharing formula.[84] But there was general agreement both about the world situation and the degree of military threat posed by the Soviet Union. Despite the Soviet Union's blockade of Berlin, Forrestal concurred with Claxton's view that although "there were no limits to the aggressive intentions of the Soviet Union," the Soviets would, "for the time being," attempt to achieve the goals short of war.[85]

On the matter of joint defense arrangements, the briefing paper prepared for Forrestal by the U.S. Section of the PJBD summed things up nicely:

Bearing in mind that the Canadians are extraordinarily sensitive about their sovereignty and independence and that they live, so to speak, under the constant shadow of the "Colossus to the South" such Canadian apprehensions have been inevitable. It has therefore behooved the United States to act with the utmost circumspection and restraint. . . . On the whole, the U.S. record . . . is good.[86]

It was an accurate observation.

By the end of 1948 about 1,000 U.S. service personnel were stationed in Canada operating or helping to staff a variety of defense facilities from the air strips of the old Northwest Staging Route to the weather stations in the high Arctic.[87] In the following year the RCAF took over the operation of the Resolute air strip and began to assume a larger share of the northern supply burden. The weather station program continued through the year with an additional station, completing the chain, constructed at Alert in 1950. In each case the principles for joint-defense operations first laid out in the Spry paper were applied.[88] The key event of 1949 was the Soviet explosion of an atomic bomb in August—much to the surprise of both the Americans and Canadians—which forced the military in both countries to begin to reevaluate their assessments of Soviet plans and capabilities. Russian possession of the A-bomb, coupled with the communist invasion of South Korea in June 1950, marked a new increase in Cold War tensions.

These developments did not, at first, affect joint defense projects in the Arctic. If anything, they tended to focus Canadian and U.S. attention more on solving the problems associated with the U.S. desire to build up SAC's strength in Newfoundland and Labrador. Toward the end of 1950, however, the Americans grew increasingly concerned about the lack of effective continental radar warning facilities and negotiations leading to the completion of the Pinetree radar network began.

The story of the radar chains spanning three continents has been effectively told elsewhere[89] and, in any case, northern sovereignty was not at issue either in the construction of the Pinetree chain or the Mid-Canada Line because in both cases, the radars were built on territory that was clearly Canadian. What should now be clear, however, is that it was no longer an issue in negotiations leading to the DEW Line agreement either. That agreement contained provisions that were unambiguous in their reflection of Canada's sovereign title to the region,[90] provisions that had been part of every joint-defense agreement concluded since 1946. Although U.S. influence in the far north increased greatly during the construction phase of the DEW Line, that influence was temporary, and Canadian rights to the area were not challenged.[91]

Assuming that the struggle to maintain sovereignty must of necessity be a continuing one, even for a great power,[92] Canada fared well in protecting its claim to the north in these early years of the Cold War. Through trial and error, Canada established the policies and procedures by which it safeguarded its interests and protected its sovereignty while still satisfying the defense needs of its superpower partner. In effect, Canadian control over the far north was systematically challenged for the first time since Canada had acquired the region, and, in effect, Canada's claim to the far north emerged stronger than ever. Given the stakes involved, it was a remarkable success.

NOTES

1. National Archives of Canada (NAC), Claxton papers, vol. 102, "Continental Defence," Canadian ambassador to the United States to Secretary of State for External Affairs, August 12, 1953, August 26, 1953; Joseph T. Jockel, *No Boundaries*

Upstairs: Canada, the United States, and the Origins of North American Air Defence, 1945-1958 (Vancouver, 1987), 75.

2. National Security Council, "A Report to the National Security Council by the Executive Secretary on Continental Defense" (Washington, September 25, 1953).

3. Jockel, *No Boundaries*, 96.

4. Curtin R. Nordman, "The Army of Occupation: Malcolm MacDonald and the U.S. Military Involvement in the Canadian Northwest," in Kenneth Coates, (ed.), *The Alaska Highway: Papers of the 40th Anniversary Symposium* (Vancouver, 1985), 83-101.

5. R. J. Sutherland, "The Strategic Significance of the Canadian Artic," in R. St. J. Macdonald (ed.), *The Arctic Frontier* (Toronto, 1966), 271.

6. See Canada, *Treaty Series 1955 no. 8*, "Establishment of a Distant Early Warning System . . . in Force May 5, 1955."

7. See Gordon W. Smith, "Sovereignty in the North: The Canadian Aspect of an International Problem," in Macdonald, *Arctic Frontier*, 214-26. Smith defines the sector principle this way: "Each state with a continental Arctic coastline automatically falls heir to all the islands lying between this coastline and the North Pole, which are enclosed by longitudinal lines drawn from the eastern and western extremities of the same coastline to the Pole."

8. Ibid., 201-2.

9. Ibid., 218-20.

10. A dissenting view is given by Don Page and Don Munton, "Canadian Images of the Cold War 1946-7," *International Journal* (Summer 1977), 577-604. I have recently analyzed Canadian views and their similarity with U.S. perceptions in "A People So Ruthless as the Soviets: Canadian Images of the Cold War and the Soviet Union—1946-1950," a paper presented to the Conference on Canada and the Soviet Union, Elora, Ontario, August 1987.

11. NAC King Papers, Series J1, vol. 422, Claxton to King, January 7, 1947, 382598-382599.

12. NAC RG 2, 16, vol. 3 (Cabinet Conclusions), December 19, 1945; Department of National Defence, Directorate of History (DHist), File 112.3M2 (565) Memorandum for Cabinet Defence Committee included in materials for Special Meeting of August 12-13, 1947.

13. DHist, File 112.2M2 (D212) PJBD, "Canada-U.S. Collaboration," Memo to CGS, January 20, 1946, with attachments.

14. William Lyon Mackenzie King, *Mackenzie King Diaries* (Toronto, 1980), Sheet 229, May 9, 1946 (King diary).

15. Cabinet Conclusions, May 9, 1946.

16. King diary, Sheet 229, May 9, 1946.

17. Department of External Affairs, *Documents on Canadian External Relations, vol. 12, 1946* (Ottawa, 1977), no. 954, 1613 (DCER).

18. Ibid., no. 907, 1541-42; no. 915, 1564-65.

19. Ibid., no. 920, 1568-69. These were the same waters transited by the U.S. navy icebreaker *Polar Sea* in 1985 *without* first seeking Canadian permission.

20. Ibid., no. 907, 1543-44.

21. Ibid.

22. Ibid., no. 908, 1545-46.

23. Ibid., 1546.

24. Ibid., no. 912, 1549-54.

25. Ibid., no. 916, 1565-66.

26. Ibid., no. 919, 1568.

27. One officer in External Affairs challenged this view. See ibid., 1555n.

28. DHist, File 112.3M2 (565), Cabinet Defence Committee Papers, Memo on "Sovereignty in the Canadian Arctic in Relation to Joint Undertakings," n.d., attached to documents prepared to Special CDC/PJBD meeting, August 12-13, 1947.

29. Ibid.

30. Cabinet Conclusions, June 12, 1946.

31. Joseph T. Jockel, "The Canada-United States Military Cooperation Committee and Continental Air Defence, 1946," *Canadian Historical Review*, September 1983, 352-77.

32. Ibid.

33. King diary, Sheet 231, June 27, 1946.

34. Cabinet Conclusions, June 27, 1946: NAC Department of External Affairs Records, Acc 84–85/226, vol. 11, File 9061–40, Memo on "U.S. Request for Arctic Weather Station," June 28, 1946.

35. DCER, no. 924, 1571-72.

36. *New York Times*, May 18, 1946, 1-2.

37. *Financial Post*, June 29, 1946, 1-2.

38. King papers, Series J4, File 3365 "PJBD 1946–48," untitled typescript statement dated June 28, 1946.

39. See, for example, Blair Fraser, "The Watch on the Arctic," *Maclean's Magazine*, December 1, 1946.

40. Leslie Roberts, "Canada Fears Being Ham in U.S.-Soviet Sandwich," *PM*, December 22, 1946.

41. National Archives, Washington (NAW), General Records of the Department of State (State Department Records), RG 59, Correspondence of the Permanent Joint Board on Defense, File "Goose Bay–1942–19047," Memorandum for File, September 25, 1946.

42. DCER, no. 925, 1572ff.

43. Cabinet Conclusions, September 26, 1946.

44. Ibid.

45. NAC, Privy Council Office Records (PCOR), vol. 74, File D–19–2 (September-December 1946), Memorandum for the Cabinet, October 21, 1946.

46. Jockel, *No Boundaries*, 25-26.

47. PCOR, vol. 74, File D–19–2 (September-December 1946), "Oral Message" attached to "Memorandum for the Prime Minister," October 29, 1946.

48. King diary, October 28, 1946.

49. Claxton papers, vol. 122, File "P.M. Joint Defence Policy," Memo of November 15, 1946.

50. Cabinet Conclusions, November 14, 15, 1946.

51. PCOR, Interim Box no. 12, vol. 246, "Memorandum for the Prime Minister," December 23, 1946.

52. King papers, Series J4, vol. 380, File "Defence, 1946-47, vol. 1," Memorandum for the Prime Minister, December 23, 1946, C273542-C273547.

53. State Department Records, Files of the Policy Planning Staff, Box 13, File "Canada," Kennan to Acheson, May 7, 1948.

54. Cabinet Conclusions, January 16, 1947.

55. House of Commons, *Debates (Hansard)*, February 12, 1947, 359-61.

56. King Papers, Series J4, vol. 380, File "Defence 1946-47, vol. 1," Memorandum on "Sharing of Defence Costs," December 6, 1946.

57. PCOR, vol. 74, File "D-19-2 (1947 July-December)," Memorandum for Cabinet Defence Committee, August 5, 1947.

58. King Papers, Series J4, vol. 380, File "Defence 1946-47, vol. 1," Memorandum on "Sharing of Defence Costs," December 6, 1946.

59. DHist, File 112.3M2 (D214), Memorandum for the Canadian Section of the PJBD, September 3, 1947; Memorandum on Cost-sharing for the CGS, July 3, 1947.

60. PCOR, vol. 60, File "C-10-9-M, 1945-47," Cabinet Defence Committee, Minutes of August 12, 1947.

61. See, for example, King Papers, Series J4, vol. 421, File "PCO Defence Committee, January 1947-April 1948," Cabinet Defence Committee Minutes, March 31, 1947; PCOR, vol. 60, File "C-10-9M, 1945-47," Cabinet Defence Committee Minutes, February 11, 1947; Cabinet Conclusions, February 27, 1947; PCOR, Interim Box no. 12, vol. 246, Memorandum on "Division of Responsibility," January 7, 1948. (Note: There is no complete set of Cabinet Defence Committee minutes for this period.)

62. PCOR, vol. 74, File "D-19-2 (1947 July-December)," Memorandum for Cabinet Defence Committee, August 5, 1947.

63. A list of facilities established or expanded in 1947 can be found in Department of External Affairs Records, Acc. 84/85/226, vol. 11, File 9061-40, Memorandum on "Defence Relations with the United States, United States Troops in Canada," December 3, 1947.

64. King Papers, Series J4, vol. 421, File "PCO Defence Committee, January 1947-April 1948," Cabinet Defence Committee Minutes, March 31, 1947.

65. *Winnipeg Free Press*, April 4, 1947, 1.

66. Cabinet Conclusions, January 29, 1947; State Department Records, RG 84, Ottawa Conference Files, Box 1517, vol. 129, Memorandum on "Jurisdiction over Armed Forces of the United States in Canada," April 29, 1947.

67. *Hansard*, June 4, 1947, 3797.

68. PCOR, vol. 60, File "C-10-9-M, 1945-47," Cabinet Defence Committee Minutes, August 12, 1947.

69. PCOR, vol. 74, File "D-19-2, 1947 (July-December)," November 19, 1947.

70. Ibid., McNaughton to Heeney, November 26, 1947.

71. Ibid., Interim Box no. 12, vol. 246, Memorandum on "Division of Responsibility," January 7, 1948.

72. NAC, Pearson papers, vol. 35, File "Korea—Canadian Membership," "Points to be Taken Up in Washington," December 31, 1947.

73. PCOR, Interim Box no. 12, vol. 246, Memorandum on "Division of Responsibility," January 7, 1948.

74. Ibid., vol. 243, File "C-10-9," Memorandum to Cabinet Defence Committee, January 7, 1948.

75. Ibid.

76. Ibid.

77. Cabinet Conclusions, March 11, 1948; King papers, Series J4, vol. 249, File 2579, Cabinet Defence Committee, minutes of June 2, 1948.

78. King papers, Series J4, vol. 249, File 2579, Cabinet Defence Committee, minutes of June 2, 1948.

79. Cabinet Conclusions, June 1948.

80. Canada, *External Affairs*, vol. 4, August 1952, "North of Seventy Four," 281.

81. Larry Milberry, *The Canadair North Star* (Toronto, 1982), 141.

82. Ibid., 140-43; Canada, *External Affairs*, "North of Seventy Four," 280-81.

83. PCOR, vol. 145, File "D–19–2 (vol. 1) DND 1950," Harrington to Secretary of State for External Affairs, July 10, 1950.

84. NAW RG 330, Records of the Office of the Secretary of Defense, (OSD) File CD–3–1–20, Memorandum for Secretary Forrestal, August 13, 1948.

85. King papers, Series J4, vol. 239, File 2384, Cabinet Defence Committee minutes, August 16, 1948.

86. OSD, File CD–3–1–20, Memorandum for Secretary Forrestal, August 13, 1948.

87. PCOR, vol. 60, File "C–10–9-D 1948," Memorandum for the Cabinet Defence Committee, August 11, 1948.

88. Canada, *External Affairs*, "North of Seventy Four," 281ff.

89. See Jockel, *No Boundaries*, 30-90.

90. Ibid., 83-84; Canada, *Treaty Series 1955 no. 8*, "Establishment of a Distant Early Warning System . . . in Force May 5, 1955."

91. Jockel, *No Boundaries*, 84.

92. News reports during the week of February 8-12, 1988, indicate that Soviet commandos may have been using U.S.-owned islands in the Bering Strait to practise covert landing techniques.

7

Canada and NATO: Adjusting the Balance

Denis Smith

Forty years ago, on March 11, 1948, Prime Minister Mackenzie King received an urgent message from the British Prime Minister, Clement Attlee, expressing the British government's alarm at the consolidation of Communist power in Czechoslovakia two weeks earlier, and its anxiety over where and when Soviet pressures might next be revealed. Attlee wrote that "events are moving ever quicker than we at first apprehended and there are grave indications from many sources that the next Russian move will be to make demands on Norway. . . . Norwegian Government have consulted United States and ourselves as to the help that we could expect if attacked."[1] While he said that the Norwegians had been advised to resist Soviet demands, Attlee was uncertain whether "encouragement of this kind will alone induce Norwegian Government to hold out." Its defection, however, "would not only involve the collapse of the whole Scandinavia system but would also prejudice our chances of calling a halt to expansion of Soviet influence over Western Europe and would in fact mean the appearance of Russia on the Atlantic." The British concluded from this alarming prospect that "only a bold move can avert the danger and the pace already set by Russia tells us that there is no time to lose." What was necessary was "a regional Atlantic pact of mutual assistance" to be joined by "all the countries threatened by a Russian move on the Atlantic," including the United States, Canada, and Western Europe. Attlee warned that Nazi Germany offered the historic parallel: "Failure to act now may mean a repetition of our experience with Hitler and we should again have to witness the slow deterioration of our position until we were forced to resort to war in much less favorable circumstances."

The British Prime Minister proposed to King (and simultaneously to

President Truman) the immediate convening of secret talks between Britain, the United States, and Canada to explore the creation of an Atlantic security system. Its purpose would be, in Attlee's words, to "inspire necessary confidence to consolidate west against Soviet infiltration and at the same time inspire the Soviet Government with sufficient respect for the west to remove temptation from them and so ensure a long period of peace." The three foreign offices had been preparing the mood for such talks for several months, in an atmosphere of increasing fear over Soviet diplomatic belligerence and heavy-handedness in the occupied countries of Eastern and Central Europe. Mackenzie King had already passed through several interludes of cold panic since 1945 over the prospect of a new world war that would this time be fought, he was certain, on Canadian as well as European soil. The U.S. administration would not itself initiate talks on a peacetime alliance, because it was still shepherding the Marshall Plan through Congress and was worried about an isolationist reaction against further, potentially unlimited, international obligations. What it needed in order to proceed was some kind of unusual justification—preferably a European request based on a fresh and apparently tangible threat to Western security.

Mackenzie King, too, needed unusual justification to commit Canada to any continuing peacetime obligations abroad. Attlee's message to King provided the necessary alarm from the appropriate source, for King deferred more easily to the British than to the Americans on postwar international issues. When Attlee's message arrived, King consulted three persons: Louis St. Laurent (Secretary of State for External Affairs), Brooke Claxton (Minister of Defense), and Mike Pearson (Under-Secretary of State for External Affairs). Pearson drafted a reply which was agreed upon and dispatched that evening. In it King offered Canada's commitment to join in a treaty of mutual assistance under Anglo-American sponsorship.

There followed ten days of hectic Anglo-American-Canadian diplomacy. On March 12 the United States accepted the British suggestion; on March 17 President Truman announced publicly the U.S. commitment to the political integrity of Western Europe; and on March 22, 1948, representatives of the three powers met at the Pentagon to begin planning for a security system. These talks led to broader consultations over the summer and autumn, and eventually, on April 4, 1949, to the signing in Washington of the North Atlantic Treaty.[2]

In retrospect, there were at least two curiosities about the appeal made by Clement Attlee to Mackenzie King that led to the initial treaty discussions. The first was that the assumption of power by the Communist party in Czechoslovakia occurred in a country already considered by Western diplomats to be within the Soviet sphere of influence, and conceded to be an inevitable target for an exclusive Communist takeover. (But the diplomats had not anticipated the strength of Western emotional identification with Czechoslovakian democracy when the takeover came, a sympathy that

contained a strong remnant of guilt for Czechoslovakia's previous abandonment to the Nazis in 1939. Once again, however, the belated diplomatic
reaction in the democracies did not benefit the unfortunate Czechoslovaks.)
While the coup did not obviously alter the existing balance of power, it
created unexpected panic in Western capitals. The second curiosity was the
nature (or indeed quite possibly the existence) of Soviet pressure on Norway. Attlee described this variously as demands made along the Nazi model,
pressure, aggression, attack, or the potential appearance of Russians on the
Atlantic. His account seemed to arise from a British embassy dispatch from
Oslo reporting vague rumors that the Soviets had asked for treaty discussions with the Norwegians after the conclusion of their recent negotiations
with Finland—something considerably less alarming than Attlee's account
of it.[3] According to Escott Reid and Mike Pearson, the Norwegian factor
strongly influenced the Canadian government's mood of fear and assisted
in the decision to join the talks on a security treaty.[4] But it was never
mentioned publicly at the time, subjected to analysis, or apparently referred
to again in the urgent consultations that followed.[5] Can we speculate, perhaps, that it was a bit of black propaganda produced conveniently by the
Foreign Office to prompt a decision that Britain now urgently desired and
knew how to promote? From this distance, given our knowledge of later
occasions of deception and disinformation in what were seen to be good
causes, the thought might occur to skeptical historians. Or perhaps it was
merely the exaggeration of panic. It was curious nonetheless, and, at the
least, evidence of blurred perception of a kind that became familiar as the
Cold War intensified.

For 40 years thereafter, this initial undertaking of March 11, 1948, had
guided, framed, or straightjacketed Canadian strategic policymaking and
effectively suspended Canadian debate on matters of high foreign policy.
What Canada encouraged and agreed to was the declaration of a U.S. military
guarantee of the political independence of Western Europe, decked out in
the paraphernalia of a mutual security treaty and later, in the 1950s, reinforced by the creation of a collective military command on the ground in
Europe. By endorsing the U.S. commitment and entering the alliance,
Canada chose loyalty to U.S. strategic policy over any effort to think and
act on its own in the realm of East–West relations. (For the Europeans, the
choice was more complex and, since the 1960s, more creative.)

Only once in those 40 years, in 1968 and 1969, has a Canadian government
been prepared to reopen the question of Canada's fundamental commitment
to the North Atlantic Treaty. That reassessment, undertaken at the whim
of a new Prime Minister ignorant of foreign policy, was predictably compromised away under the pressure of Canada's allies, the bureaucracy, and
Pierre Trudeau's own cabinet.[6] Although the Trudeau government did not
treat Canada's NATO role (or its defense policy in general) as a matter of
priority during the following 15 years, neither did it attempt again to alter

that role in principle. Now the new government of Brian Mulroney has reaffirmed Canada's NATO commitment as the central element of its foreign policy, based on the bedrock of a traditional view of the intentions and capabilities of the Soviet Union.[7]

While the issue of NATO's purpose and strategy has generated a continuous flow of analysis and commentary in the United States and Europe since the 1960s, there is virtually no Canadian equivalent. (There was a burst of discussion in the late 1960s which exhausted itself by the settlement of the Trudeau policy in 1971.) Canada's fitful defense debate has tended to focus on North American defense, North American Air Defense (NORAD), and the Arctic rather than on NATO and European defense; that balance in the domestic debate probably reflects the essentially marginal or subordinate role that Canada chose to take in the alliance from the beginning.

That judgment perhaps needs some reflection, because it would certainly be disputed by most Canadian governments since 1949. In their rhetoric, NATO has been the most significant part of the country's foreign policy, a historic departure from its previous peacetime isolationism. It has involved, they would say, a fundamental acceptance of collective security in principle and, since 1950, a major burden of defense spending and military participation as well. And it has been an emphatic expression of Canada's perception of the world conflict. More subtly, the professional diplomats first hoped, and then asserted, that NATO would give—had given—Canada a privileged place at the table in making Western policy, and a multilateral means of restraining the ambitions and impulses of the Americans. These claims have some weight, but they are devalued by the realities that the rhetoric ignores.

What really distinguishes Canadian membership in NATO is not its historic boldness and novelty but its caution and conventionality. The principle of Mackenzie King's diplomacy before 1948, when he allowed Canada to act in the world at all, was to do so with the approval and protection of the United Kingdom and the United States. The principle of Canada's entry into NATO was identical. NATO provided the traditional umbrella for Canadian diplomacy. An Anglo-American initiative was King's prerequisite for Canadian participation in a security treaty; for Norman Robertson it was "a providential solution for so many of our problems."[8] Put in other words, the creation of NATO meant that Canada could leave the thinking about the big questions to others, as it had always done before, but now with the comfortable illusion of participation in high decisions.

NATO was Canada's new fireproof house. If the existence of strategic weapons and long-range air power made Canada physically less secure from attack than it had been in the 1930s, the country was made more secure in another sense by the resolute guarantee of the United States and the United Kingdom to deter aggression—a guarantee previously missing and whose absence had apparently brought on World War II. The new guarantee was directed against a single great power, which was taken to offer the only serious threat to peace.

Within NATO Canada gained the satisfaction of consultation about the alliance's European strategy, and a measure (more apparent than real) of U.S. military guarantee to Europe. President Truman's declaration of March 17, 1948, did not require a treaty of alliance for its effect, and there were influential voices in the State Department and the Congress (not necessarily isolationist) who argued against the creation of a formal alliance. But the Europeans, with their memories of U.S. isolationism, did not find the President's promise sufficient. The treaty of 1949 was thus an elaborate device of psychological reassurance to the governments of Western Europe, a means of convincing a weak and ravaged continent that America's presence as a counterweight to the Soviet Union was real and long term. Despite the elaboration of its political and military structure in the 1950s, NATO has remained, behind the facade, simply the formal expression of this original guarantee—as David Calleo describes it, a U.S. military protectorate.[9] The various efforts throughout the 1950s, 1960s, and 1970s (usually promoted by the relentlessly idealist Canadians) to turn NATO into something broader than a system of U.S. guarantee uniformly failed.

Forty years on, the strategic and political situation of Western Europe has been transformed, but the organization that proved so comforting a device in European recovery has somehow become a sacred and untouchable element in Western mythology. It should not be regarded that way.

In the beginning NATO was the outcome, in part, of misunderstanding. That misunderstanding was entrenched in the Western mind in the late 1940s, lingers on, and is probably the main source of NATO's immunity from change today. The misunderstanding, as I hinted in my remarks on Czechoslovakia and Norway, related to the objectives and immediate intentions of the Soviet Union. It was a product of fear, postwar exhaustion, the misapplication of a historical lesson, and opportunist political calculation.

Europe was physically, economically, and morally devastated by World War II. The influences of Germany, France, and the United Kingdom as great powers were destroyed. There was a vast and premature power vacuum on the continent, and just one continental power that could conceivably fill it in the short run—the Soviet Union. The other remaining great power, the United States, was engaged in rapid demobilization and, for a few years after 1945, was confused and uncertain about whether and how to commit itself firmly to a forward international role. The condition of Europe in 1945 was unstable and, if a new balance of power was to be established that restored the independence of the European countries and avoided Soviet hegemony by default, the United States would have to be a prominent player. (By hegemony I mean dominant influence, not conquest and military occupation.) But utopian U.S. objection to, and failure to understand, the politics of international balance meant that the United States could not be appealed to for support in such old-fashioned diplomatic terms.

In Britain, the United States, and Canada two lessons above all were drawn from the Nazi experience: that aggressive dictatorship should not be appeased and bought off, but rather confronted early with real military force; and that the United States, which might have restrained the dictators if it had not chosen renewed isolation after 1919, should be brought permanently into the system of postwar guarantee. These beliefs, accompanied by a commitment to the international free market and expanding world trade as the other source of peace, freedom, and prosperity, formed the core of the liberal internationalist consensus.

By one of the ironies of history, this accidental pattern of convictions became fixed together in a rigid ideological grid as the dogmatic foundation for the postwar system. The means by which the U.S. Congress and public were persuaded to join the world was to threaten them with Communism, catastrophe, and war if they did not do so. The Marshall Plan was devised in 1947 to promote European economic recovery and thus to avoid another great economic depression; NATO was devised in 1948 to confront the new manifestation of an evil aggressor in the Nazi pattern—the Soviet Union. The real benefits of economic prosperity and a stable balance of power (both of them desirable objects of policy) were transformed, for Americans and Canadians, into cosmic necessities whose alternative was apocalyptic. The product was oversold.

What was going on in the late 1940s in the effort to bring the United States into a permanent activist role in international affairs was well understood by the managers of the process in Congress and the Truman administration.[10] It was understood as well by close diplomatic observers in Washington, by observant members of the press, and by political skeptics. But the success of the campaign of 1947 and 1948 in Washington, and the rigid fixation it created in Western foreign policy for the succeeding 40 years, have tended to disguise from public understanding the degree of self-conscious exaggeration and easy deception that was involved.

The new pattern of domestic explanation for an activist U.S. foreign policy was established before the creation of NATO, in the Truman administration's unexpectedly hasty effort to take over the role of protector for Greece and Turkey when that role was suddenly abandoned by Britain early in 1947. The epoch-making shift in U.S. perception and policy can be precisely dated: it occurred in a meeting on February 27, 1947, of President Truman, Secretary of State Marshall, Assistant Secretary of State Dean Acheson, and Congressional leaders. According to Joseph Jones, Secretary Marshall made a "summary and cryptic" presentation at that meeting of the strategic case for U.S. aid to Greece and Turkey which failed to convince the Congressional delegation. Dean Acheson intervened to speak as the "fervent advocate" of the U.S. mission to defend democracy and liberty

throughout the world against Soviet aggression, to which Senator Vandenberg replied gravely that the request to Congress for aid should be
accompanied by a presidential message "in which the grim facts of the
larger situation should be laid publicly on the line as they had been at their
meeting there that day." The administration's policy, expressed in the President's speech to Congress of March 12, 1947, and subsequently known as
the Truman Doctrine, was thus framed in those terms. Jones wrote: "It
was Vandenberg's 'condition' that made it possible, even necessary, to
launch the global policy that broke through the remaining barriers of American isolationism."[11] Acheson told the same story at the time to Hume
Wrong (the Canadian ambassador), reaffirming his own decisive role in
linking U.S. aid to "the openly anti-Communist aspects which were incorporated in the President's speech to Congress."[12]

"The grim facts of the larger situation" which Dean Acheson presented
to the Congressional delegation that day did not consist of any secret intelligence about Soviet plans or intentions, but rather Acheson's dramatic
early version of the domino theory.[13] Already, and increasingly, the attention to fact in analyzing Soviet policy and the desirable U.S. response were
giving way to reactions of instinct and assertions of faith. The fateful discovery of February 27, 1947, was that this was the way to sell U.S. global
activism to Congress.[14] By the time of the North Atlantic treaty discussions
the predisposition was well established, and NATO was marketed by the
same overwrought appeal to prejudice and fear.

I do not suggest that U.S. aid was unnecessary for Europe's economic
recovery. It was essential. I do not suggest that a U.S. guarantee to Western
Europe was superfluous. There was a vacuum of power. Soviet intentions
were unclear, its actions in Eastern Europe were brutal, and its rhetoric was
menacing. But, regarded closely, its acts beyond the limits of its established
sphere of influence were much less threatening to the West than its rhetoric.
In order to make and elaborate its military guarantee, the United States and
its allies progressively misrepresented the nature of the Soviet challenge.
The challenge was diplomatic, in the fullest sense of that word, rather than
military.

The evidence is strong that there was no Soviet military threat to Western
Europe in the late 1940s and 1950s. The lesson of Soviet deeds was that,
except in the areas of wartime occupation by the Red Army, where Soviet
dominance was imposed (Finland and eastern Austria were notable excep-
tions to that note, where the Soviets withdrew and permitted the creation
of independent governments), the Soviet Union was a cautious power,
probing the limits of its influence as great powers invariably do, but acting
with restraint when firmly challenged. Its greatest respect was reserved for
U.S. power, or U.S. and British power in combination, when it was applied
clearly and with determination—as it was in Iran in March 1946 and Berlin
in 1948–1949.

And yet the Soviet challenge was explained to the parliaments and publics of the NATO countries as an unprovoked military threat based upon a coherent plan and aimed at world domination. After the outbreak of the Korean War in the summer of 1950, the NATO military structure was erected in Central Europe to resist such anticipated aggression. The vast panoply of U.S. forces and arms in Europe, under the seas, and in the missile silos on the U.S. plains, was created to reassure Americans and Europeans that they were under the protective care of the U.S. deterrent against Soviet military attack. On the other side of the line, the response was the Warsaw Pact, which was popularly taken in the West to confirm the claim of Soviet aggressive intent. On both sides, as the arms proliferated, the forces and weapons themselves (when combined with the fixed ideas that justified them) became the primary source of danger, more real in the 1980s than in the 1940s.

We, the Canadians, with our few dozen F–18s and our 6,000 ground troops in Europe, went to Europe to help encourage the Americans to go, and we remain to help keep the Americans there. Given Canada's other defense undertakings, our European units could not be maintained and supplied during real hostilities; their presence in Europe is symbolic and potentially sacrificial.[15] It always has been. In 1948 it was essential for European morale to ensure the U.S. presence. Now, in 1988, that should no longer be true: Europe is prosperous, and can, if it must, defend its own interests wholly by its own means. But it is also financially and politically comfortable under U.S. protection, and will have to be firmly pushed to allow the Americans to depart. For us in Canada in 1948 there was palpable relief at being able to slip under the British-American security blanket, as there was for the more desperate Europeans. Canada, in contrast, had no record of bold activity in foreign policy, no domestic lobby for it, no expression of an alternative. In foreign policy we were just emerging from the womb. The European nations, old and wounded, were being treated in the emergency ward, but with every intention of reentering the world of international decision when they could. It seems strange that, 40 years later, we Canadians are still resting snugly in the delivery room while the West Europeans have long ago checked themselves out of hospital and resumed their role in high policymaking.

For them, the debate on NATO doctrine and strategy has been vigorous since the early 1960s, when the United States substituted "flexible response" for "massive retaliation" and began to place tactical nuclear weapons with NATO ground forces in Europe. The Canadian government of John Diefenbaker stumbled into that controversy by arming its European contingents at U.S. persuasion with weapons designed to use nuclear warheads—and then refusing to accept the warheads. But Canadian politicians did not confront the strategic issues with any clarity, and in the end the country sidestepped the debate by replacing Diefenbaker with Pearson, who accepted the nuclear commitment (but with a never-never promise to renegotiate it). Finally, in the late 1970s the Trudeau government quietly ended Canada's tactical nuclear role in Europe, again without contributing anything to the broader discussion of policy. Since then Canada has supported NATO's two-track policy and the various arms reduction negotiations, but without any related effort to think through its role in the alliance. As Rod Byers writes:

Canada's political leaders have not sufficiently appreciated the need to base . . . policy on national assessments of those strategic issues which directly and indirectly affect Canada's security interests. The inclination has been to rely on European or U.S. assessments and perspectives. The major military-strategic issues of the last 20 years have not been influenced by Canada.[16]

The new international stance of the Soviet Union since 1985, the growing problems of U.S. economic and military overextension, and the undoubted ability of the Europeans now to provide for their own defense together throw the continuing role of NATO into doubt. The clear outlines of an altered and less dangerous balance of power, which responds to such challenges, are emerging. It is not obvious what place Canada would have in that balance, unless we Canadians make it for ourselves. But the existence of a problem seems not to have occurred to the Canadian government, if we can judge from the recent External Affairs Green Paper and Defense White Paper. They stand for all the good things, including arms reduction and the honorable fulfillment of commitments; but their image of NATO and its purposes springs from the exaggerations of the 1940s rather than the 1980s. The Defense White Paper simply asserts as

a fact, not a matter of interpretation, that the West is faced with an ideological, political and economic adversary whose explicit long-term aim is to mould the world in its own image. That adversary has at its disposal massive military forces and a proven willingness to use force, both at home and abroad, to achieve political objectives. . . . [U]nless and until there is concrete progress, the West has no choice but to rely for its security on the maintenance of a rough balance of forces, backed up by nuclear deterrence.[17]

The paper follows that statement with proposals for a modest consolidation, and strengthening, of the Canadian military commitment in Europe (not to speak of its substantial recommendations for enhanced naval and air forces on and around Canadian territory, including nuclear submarines, which have received the bulk of public comment).

There is something half-hearted about the White Paper's presentation of the security challenge, as though the authors themselves did not believe it. The call for military balance, and the recognition of the existence of the nuclear deterrent, are unexceptional platitudes. But they get us nowhere in the consideration of policy for Canada—except, fuzzily, to sustain the status quo in NATO. (The whole statement could be turned around to apply, with equally empty effect, to what the Soviet Union perceives when it regards the U.S. alliance—an adversary hoping to mold the world eventually in its image, with a proven willingness to use force for political ends, and giving the Soviet Union no choice but to maintain a stable balance of forces and its own nuclear deterrent.) It masks totally the needs and possibilities faced by both NATO and the Warsaw Pact in the 1980s.

The forces of strategic deterrence are vastly redundant on both sides, and inherently paradoxical: they depend for their effect on the willingness to use them, but both Soviets and Americans admit that they cannot be used. If both sides know that, and yet the peace in Central Europe has nevertheless lasted for four decades, it is probably the result of mutual restraint that has much more complex sources than the existence of the nuclear deterrent— such as a strong disinclination to engage in any kind of war on that battleground, where so much has already been suffered. The present military balance strains both U.S. and Soviet treasuries to an unacceptable extent, from which they seek relief; the balance could be maintained at a dramatically lower level of armament and expense. In Central Europe the concentration of massive forces and weapons on both sides creates unusual danger, inconvenience, and uncertainty. The overwhelming and widely accepted need is to reduce both strategic and tactical nuclear armories and conventional forces in Central Europe in a series of arms control agreements that is now under active negotiation.

There is now, for the first time since 1948, a reasonable possibility that the frozen assumptions of 40 years can at last be thawed by actions that will gradually create a reduced, more plural, more stable, less ideological disposition of forces in Europe and the world. Canada wastes its influence if it avoids participating in the creation of that new balance.

To participate effectively we Canadians will have to think coherently about strategic policy as we have not done since the 1940s; and then we will have to take initiatives. Increasing and concentrating our military contribution to NATO, as the Mulroney government now proposes, does nothing to encourage movement in the right direction. However, a withdrawal from NATO is not the only alternative, and it is perhaps unwise as well. Canada gains from the political connection, and there is no reason why it should not continue to do so. We should emulate the French, who withdrew from the integrated military command in 1966 and threw NATO headquarters out of the country, but remained active as political members of the alliance; or the Spanish, who followed their recent entry into NATO by refusing to renew their bilateral treaty to permit the stationing of U.S. fighter-bombers on Spanish soil; or the Danes and Norwegians, who refuse bases on their territory for their NATO allies. It is quite possible for members of this alliance to judge for themselves the state of East–West relations, the collective needs of the organization, and their own national interests—and to act on them, if necessary against the judgments of other members. Canada must be unique among the members of NATO in believing that membership entails the surrender of independent judgment.

A prudent Canadian reassessment of the strategic situation and its own interests would, I believe, lead Canada to conclude that its military contribution to NATO in Europe no longer serves any understandable purpose. As a fighting force it is negligible; the circumstances in which it might be called upon to fight are now almost inconceivable, and its contribution to something called "the deterrent" is implausible.

Both Europeans and Americans still hesitate to consider large reductions in the U.S. military presence in Europe, and they link the Canadian contingent (despite its tiny scale) to the Americans. Talk of its departure would give the Americans ideas. A Canadian decision to withdraw its forces, announced with sufficient warning of the timetable (perhaps spread over five years) and justified as a contribution to the scaling down of the military balance, could thus be a significant stimulus to creative thought in Washington and the European NATO capitals. If the U.S. tripwire forces were no longer to be present, the American guarantee of 1948 would seem less secure, and that would require the West European nations to provide adequately for their own defense (within whatever limits could be agreed on with the Soviet Union). More than 40 years after the end of World War II that seems a reasonable expectation. For Canada the direct benefit would be to give that country greater flexibility in arranging its defense priorities to meet Canadian needs adequately on and around this continent.

As a complement to such action, Canada should pursue active discussion with the Soviets on measures of arms control and other common purposes in the area of our greatest mutual concern (the Arctic), with Canadian national interests firmly in mind—just as the Americans and the Europeans have pursued their own bilateral arrangements for detente with the Soviets, according to their own calculations of interest, since the early 1970s. We should begin in earnest, too, the complex task of reassessing the whole range of our intricate North American defense arrangements with the United States, with the clear objective of assuming, where technically and economically feasible, a greater measure of autonomy in our policies than we have permitted ourselves since 1945. Canada should begin at home, that is, to weigh and assert its strength in its own national interest, just as other confident and mature nations expect to do. In the present international atmosphere, handled skillfully, that would be a contribution to stability. But Canada's long membership in NATO has given us the debilitating illusion that we need never act in defense of our own perception of our highest interests.

To be practical, this is not an approach that the Mulroney government is now likely to endorse. It has chosen, instead, to discourage change in the alliance, and to do essentially nothing in any field of policy to disturb the evolution of former President Reagan's cloud-cuckoo world. Independent Canadian action in NATO of the kind I suggest would certainly disturb slumbers on the Canadian watch in Washington. (But many in the United States, more discerning about the real world than the present administration, would welcome such Canadian prodding.) At home, an initiative of this kind would not be entirely at odds with the Mulroney government's own rhetoric. There are elements of its northern, defense, and disarmament policies that are more consistent with this approach than with its intellectual sterility on NATO and the Soviet threat. At least it should recognize that a serious debate on foreign policy is desirable as the U.S.-Soviet relationship of 40 years transforms itself. Such a debate, for Canada, must start with the nature of the Soviet challenge and the NATO connection—the very points that mesmerized us and halted our thinking after 1948.

NOTES

1. Secretary of State for Commonwealth Relations to High Commissioner for United Kingdom, Ottawa, no. 220, March 10, 1948, DEA files 283(s).
2. See Escott Reid, *Time of Fear and Hope* (Toronto, 1977), for a detailed account of the making of the treaty.
3. Secretary of State for Commonwealth Relations to High Commissioner for United Kingdom, Ottawa, no. 217, March 10, 1948, DEA files 283(s). See also Denis Smith, *Diplomacy of Fear* (Toronto, 1988), 223–24.
4. See Reid, *Time of Fear and Hope*, 42–43, 49–50, 70; and Lester B. Pearson, *Mike* (Toronto, 1972), vol. 2, 39.
5. Escott Reid says: "The fact that the incident which precipitated the talks on the treaty was a Soviet threat to Norway seems to have been kept secret for ten years or more"; *Time of Fear and Hope*, 70.
6. See D. C. Thomson and R. F. Swanson, *Canadian Foreign Policy: Options and Perspectives* (Toronto, 1971), 48–56.
7. See the 1987 Defense White Paper, *Challenge and Commitment*, passim.
8. Canadian High Commissioner to Secretary of State for External Affairs, April 2, 1948, DEA files, 264(s), quoted in Escott Reid, *Time of Fear and Hope*, 132; J. L. Granatstein, *A Man of Influence* (Ottawa, 1981), 236; and Smith, *Diplomacy of Fear*, 229.
9. See David Calleo, *Beyond American Hegemony* (New York, 1987), passim; Theodore Draper, *Present History: On Nuclear War, Detente, and Other Controversies* (New York, 1984), 106–94.
10. See, for example, the account by Joseph Jones of the genesis of the Truman Doctrine in *The Fifteen Weeks* (New York, 1965).
11. Jones, *The Fifteen Weeks*.
12. See Smith, *Diplomacy of Fear*, 185.
13. Ibid., 197.
14. Ibid., 184–89.
15. The Minister of National Defense was reported in April 1984 to have told

the cabinet: "If a major national crisis were to occur, the Canadian Forces could not make a credible contribution to deterrence; and in the event of hostilities, the Canadian Forces would not be sufficiently manned and equipped to carry out the tasks expected of them in support of the Allied effort and consequently would be overly vulnerable to enemy attack"; *Calgary Herald*, April 14, 1984, quoted in R. B. Byers, *Canadian Security and Defence: the Legacy and the Challenges* (Adelphi Papers 214, Winter 1986), 11.

16. R. B. Byers, *Canadian Security and Defence*, 13.
17. Defense White Paper, *Challenge and Commitment*, 5.

Afterword: Foreign Policy and Military Planning—The Cold War and National Defense, 1945–60

B. J. C. McKercher

The history of the Cold War is an extremely complex subject, but for too long historians and others have been preoccupied with seeking to apportion blame for the crisis in East–West relations that has dominated international politics since the end of World War II. Although an alluring academic exercise in its own right, admittedly one fraught with important political considerations, the affixing of responsibility has proven difficult to achieve. The interpretations vary widely, most often reflecting the ideological bias of whoever has done the analysis; and because of their implications about innocence and guilt which have produced vituperative debate, these interpretations have tended to create a kind of historical tunnel vision that ignores wider historical questions that are just as interesting and, certainly, just as important. Happily, the chapters in this volume are an attempt to go beyond the search for responsibility. With the existence of the Cold War accepted simply as a fact of international life after 1945, the participants in the Fourteenth Military History Symposium have undertaken an examination of the national defense policies of several key Western powers. Admittedly, the origins of the Cold War are addressed obliquely in some of the chapters, but the purpose of this collection is to look at a specific aspect of the Cold War's development in its first decade and a half. By doing so, these historians are part of a recent and much-needed trend to break away from the one-dimensional focus of extant Cold War historiography.[1] In this way, they are helping to unravel one of the most labyrinthine chapters of modern international history by considering other aspects not only of East–West relations but of intra-alliance relations as well.

The problem has been that much Cold War historiography has been

conditioned by the responsibility debate. Interestingly, however, the kind
of work done to attach blame for the Cold War parallels in many ways that
earlier debate of this century over war guilt: the so-called *Kriegschuldfrage*
after World War I. For most of the interwar period, a range of historians
in several countries became preoccupied with determining who precisely
bore the responsibility for July 1914, their work filling endless bookshelves.
No one can deny that the *Kriegschuldfrage* possessed an intrinsic value all of
its own. Article 231 of the Treaty of Versailles stated flatly that Germany
caused the war and, it followed from this, that Germany was forced to pay
heavy reparations and suffer the loss of territory which, though earlier taken
by the sword, touched Germany's *amour propre* as a first-class power. Initially, British and French historians endeavored to write histories that
showed German culpability—the established view as enshrined in Versailles.[2] German historians, however, sought to prove that the other powers,
or at least the statesmen of other powers, were at fault—the revisionist
interpretation.[3] As time passed, and as disillusionment with the Paris Peace
Settlement set in on both sides of the Atlantic, a school of thought arose
that argued that responsibility should probably be shared—though the degree of blame then became important; this was the postrevisionist view.[4]

   The advent of World War II, and the obvious aggression of Hitler's
Germany in the run-up to this struggle, saw an eclipse of interest in World
War I origins until the publication of Fritz Fischer's monumental studies
rekindled interest in the early 1960s. This has led to more study of the
origins of the 1914–18 war but, importantly, as just part of a wider examination of great-power politics that has looked at a range of foreign
factors, domestic influences, intra-alliance politics, and more in reaching
conclusions about how and why events happened as they did.[5]

   In the West at least, Cold War historiography has paralleled this earlier
paradigm—Soviet historiography until the past two or three years has been
uniformly consistent on where guilt lies.[6] At first, Western scholars adopted
what became the established interpretation—that Soviet policy was responsible for the tension in international relations that arose in the dying months
of World War II and continued thereafter in crises in Germany, Iran, Eastern
Europe, China, Korea, and so on.[7] This remained at the fore until, in the
latter half of the 1950s, revisionist studies began to appear—revisionism
meaning that the United States and its allies held the responsibility for
initiating and sustaining Cold War tensions. Opposed to the domestic policies of the Truman and Eisenhower administrations, these critics extended
their dialectical differences with the prevailing internal political atmosphere
of the United States, compounded by the hysteria of McCarthyism and its
aftershocks, to castigate U.S. foreign policy from the end of World War II
onward.[8] The debate between the traditional and revisionist interpretations
raged for almost 20 years, with U.S. involvement in the war in Vietnam
sharpening the differences between the two schools of thought.[9] But with

the end of U.S. involvement in Southeast Asia, and the advent of Soviet adventurism in Africa and other places (beginning in 1975 and culminating in the invasion of Afghanistan), a postrevisionist interpretation has emerged.[10] This holds that the blame for the Cold War can be shared to a degree, though the Soviets are probably more culpable than the Western powers because of the nature of Stalin's foreign policy, which was pursued with relative consistency until the early 1980s and the death of Leonid Brezhnev. This newer interpretation has been enhanced somewhat by the changing political climate in the Soviet Union, the denunciations of Stalin and all his works by Mikhail Gorbachev and his reformers, and the announced intention of these reformers to throw light upon the "dark holes" of Soviet Russian history via *glasnost*. Admittedly, should *perestroika* fail and Gorbachev fall, *glasnost* might quickly become a thing of the past as a new Soviet leadership seeks to discredit Gorbachev by suggesting that perhaps all was not so bad before he rose to power.

Nonetheless, the result of these developments in the West is that the question of responsibility for the Cold War, its origins and sustenance, is becoming less and less important. Admittedly, some old revisionists still produce works that look at Cold War issues through the flawed lens of sole Western responsibility for the post–1945 international situation.[11] However, they are in the minority, the more so as a younger generation of historians is looking at other aspects of international history since 1945. One of the most important instances of this is the investigation into the matter of Anglo-American relations as the linchpin of the Western alliance, tied to the seemingly insoluble conundrum of whether a special relationship between the two chief North Atlantic powers exists or ever existed.[12] At the same time a growing body of recent historiography is examining important milestones in the course of the Cold War, from the Marshall Plan through the changing nature of containment to the integration of Western Europe.[13] This work is being enhanced by other studies focusing on issues outside the North American–European axis: assessments of the problems touching Sino-American relations, the position of Japan, the Korean War, and more, all pursued within the context of a multidimensional historiography.[14] Like the debate earlier in this century, the more recent one surrounding the Cold War has seen the beginning of a change of emphasis that has moved away from the question of responsibility. To understand this shift is to appreciate that the origins and early course of the Cold War at least up to the early 1960s are now viewed as distinct phases of modern history and not as contemporary events. The result is a recognition of the rich and varied pattern of this period of modern international history, or, to be more precise, the complexity of the Cold War.

Ernest May and his colleagues in this Symposium have shown this by their analysis of the national defense policies of several leading Western powers in the 15 years after 1945. In doing so, they are part of a normal trend in historical scholarship, whether it concerns the *Kriegschuldfrage*, the "guilty men" debate after 1940, or the Cold War. This tendency was made clear in a recent historiographical survey of the Yalta Conference and the development of the Cold War in which a perceptive historian observed the existence of a developmental typology of six stages in any study of contemporary events.[15] The first two stages encompass the production of "first narratives," statements of government policy and immediate academic analysis of this policy, plus the production of memoirs and apologia that either agree or disagree with the "first narratives." The third stage sees revised versions of events emerge as a result of the mass of material produced during the first two. While these first three levels of analysis are nearly always polemical, a consequence of the continuing political importance of this recent history to contemporary events that might not have run their course, the fourth is less so. It develops out of the publication of official documents and the opening of archives which permits the amassing of an empirical basis for more—but not always—objective analysis. The fifth stage is marked by the advent of younger historians who explore the archives and sift through the material available in the first four phases to "view the material through the lens of the past that preceded it and gave it birth." Generally, so this argument runs, these historians look at events by concentrating on the extant material to produce a truthful account of events, while downplaying "the myths, misrepresentations, and misperceptions" that were prominent in the earlier stages and were part and parcel of the historical process. Finally, the sixth stage is reached, in which those myths, misrepresentations, and misperceptions are exhumed, analyzed, and incorporated into the historiography of the period under consideration. By this time the events that made the original issues so contentious are long past and, unless some new and startling piece of evidence emerges to change the interpretations of the sixth stage, the view thus derived is accepted generally as *the* version of events. As the contributions in this volume attest, the historiography of the early Cold War in terms of military planning seems now to be entering the sixth stage of this typology.

There seems to be little that is unknown about the general lines of international events in the 15 years after the Allied powers defeated Germany and Japan and then, because of the incompatibility of the national interests of the Western powers and those of the Soviet Union, drifted into the Cold War. The availability of archives, plus the mass of material from the first five stages, is staggering. World War II transformed the United States into the leading economic, financial, and, with its monopoly of atomic weapons, military power in the world. But this was a new world wrought by that war and the forces it had unleashed. The United States had replaced Great Britain—now not so "Great"—as the only truly global power. In addition, Britain and France, the two leading states with which the United States found itself loosely allied by 1945, were weakened severely in Europe and beyond. As a result, the United States suddenly found itself having the leadership of the Western powers thrust upon it. Moreover, in this new world, buoyed up by its success at arms after 1941 and desirous of security at the expense of weaker states on its European and Asian periphery, the Soviet Union emerged as a threat to the Western powers ideologically, strategically, and in other ways. Led by the United States, Western leaders now confronted the economic, diplomatic, and military problems that this threat entailed, and until at least the early 1960s—the purview of this collection—sought to mesh foreign and defense policy so as to better protect their national interests and those of the West against Soviet inroads.

The historians who have contributed to this Symposium have added significantly to the understanding of the Cold War by delving deeply into an area that has heretofore been largely ignored. In doing so, they have taken existing work, added new material, considered earlier myths, misrepresentations, and misperceptions, and produced cogently argued pieces that throw light on the ways in which national defense policy in the West was devised between 1945 and 1960. Although by no means comprehensive—these chapters deal with the policies of Britain, Canada, the United States, and Australia—they illuminate a number of issues that have not been adequately addressed in earlier writings; this is because, as these chapters accept the fact that the Cold War had begun, they are not really conditioned by the question of responsibility.

May looks at the structure of the decision-making process in the United States that emerged in the early days of the Truman administration and lasted with minor changes until at least the end of its Eisenhower successor. During these years, successive U.S. leaders, in the White House, the State Department, and the armed services, realized that the United States had responsibilities as the leading state among the Western powers in meeting the Soviet challenge. These men confronted a daunting task. They had to determine precisely what U.S. interests were diplomatically and militarily; they had to come to some sort of consensus with their allies, who were not always willing to follow a U.S. lead; and they had to present all of this in such a way as to win over Congressional support and conform to the strictures imposed by U.S. public opinion. In essence, this meant that the foreign policy and military planning of the pre–1941 isolationist United States—isolationist in the sense of political commitments abroad—had to be redefined in the context of the Cold War. By extension, it also meant that seeing the United States as the dominant power within their coalition, U.S. allies had to redefine their policies and planning. May's colleagues examine various aspects of this redefining process. The Marshall plan, for instance, is seen as an endeavor by the Truman administration that contained specific U.S. strategic goals designed to augment the national defense interests of the United States' European allies. There was nothing altruistic in this; rather, the Marshall offer was designed to protect those redefined

U.S. interests by strengthening the economies of Western Europe so as to balance the apparently overwhelming strength of the Soviet Union.

But the United States could not dictate to its allies. Britain and Canada provide two examples of Western powers that, although allied to the United States, had their own interests to consider, interests that did not necessarily coincide with those being determined at Washington. Thus, London and Ottawa had to balance their own foreign policy and military planning with those of the United States and, after 1949, within the confines of the North Atlantic Treaty Organization. Results all around were mixed, especially as British leaders in the 1950s still had pretensions about their state's having a world role. Outside the North Atlantic triangle, the line between what was in the national defense interests of the Americans and their allies in meeting and containing the perceived communist threat was even more blurred. In the Middle East and in Southeast Asia, decided tensions existed in finding common ground between what Washington thought possible and desirous, and what other Western powers reckoned to be essential. As Peter Dennis observes in Chapter 5 about Southeast Asia:

The inequality of obligation thus enshrined in SEATO reinforced Australian insecurity. In theory at least, the United States could choose whether or not to define a threat to the region as emanating from a communist source, whereas territorially based members such as Australia had to respond to every threat.

What was true in that area of the globe remained equally true in the Middle East, in Europe, or even in the Canadian Arctic. Foreign policy and military planning had to go hand in hand, but with differing interests, differing perceptions of threat, and differing ideas about the value of U.S. leadership of the Western alliance and of U.S. commitments. The general response of the Western powers to the Cold War in this respect remained a complicated issue.

The attempt to look objectively at the Cold War is not of recent vintage. On the twentieth anniversary of the Truman Doctrine, the liberal U.S. historian Arthur Schlesinger sought to do this, writing when U.S.-Soviet relations were in a quiescent phase and the United States was coming to the recognition that it was bogged down in Vietnam:

As the Cold War has begun to lose its purity of definition, as the moral absolutes of the fifties become the moralistic clichés of the sixties, some have begun to ask whether the appalling risks which humanity ran during the Cold War were, after all, necessary and inevitable; whether more restrained and rational policies might not have guided the energies of man from the perils of conflict into the potentialities of collaboration.[16]

But greater objectivity proved to be elusive. Increasing difficulty in Vietnam, the Czechoslovakian crisis in 1968, and continuing strain in Sino-

American relations militated against this. Since then, however, the U.S. international self-doubt that marked the 1970s has come and gone, followed by the renewed moral absolutes of the 1980s personified generally in the West by Ronald Reagan and Margaret Thatcher. This has occurred while Stalinist foreign policy experienced its death rattle in Afghanistan and a different, less rigid leadership has arisen in Moscow. Added to this has been the reemergence of Germany—or at least its Western half—and Japan as major economic powers, tied to the amelioration of Sino-American relations and other legacies of the Nixon Doctrine.

Although there seems to be a return to the old moral absolutes of the 1950s in the West (especially in the United States, which had been the de facto leader of the Western powers for at least three decades after 1945), this has not led to a revival of the traditional view of the Cold War. The reason is compelling. While Schlesinger correctly pointed out that the risks of the first years of the Cold War might not have been necessary, the development of national defense policies in the West at that time, at least as this volume shows, were reasonably restrained and rational. This is the result of the recognition today, except among a diminishing band of historians and others, that the Cold War was not simply a matter of black and white, or right and wrong. Instead, there is more objectivity about the origins of the Cold War and its early course. These events are squarely in the past; having ceased to have contemporary relevance, they are history. With a different political agenda for the 1980s and 1990s involving issues like the North–South dialogue, and with the seemingly profound changes occurring in the political and economic structure of Europe, the Far East, and within the crucial U.S.-Soviet relationship, the tense political and military milieu in which earlier studies of the Cold War were written is disappearing. A different world is evolving, one in which bipolarity has been superseded by multipolarity. It is this, coupled with the rise of a new generation of leaders and historians, that has led to the prevailing idea that the events from 1945 to at least the early 1960s fall within a distinct historical period. This allows modern historians, finally, to treat this phase of the Cold War as history,[17] permitting the exploration in depth of issues like national defense planning. History is rich and varied no matter the period, and it is clear that historians can now pursue their study of the Cold War, or at least its early phase, as the multidimensional era it really is.

NOTES

1. One of the pioneers in this respect is Lawrence Kaplan. See his *A Community of Interests: NATO and the Military Assistance Program, 1948–1951* (Washington, 1980); and *The United States and NATO: The Formative Years* (Lexington, 1984).

2. For instance, see R. C. K. Ensor, *England, 1870–1914* (Oxford, 1936), 469–71; and P. Renouvin, *The Immediate Origins of the War* (New Haven, 1928). This

does not ignore the bulk of memoir material which follows the same line; see, as an example, H. H. Asquith, *The Genesis of the War* (New York, 1923).

3. The best example is H. Delbrück, *Vor und nach dem Weltkrieg. Politische und historische Aufsätze, 1902–1925* (Berlin, 1926). As in the entente case, there was an abundance of memoir literature to show a lack of German culpability; see, as an example, A. Von Tirpitz, *My Memoirs*, vol. 1 (London, 1919).

4. Cf. S. B. Fay, *Origins of the World War*, 2nd edn (New York, 1930); and G. P. Gooch, *Before the War*, 2 vols. (London, 1936, 1938).

5. See F. Fischer, *Germany's Aims in the First World War* (London, 1967). Cf. J. A. Moses, *The Politics of Illusion: The Fischer Controversy* (London, 1975).

6. For example, A. A. Gromyko and B. N. Ponomarev, *Soviet Foreign Policy, 1917–1980*, vol. 2: *1945–1980* (Moscow, 1980); and A. Zhdanov, *The International Situation* (Moscow, 1947).

7. For example, H. Feis, *Churchill, Roosevelt, Stalin: The War They Waged and the Peace They Sought* (Princeton, 1957); Feis, *Between War and Peace: The Potsdam Conference* (Princeton, 1960); and Feis, *The Atomic Bomb and the End of World War II* (Princeton, 1966). These are classic analyses of Soviet responsibility, although there are many more. Memoir material augmented this "historical" writing; for instance, see J. Deane, *The Strange Alliance: The Story of Our Efforts at Wartime Co-operation With Russia* (New York, 1947).

8. See, for instance, D. F. Fleming, *The Cold War and Its Origins, 1917–1960*, 2 vols. (Garden City, New York, 1961); and W. A. Williams, *The Tragedy of American Diplomacy*, rev. edn (New York, 1962).

9. Cf. G. Alperowitz, *Atomic Diplomacy: Hiroshima and Potsdam* (New York, 1965); H. Feis, *From Trust to Terror: The Onset of the Cold War, 1945–1950* (New York, 1970); L. J. Halle, *The Cold War as History* (New York, 1967); D. Horowitz, *The Free World Colossus: A Critique of American Foreign Policy in the Cold War*, 2nd edn (New York, 1971); G. Kolko, *The Politics of War: The World and United States Foreign Policy, 1943–1945* (New York, 1968); and R. J. Maddox, *The New Left and the Origins of the Cold War* (Princeton, 1973).

10. Cf. F. J. Harbutt, *The Iron Curtain: Churchill, America, and the Origins of the Cold War* (New York, 1986); E. Mark, "American Policy Toward Eastern Europe and the Origins of the Cold War, 1941–1946: An Alternative Explanation," *Journal of American History*, 68 (1981), 313–36; and D. Yergin, *Shattered Peace: The Origins of the Cold War and the National Security State* (Boston, 1977).

11. For instance, G. Kolko, *Anatomy of a War: Vietnam, the United States and the Modern Historical Experience* (New York, 1985).

12. Cf. T. H. Anderson, *The United States, Great Britain and the Cold War, 1944–1947* (Columbia, MO, 1981); R. Hathaway, *Ambiguous Partnership: Britain and America, 1944–1947* (New York, 1981); H. B. Ryan, *The Vision of Anglo-America: The US–UK Alliance and the Emerging Cold War, 1943–1946* (Cambridge, 1987); and D. C. Watt, *Succeeding John Bull: America in Britain's Place, 1900–1975* (Cambridge, 1984).

13. For instance, see J. L. Gaddis, *Strategies of Containment: A Critical Appraisal of Postwar American National Security Policy* (New York, 1982); M. J. Hogan, *The Marshall Plan: America, Britain, and the Reconstruction of Western Europe, 1947–1952* (Cambridge, 1987); and A. S. Milward, *The Reconstruction of Western Europe, 1945–1951* (London, 1984).

14. For instance, C. A. MacDonald, *Korea: The War Before Vietnam* (London, 1986); M. Schaller, "Securing the Great Crescent: Occupied Japan and the Origins of Containment in Southeast Asia," *Journal of American History*, 69 (1982), 392–414; and N. B. Tucker, *Patterns in the Dust: Chinese-American Relations and the Recognition Controversy, 1949–1950* (New York, 1983).

15. D. Cameron Watt, "Britain and the Historiography of the Yalta Conference and the Cold War," *Diplomatic History*, 13 (1989), 67–98.

16. A. Schlesinger, Jr., "Origins of the Cold War," *Foreign Affairs*, 46 (1967), 22–52, specifically, 23. Although this was technically Professor Schlesinger's musings on the fiftieth anniversary of the Russian Revolution, its publication on the twentieth anniversary of the issuing of the Truman Doctrine is not really coincidental.

17. This is with all deference to Professor Halle's *The Cold War as History* which, although it is good history, is more precisely a memoir.

Bibliography

BOOKS

Anderson, Terry H. *The United States, Great Britain, and the Cold War, 1944–1947.* Columbia, MO: University of Missouri Press, 1981.

Andrews, E. M. *Australia and China: The Ambiguous Relationship.* Carleton: Melbourne University Press, 1985.

Backer, John H. *Winds of History: The German Years of Lucius DuBignon Clay.* New York: Van Nostrand Reinhold, 1983.

Berman, Larry M. *Planning a Tragedy: the Americanization of the War in Vietnam.* New York: W. W. Norton, 1982.

Best, Richard A., Jr. *"Cooperation with Like-Minded Peoples": British Influences on American Security Policy, 1945–1949.* Westport, CT: Greenwood Press, 1986.

Bialer, Seweryn, ed. *Stalin and His Generals: Soviet Military Memoirs of World War II.* New York: Pegasus, 1969.

Bullock, Alan. *Ernest Bevin, Foreign Secretary, 1945–1951.* New York: Oxford University Press, 1983.

Bundy, McGeorge. *Danger and Survival: Choices about the Bomb in the First Fifty Years.* New York: Random House, 1989.

Cheong, Yong Mun. *H. J. van Mook and Indonesian Independence: A Study of His Role in Dutch-Indonesian Relations, 1945–1948.* The Hague: Martinus Nijhoff, 1982.

Cline, Roy S. *Secrets, Spies and Scholars: The Essential CIA.* Washington, DC: Acropolis Books, 1976.

Coletta, Paolo E. *The United States Navy and Defense Unification, 1947–1953.* Newark, DE: University of Delaware Press, 1981.

Condit, Kenneth W. *The Joint Chiefs of Staff and National Policy, 1947–1949.* Wilmington, DE: Michael Glazier, 1979.

Darby, Philip. *British Defence Policy: East of Suez 1947–1968.* London: Oxford University Press, 1973.

Dennis, Peter. *Troubled Days of Peace: Mountbatten and South East Asia Command, 1945–1946*. Manchester: Manchester University Press, 1987.

De Santis, Hugh. *The Diplomacy of Silence: The American Foreign Service, the Soviet Union, and the Cold War, 1933–1947*. Chicago, IL: University of Chicago Press, 1980.

Dinerstein, Herbert S. *War and the Soviet Union: Nuclear Weapons and the Revolution in Soviet Military and Political Thinking*. New York: Praeger, 1958.

Djilas, Milovan. *Conversations with Stalin*. New York: Harcourt Brace, 1962.

Donovan, Robert J. *The Presidency of Harry S. Truman, 1949–1953: Tumultuous Years*. New York: W. W. Norton, 1982.

———. *The Presidency of Harry S. Truman, 1945–1948: Conflict and Crisis*. New York: W. W. Norton, 1977.

Draper, Theodore. *Present History: On Nuclear War, Detente, and Other Controversies*. New York: Random House, 1984.

Etzold, Thomas H. *The Conduct of American Foreign Relations: The Other Side of Diplomacy*. New York: New Viewpoints, 1977.

Fursdon, Major-General Edward. *The European Defence Community: A History*. London: Macmillan, 1980.

Gaddis, John Lewis. *The United States and the Origins of the Cold War, 1941–1947*. New York: Columbia University Press, 1972.

Garthoff, Raymond L. *Soviet Strategy in the Nuclear Age*. New York: Praeger, 1958.

———. *Soviet Military Doctrine*. Glencoe, IL: The Free Press, 1953.

George, Margaret. *Australia and the Indonesian Revolution*. Carleton: Melbourne University Press, 1980.

Gimbel, John. *The Origins of the Marshall Plan*. Stanford, CA: Stanford University Press, 1976.

Granatstein, J. L. *A Man of Influence*. Ottawa: Deneau Publishers, 1981.

Grosse, Peter. *Israel in the Mind of America*. New York: Alfred A. Knopf, 1983.

Hogan, Michael J. *The Marshall Plan: America, Britain, and the Reconstruction of Western Europe, 1947–1952*. Cambridge: Cambridge University Press, 1987.

Hudson, W. J. *Casey*. Melbourne: Oxford University Press, 1986.

Ireland, Timothy P. *Creating the Entangling Alliance: The Origins of the North Atlantic Treaty Organization*. Westport, CT: Greenwood Press, 1981.

Isaacson, Walter and Evan Thomas. *The Wise Men: Six Friends and the World They Made—Acheson, Bohlen, Harriman, Kennan, Lovett, McCloy*. New York: Simon and Schuster, 1986.

Jockel, Joseph T. *No Boundaries Upstairs: Canada, the United States, and the Origins of North American Air Defence, 1945–1958*. Vancouver: University of British Columbia Press, 1987.

Jones, Joseph. *The Fifteen Weeks*. New York: Harcourt Brace Jovanovich, 1965.

Kaplan, Fred. *The Wizards of Armageddon*. New York: Simon and Schuster, 1983.

Kaplan, Karel. *Dans les archives du comité central: Trente ans de secrets du bloc soviétique*. Paris: Michel, 1978.

Kaplan, Lawrence. *The United States and NATO: The Formative Years*. Lexington, KY: University of Kentucky Press, 1984.

Keiser, Gordon W. *The U.S. Marine Corps and Defense Unification, 1944–47: The Politics of Survival*. Washington, DC: National Defense University Press, 1982.

Keohane, Robert O. and Joseph Nye, eds. *Transnational Relations and World Politics.* Cambridge, MA: Harvard University Press, 1972.

Kolodziej, Edward A. *The Uncommon Defense and Congress, 1945–1963.* Columbus, OH: Ohio State University Press, 1966.

Kuniholm, Bruce R. *The Origins of the Cold War in the Near East: Great Power Conflict and Diplomacy in Iran, Turkey, and Greece.* Princeton, NJ: Princeton University Press, 1980.

Larson, Deborah Welch. *Origins of Containment: A Psychological Explanation.* Princeton, NJ: Princeton University Press, 1985.

Lee, William T. and Richard F. Staar. *Soviet Military Policy Since World War II.* Stanford, CA: Hoover Institution, 1986.

LeMay, Curtis E. (with Dale O. Smith). *America is in Danger.* New York: Funk and Wagnalls, 1968.

Louis, William Roger. *The British Empire in the Middle East 1945–1951.* Oxford: Clarendon Press, 1984.

Mastny, Vojtech. *Russia's Road to the Cold War: Stalin's War Aims, 1941–1945.* New York: Columbia University Press, 1979.

May, Ernest R. *Imperial Democracy: The Emergence of the United States as a Great Power.* New York: Harcourt Brace, 1961.

McCagg, William O. *Stalin Embattled, 1943–1948.* Detroit, MI: Wayne State University Press, 1978.

McGwire, Michael. *Military Objectives in Soviet Foreign Policy.* Washington, DC: The Brookings Institution, 1987.

McLellan, David S. *Dean Acheson: The State Department Years.* New York: Dodd, Mead, 1976.

McMahon, Robert J. *Colonialism and Cold War: The United States and the Struggle for Indonesian Independence, 1945–1949.* Ithaca, NY: Cornell University Press, 1981.

Messer, Robert L. *The End of an Alliance: James F. Byrnes, Roosevelt, Truman, and the Origins of the Cold War.* Chapel Hill, NC: University of North Carolina Press, 1982.

Midgley, John J., Jr. *Deadly Illusions: Army Policy for the Nuclear Battlefield.* Boulder, CO: Westview Press, 1986.

Milberry, Larry. *The Canadair North Star.* Toronto: Canav Books, 1982.

Milward, Alan S. *The Reconstruction of Western Europe, 1945–1951.* London: Methuen, 1984.

Neustadt, Richard E. *Presidential Power: The Politics of Leadership from FDR to Carter.* New York: John Wiley, 1980.

O'Neill, Robert. *Australia in the Korean War 1950–1953.* Vol. 1: *Strategy and Diplomacy.* Canberra: Australian War Memorial/Australian Government Printing Service, 1981.

Pastor, Robert A. *Congress and the Politics of U.S. Foreign Economic Policy.* Berkeley, CA: University of California Press, 1980.

Pemberton, Gregory. *All the Way: Australia's Road to Vietnam.* Sydney: Allen & Unwin, 1987.

Pemberton, William E. *Bureaucratic Politics: Executive Reorganization during the Truman Administration.* Columbia, MO: University of Missouri Press, 1979.

Pogue, Forrest C. *George C. Marshall, III: Statesman, 1945–1959*. New York: Viking Press, 1987.

Poole, Dewitt C. *The Joint Chiefs of Staff and National Policy, 1950–1952*. Wilmington, DE: Michael Glazier, 1980.

Potter, E. B. *Nimitz*. Annapolis, MD: Naval Institute Press, 1976.

Putnam, Robert D. *The Beliefs of Politicians: Ideology, Conflict, and Democracy in Britain and Italy*. New Haven, CT: Yale University Press, 1973.

Reid, Escott. *Time of Fear and Hope*. Toronto: McClelland, 1977.

Riste, Olav, ed. *Western Security: The Formative Years: European and Atlantic Defence 1947–1953*. Oslo: Universitetslforlaget, 1985.

Rosenfeldt, Niels Erik. *Knowledge and Power: The Role of Stalin's Secret Chancellory in the Soviet System of Government*. Copenhagen: Rosenkilde and Bagger, 1978.

Rothwell, Victor. *Britain and the Cold War, 1941–1947*. London: Cape, 1982.

Ryan, H. B. *The Vision of Anglo-America. The US–UK Alliance and the Emerging Cold War, 1943–1946*. Cambridge: Cambridge University Press, 1987.

Sbrega, John J. *Anglo-American Relations and Colonialism in East Asia, 1941–1945*. New York: Garland, 1983.

Schlesinger, Arthur M., Jr. *The Age of Roosevelt, I: The Crisis of the Old Order, 1919–1933*. Boston, MA: Houghton Mifflin, 1957.

Schmitt, Hans A., ed. *U.S. Occupation in Europe after World War II*. Lawrence, KS: Regents Press of Kansas, 1978.

Scott, Harriet Fast and William F. Scott, *The Armed Forces of the USSR*, 3rd edn. Boulder, CO: Westview Press, 1984.

Sherry, Michael S. *Preparing for the New War: American Plans for Postwar Defense, 1941–45*. New Haven, CT: Yale University Press, 1977.

Shlaim, Avi. *The United States and the Berlin Blockade, 1948–1949: A Study in Crisis Decision-Making*. Berkeley, CA: University of California Press, 1983.

Smith, Denis. *Diplomacy of Fear*. Toronto: University of Toronto Press, 1988.

Stueck, William Whitney, Jr. *Road to Confrontation: American Policy Toward China and Korea, 1947–1950*. Chapel Hill, NC: University of North Carolina Press, 1981.

Taubman, William. *Stalin's American Policy: From Entente to Detente to Cold War*. New York: W. W. Morrow, 1982.

Thorne, Christopher. *Allies of a Kind: The United States, Britain and the War against Japan, 1941–1945*. London: Hamish Hamilton, 1978.

Tucker, Nancy B. *Patterns in the Dust: Chinese-American Relations and the Recognition Controversy, 1949–1950*. New York: Columbia University Press, 1983.

Ulam, Adam B. *The Rivals: America and Russia Since World War II*. New York: Viking, 1971.

Walker, J. Samuel. *Henry A. Wallace and American Foreign Policy*. Westport, CT: Greenwood Press, 1976.

Watt, D. Cameron. *Succeeding John Bull: America in Britain's Place, 1900–1975*. Cambridge: Cambridge University Press, 1984.

Weil, Martin. *A Pretty Good Club: The Founding Fathers of the U.S. Foreign Service*. New York: W. W. Norton, 1978.

Weiler, Peter. *British Labour and the Cold War*. Stanford, CA: Stanford University Press, 1988.

Wolfe, Thomas W. *Soviet Power and Europe, 1945–1970*. Baltimore, MD: Johns Hopkins Press, 1970.

Wyden, Peter. *Bay of Pigs, The Untold Story*. New York: Simon and Schuster, 1979.

Yergin, Daniel. *Shattered Peace: The Origins of the Cold War and the National Security State*. Boston, MA: Houghton Mifflin, 1977.

Young, John W. *Britain, France, and the Unity of Europe, 1945–1951*. Leicester: Leicester University Press, 1984.

ARTICLES

Baylis, J. "Britain, the Brussels Pact, and the Continental Commitment," *International Affairs*, 60 (1984).

Bell, Roger. "Australian-American Discord: Negotiations for Post-war Bases and Security Arrangements in the Pacific, 1944–1946," *Australian Outlook*, 27:1 (1973).

Denoon, Donald. "The Isolation of Australian History," *Historical Studies*, 22:87 (1986).

Edwards, P. G. "Evatt and the Americans," *Historical Studies*, 18:73 (1979).

Edwards, Peter. "The Australian Commitment to the Malayan Emergency, 1948–1950," *Historical Studies*, 22:89 (1987).

Evangelista, Matthew. "Stalin's Postwar Army Reappraised," *International Security*, 7 (1982–83).

Gaddis, John Lewis. "The Emerging Post-Revisionist Synthesis on the Origins of the Cold War," *Diplomatic History*, 7:3 (1983).

Gardner, Lloyd C. "Lost Empires," *Diplomatic History*, 13 (1989).

Greenwood, Sean. "Ernest Bevin, France and 'Western Union': August 1945–February 1946," *European History Quarterly*, 14 (1984).

Hammond, Paul Y. "Super Carriers and B–36 Bombers," in Harold Stein, ed., *American Civil-Military Decisions: A Book of Case Studies*. Birmingham, AL: University of Alabama Press, 1963.

Hogan, Michael J. "American Marshall Planners and the Search for a European Neocapitalism," *American Historical Review*, 90 (1985).

Jockel, Joseph T. "The Canada–United States Military Cooperation Committee and Continental Air Defence, 1946," *Canadian Historical Review* (1983).

Kahin, George M. "The United States and the Anticolonial Revolutions in Southeast Asia, 1945–1950," in Yonosuke Nagai and Akira Iriye, eds., *The Origins of the Cold War in Asia*. New York and Tokyo: Columbia University Press, 1977.

Kirby, Stephen. "Britain, NATO and European Security," in John Baylis, ed., *British Defence Policy in a Changing World*. London: Croom Helm, 1979.

Knight, Jonathon. "American Statecraft and the 1946 Black Sea Straits Controversy," *Political Science Quarterly*, 90 (1975).

LaFeber, Walter. "Roosevelt, Churchill, and Indochina: 1942–1945," *American Historical Review*, 80 (1975).

Lee, R. Alton. "The Army 'Mutiny' of 1946," *Journal of American History*, 52 (1966).

Leffler, Melvyn. "Strategy, Diplomacy, and the Cold War: The United States, Turkey, and NATO, 1945–1952," *Journal of American History*, 71:4 (1985).

———. "Expansionist Impulses and Domestic Constraints," in William H. Becker and Samuel F. Wells, Jr., eds., *Economics and World Order: An Assessment of American Diplomacy Since 1789*. New York: Columbia University Press, 1984.

———. "The American Conception of National Security and the Beginnings of the Cold War," *American Historical Review*, 89 (1984).

Lynch, Frances B. "Resolving the Paradox of the Monnet Plan: National and International Planning in French Reconstruction," *Economic History Review*, 37 (1984).

Mark, E. "American Policy Toward Eastern Europe and the Origins of the Cold War, 1941–1946: An Alternative Explanation," *Journal of American History*, 68 (1981).

Mastny, Vojtech. "Stalin and the Militarization of the Cold War," *International Security*, 9 (1984–85).

May, Ernest R. "Changing International Stakes in Presidential Selection," in Alexander Heard and Michael Nelson, eds., *Presidential Selection*. Durham, NC: Duke University Press, 1987.

Nelson, Anna K. "President Truman and the Evolution of the National Security Council," *Journal of American History*, 72 (1985).

Nitze, Paul. "The Development of NSC 68," *International Security* (1980).

———. "Atoms, Strategy, and Policy," *Foreign Affairs*, 34 (1956).

Page, Don and Don Munton. "Canadian Images of the Cold War 1945–47," *International Journal* (1977).

Rotter, Andrew J. "The Triangular Route to Vietnam: The United States, Great Britain, and Southeast Asia, 1945–1950," *International History Review*, 6:3 (1984).

Schaller, M. "Securing the Great Crescent: Occupied Japan and the Origins of Containment in Southeast Asia," *Journal of American History*, 69 (1982).

Van Cleave, William R. "A Garthoff-Pipes Debate on Soviet Strategic Doctrine," *Strategic Review*, 10 (1982).

Watt, D. Cameron. "Britain and the Historiography of the Yalta Conference and the Cold War," *Diplomatic History*, 13 (1989).

Weeks, Albert L. "The Garthoff-Pipes Debate on Soviet Doctrine: Another Perspective," *Strategic Review*, 11 (1983).

Wells, Samuel, Jr. "Sounding the Tocsin: NSC 68 and the Soviet Threat," *International Security* (1979).

Wettig, Gerhard. "The Garthoff-Pipes Debate on Soviet Strategic Doctrine, A European Perspective," *Strategic Review*, 11 (1983).

Index

Acheson, Dean, 12–14, 18, 20, 21–22, 24, 28, 50–51, 78, 90, 91, 114, 123, 126, 128, 133, 146, 176, 177
Attlee, Clement, 23, 102, 171, 172–173
Australia, 4, 103, 105, 107–8, 140–49, 189, 190
Austria, 100, 108, 177

Berlin blockade, 27, 49, 59, 85, 101, 107, 177
Bevin, Ernest, 82–83, 85–86, 90, 100, 117, 145
Bohlen, Charles E., 13, 21, 89
Brussels Pact, 82, 85
Byrnes, James F., 20

Cadogan, Sir Alexander, 137, 143
Canada, 4–5, 49, 88, 103, 153–66, 171–83, 189, 190
Chifley, J. B., 141, 144
China, 11, 88, 101, 121, 122, 140, 142, 143, 146, 148, 186, 191
Churchill, Winston S., 25, 56, 142
Claxton, Brooke, 155, 160, 162, 165, 172
Clay, Lucius, 28, 34, 49
Clifford, Clark, 11, 12, 25, 28
Collins, Lawton, 121, 124, 126

Connally, Tom, 19, 20, 25
containment, 3, 75, 76, 115, 131
Council of Europe, 81, 86, 91
Cripps, Sir Stafford, 83, 84
Curtain, John, 142
Czechoslovakia, 56, 57, 59, 85, 171, 172, 173, 190

de Gaulle, Charles, 80, 139
Denfield, Louis E., 33–34, 45, 51–52
Distant Early Warning (DEW) Line, 153, 154, 166
Dulles, John Foster, 11, 77, 78, 144
Dunkirk, Treaty of, 82, 87

Eden, Anthony, 102, 105, 109
Eisenhower, Dwight D., 29, 32, 42, 45, 46, 51–52, 116, 127–28, 130
European Defence Community (EDC), 102
European Payments Union (EPU), 79, 89, 91
European Recovery Program (ERP), 76, 86, 88
Evatt, H. V., 143–44

Forrestal, James, 31, 33–35, 40–41, 43, 44, 77, 120, 165

France, 3, 76, 79, 82, 85, 87, 90, 91,
  99–102, 105, 108, 109, 130, 137–38,
  180, 188

Germany, 78, 87, 90, 99, 100, 103,
  108, 171
Greece, 3, 23–25, 111, 114–20, 122–30,
  176

Harriman, W. Averell, 13–14, 28
Healey, Denis, 107, 109
Hopkins, Harry, 10, 56

India, 100, 139
Indonesia, 109, 139, 141, 145–47

Japan, 11, 29, 55, 56, 100, 103, 137–40,
  141–43, 144–45, 149, 187, 188, 191
Johnson, Louis, 45, 52
Johnson, Lyndon B., 12, 13, 108

Kennan, George F., 13, 21, 25, 50, 76,
  78, 88
Kennedy, John Fitzgerald, 13, 146–47
King, William Lyon Mackenzie, 155,
  158–60, 161, 171–72, 174
Korean War, 2, 39, 46, 53, 75, 101,
  109, 121, 122, 137, 141, 144, 166,
  178, 186, 187

Lemay, Curtis, 7–8, 48, 52, 61
Lodge, Henry Cabot, 25, 28
London, 79, 99, 101, 190
Lovett, Robert A., 14

MacArthur, Douglas, 33, 138, 140, 142
Malaya, 4, 140, 145, 148
Marshall, George C., 11, 20–21, 24,
  29, 36, 50, 76, 77, 80, 117
Marshall Plan, 2–3, 26–27, 39–40, 59,
  75–97, 100, 132, 176, 187, 189
McCarthy, Joe, 10, 186
McCloy, John J., 13, 28
McGhee, George, 125, 127, 128, 130,
  134
Menzies, R. G., 141, 144, 145, 147,
  148

Middle East, 100, 102, 108–9, 137,
  141, 145, 149
Monnet, Jean, 26, 28, 80, 81, 82, 91

National Security Council, 51–54, 78,
  92
Newfoundland, 162, 165, 166
New Guinea, 143, 146, 147
New Zealand, 105, 140, 143, 144
Nimitz, Chester W., 29, 32, 33
Nitze, Paul, 50, 51, 53
Nixon, Richard M., 11–12, 149, 191
North American Air Defense System
  (NORAD), 174
North Atlantic Treaty Organization
  (NATO), 2, 3, 5, 19, 49, 75, 81, 86,
  91, 101–2, 104, 107–8, 110, 118–21,
  122, 123, 125, 127–28, 129–30, 145,
  171–83, 190
nuclear weapons, 3, 38, 47–48, 105–7,
  178–79

Organization for European Economic
  Cooperation (OEEC), 79, 81, 86, 91
Ottawa, 156, 159, 160, 161, 162

Paris, 79
Pearson, Lester B., 172, 173, 178–79
Permanent Joint Board on Defence
  (PJBD), 155, 159–61, 163, 165
Potsdam Conference, 4, 22, 138

Resolute, 164, 166
Robertson, Norman A., 156, 174
Roosevelt, Franklin D., 10, 17, 20, 25–
  26, 56, 137, 142

Saigon, 138
Sandys, Duncan, 105–7
St. Laurent, Louis, 172
Schlesinger, Arthur, Jr., 13, 190
Schuman Plan, 80, 90, 91
Sherman, Forest P., 126
Slessor, Sir John, 102, 103, 104, 110
South-East Asia Treaty Organization
  (SEATO), 105, 148, 190
Spender, P. C., 144, 145
Spry, D. C., 157–58, 161, 166

Stalin, Joseph, 2, 56, 112, 113, 191
Suez, 3, 47–48, 100, 105, 107, 109, 118, 121, 122, 124
Symington, Stuart, 42

Truman, Harry S, 4, 14, 17–28, 36–37, 59, 60, 91, 103, 111, 112–14, 118, 122, 128, 139, 140, 146, 160, 172, 175, 176
Truman doctrine, 23, 24, 27, 28, 47, 59, 114–15, 128, 177, 190
Turkey, 3, 23–25, 104, 111, 112–21, 123–24, 125, 126–31, 176
Tydings, Millard, 42–43

Vandenberg, Arthur, 18–19, 20, 177
Vandenberg, Hoyt, 34, 40, 43
Vinson, Carl, 43

Wallace, Henry, 22
Washington, D.C., 9, 14–17, 21, 78, 82, 86–88, 90, 91, 101, 142, 144, 146, 156, 172, 176, 181, 182, 190
Wilson, Harold, 108, 109–10
Wrong, Hume, 157, 177

Yalta Conference, 188

About the Contributors

David Bercuson is Professor of History at the University of Calgary and the author of a number of books on Canadian labor history. At present he is preparing a book on U.S.–Canadian defense, 1945–56.

Peter Dennis teaches at the Australian Defense Force Academy. He has written extensively on British military matters, including studies of British defense policy 1919–39 and the Territorial Army.

Michael L. Dockrill is Senior Reader in the Department of War Studies, King's College, London. His two most recent books deal with British defense policy after 1945 and a survey of the Cold War.

Ronald G. Haycock is Professor of History at the Royal Military College of Canada. The author of a biography of Sir Sam Hughes, Professor Haycock is at present preparing a study of the imperial contribution to British munitions production, 1858–1945.

Michael Hogan is Professor of History at Ohio State University. His most recent book, *The Marshall Plan*, won the Stuart Bernath Prize of the American Society of Historians of Foreign Relations.

Bruce R. Kuniholm is author of *The Origins of the Cold War in the Near East* and teaches at Duke University. He is writing a sequel to his first book, one covering the period from 1947 to 1952.

Ernest R. May is Charles Warren Professor of History at Harvard University. He is the author of a number of books on U.S. foreign policy and has edited a number of works including *Knowing One's Enemies: Intelligence Assessment Before the Two World Wars.*

B. J. C. McKercher is Associate Professor at the Royal Military College of Canada. His most recent book is a biography of Esme Howard. At present, Dr. McKercher is preparing a book on Anglo-American relations, 1930–40.

Keith Neilson is Associate Professor at the Royal Military College of Canada. The author of *Strategy and Supply: Anglo-Russian Relations, 1914–17,* he is preparing a volume covering the same subject for the period 1894–1914.

Denis Smith is Dean of Social Science and Professor of Political Science at the University of Western Ontario.